MacPháidín
Library

Donated by
Dr. Robert J. Lifton

New York Medical College, 1948
Stonehill College Honorary Doctorate, 2008

Emotional Disturbance in Adopted Adolescents

EMOTIONAL DISTURBANCE IN ADOPTED ADOLESCENTS

Origins and Development

Ruth G. McRoy
Harold D. Grotevant
Louis A. Zurcher, Jr.

PRAEGER

New York
Westport, Connecticut
London

Library of Congress Cataloging-in-Publication Data

McRoy, Ruth G.

    Emotional disturbance in adopted adolescents : origins and
development / Ruth G. McRoy, Harold D. Grotevant, Louis A. Zurcher, Jr.
       p.   cm.
    Bibliography: p.
    Includes index.
    ISBN 0-275-92913-2 (alk. paper)
    1. Affective disorders in children. 2. Children, Adopted—Mental
health. 3. Adolescent psychotherapy—Residential treatment.
I. Grotevant, Harold D. II. Zurcher, Louis A., Jr. III. Title.
    [DNLM: 1. Adoption. 2. Affective Symptoms—in adolescence. WS
462 M478e]
RJ506.D4M36 1988
616.89'088069—dc19
DNLM/DLC
                                        88-1053

Library of Congress Catalog Card Number: 88-1053

ISBN: 0-275-92913-2

First published in 1988

Praeger Publishers, One Madison Avenue, New York, NY 10010
A division of Greenwood Press, Inc.

Printed in the United States of America

∞

The paper used in this book complies with the
Permanent Paper Standard issued by the National
Information Standards Organization (Z39.48-1984).

10 9 8 7 6 5 4 3 2 1

This book is dedicated to the memory of our friend,
colleague, and coauthor, Louis Anthony Zurcher, Jr.
(May 13, 1936 — December 10, 1987)

Contents

Tables and Figure

Acknowledgments

A study such as this cannot be brought to fruition without the contributions of many people. We would especially like to acknowledge the important contributions of Kerry L. White and Bernabe Marrero, research associates who were heavily involved in data collection throughout the project. Kerry's M.A. thesis in child development and Bernie's Ph.D. dissertation in educational psychology were developed from their special interests in these project data. Kerry also coordinated the data collection and was involved in the conceptual work of the project in its early stages.

Several other members of our research staff made significant contributions: Susan Ayers-Lopez in data reduction, computer analysis, project coordination, and conceptual discussions for the final report; Vivian Jenkins in data reduction and conceptual discussions on the topics of stress and vulnerability; Kathryn Kramer for data analysis; Kim Gibbens and William Affeldt for contributions of clinical and practice expertise; and Lisa Beranek, Ann Furuta, Tara Leo, Peggy McEntee, Paul Pousson, and Denise Wieland for project assistance.

We also acknowledge the generosity of Dr. Sandra Scarr of the University of Virginia and Dr. Richard A. Weinberg of the University of Minnesota for allowing us to analyze the interview data collected from the adoptive families in the Minnesota Adoption Project. Funding for that project was received from the National Institute of Child Health and Human Development and the William T. Grant Foundation.

We especially thank Dale Erdmann, MSW, ACSW, whose curiosity about the preponderance of adopted adolescents in his unit at the Oaks Treatment Center served as an important impetus for the launching of our study. Dale's colleagueship, moral support, and assistance in recruiting families for the study were critically important to the completion of the project. We also thank Marietta Spencer, MSW, ACSW, Director of Post-Legal Adoption Services of Children's Home Society of Minnesota for her encouragement, support, and assistance in facilitating our data collection efforts in Minnesota. In addition, we thank the directors and clinical coordinators of the other treatment centers who assisted us in locating families and in interviewing them. A complete list of participating treatment centers may be found in Appendix A.

Funding for this project was provided by the Hogg Foundation for Mental Health, the University Research Institute of the University of Texas at Austin, and Project QUEST, a joint venture of IBM and the University of Texas at Austin. We thank Jack Weatherbee of Project QUEST for his assistance with computer hardware and software issues, Dwight Brooks for his assistance with software and programming, and Bill Woodburn for developing the data-input program for the Minnesota data.

Finally, but certainly not least, we thank the families who participated in the study — the parents and adolescents who shared their histories with us in hopes that our study might help the families of the future. We hope to live up to that promise.

Emotional Disturbance in Adopted Adolescents

1
Introduction

Adoption is a social and legal process in which a parent-child relationship is established between persons unrelated by birth. Through this process a child born to one set of parents becomes the child of other parents, a member of another family, and thereby assumes the rights and duties of children in birthfamilies (Costin, 1972).

Accurate annual statistics on adoption in the United States have not been available since 1975 because of a lack of standard mandatory reporting. However, the National Committee for Adoption (NCFA, 1985) has estimated that 141,861 adoptions occurred in the United States in 1982. Of these adoptions, 50,720 involved children unrelated to their adopting parents. The NCFA estimated conservatively that 17,602 adoptions (12.4 percent of total) were adoptions of healthy infants by non-relatives. The largest number of these adoptions (5,176, or 29.4 percent) occurred in Texas. Overall, unrelated adoptions of healthy infants represented approximately 0.48 percent of U.S. live births in 1982 and 2.46 percent of live births to unmarried women. It is estimated that between 2 and 3.5 percent of children under eighteen in the United States are adopted (Kadushin, 1974; Senior and Himadi, 1985).

Researchers have paid close attention to the demographic and social-psychological factors associated with parents' decisions to adopt (Chambers, 1970; Fellner, 1968; Kadushin, 1962; Maas, 1960) or to make adoption plans for their children (Bachrach, 1986). However, much less attention has been given to adoptive family relationships and to the long-term adjustment issues in adoptive families (Brinich and Brinich, 1982; Fanshel, 1972; McRoy and Zurcher, 1983).

A major concern of adoption workers and adoptive families is whether adopted children are more at risk for emotional disturbance than non-adopted children. Research data suggest that adopted children are referred for psychological treatment two to five times more frequently than their non-adopted peers. This finding has been replicated in countries as widely dispersed as Great Britain, Israel, Poland, Sweden, and the United States (Bohman, 1971; Brinich, 1980; Eiduson and Livermore, 1953; Humphrey and Ounsted, 1963; Kadushin, 1967; Lifshitz et al., 1975; McWhinnie, 1969; Reece and Levin, 1968; Schechter, 1960; Senior and Himadi, 1985; Simon and Senturia, 1966; Sweeney, Gasbarro, and Gluck, 1963; Tousseing, 1962; Work and Anderson, 1971; Ziatek, 1974).

According to the literature, adopted children referred for treatment generally were adopted as infants and placed with childless couples. They typically exhibited behavior characterized as impulsive, provocative, aggressive, and antisocial (Brinich, 1980; Eiduson and Livermore, 1953; Goodman and Magno-Nora, 1975; Jackson, 1968; Menlove, 1965; Offord, Aponte, and Cross, 1969; Schechter et al., 1964; Simon and Senturia, 1966). Although many have been diagnosed as manifesting personality trait disorders, one recent analysis of diagnoses in a psychiatric hospital found that adoptees were more likely than non-adoptees to receive diagnoses of adolescent adjustment reaction (Weiss, 1985). Also, adopted children have been found to be more likely than non-adoptees to resist treatment by running away from the residential facility (Fullerton, Goodrich, and Berman, 1986).

When the high incidence of adopted children referred to mental health clinics was first reported (Goodman, Silberstein, and Mandell, 1963; Schechter, 1960; Sweeney, Gasbarro, and Gluck, 1963), several psychodynamic hypotheses were proposed to explain their problematic behavior. These hypotheses were provocative, but typically incorporated variables that were difficult or impossible to operationalize. Clinicians have also noted several factors that could more often predispose adoptive families than non-adoptive families to seek help for their children. For example, compared with the general population, adoptive parents tend to be socioeconomically advantaged and are more likely to provide mental health services for their children. The adoptive parents can feel unduly vulnerable to rejection by the adopted child, leading to maladaptive reactive defenses by parents and child. Furthermore, adoptive parents might be anxious about unknown hereditary factors influencing the child's development (Wilson, 1985).

Adolescence is a developmental period when children and their families can be at particular risk for the manifestation of problem behavior. Significant changes during this period include the physical changes brought about by puberty and adolescents' psychological reactions to their emerging sexuality. Cognitive changes enable adolescents to think beyond the here and now to the world of possibilities and abstractions. Significant others in adolescents' social environments encourage them to take on more responsible roles and act in a mature manner. As a result of these internal and external events and changes, adolescents are challenged to form a mature sense of identity in order to answer the adult question, Who am I?

For the adopted adolescent, questions about birthparents and origins play an important role in the identity formation process (see further discussion in Chapter 8). How these issues are handled within the adoptive family can have an important bearing on the adolescent's feelings and behaviors. In addition, behavioral problems that had been manageable during childhood can become intolerable in the family setting when the child becomes adolescent.

Although there has been speculation about the situational factors that place the adopted child at risk for developing emotional problems, most of the research has been inadequately controlled or designed. With the exception of Kirk's (1964, 1981) work, limited theoretical attention has been given to adoptive family relationships. Thus, owing to theoretical and empirical limitations, many important questions concerning the etiology of emotional disturbance in adopted adolescents remain unanswered.

PURPOSE OF THE STUDY

This study was designed to identify familial and other contextual factors associated with the placement of adopted children in residential treatment for emotional disorders during the adolescent years. Questions of particular interest include the following: What are the specific factors or clusters of factors that appear to be related to the adolescents' emotional disturbance? Once these general areas have been identified, what are the specific family processes and dynamics that initiate and maintain the problem? Adopted and non-adopted adolescents in treatment are compared in order to separate relational issues specific to adoptive families from relational issues that may lead to emotional disturbance in all types of families. Adopted adolescents in treatment are also compared with a non-clinical sample of adopted adolescents in order to explore whether adoption issues have been dealt with differently in the two groups.

THEORETICAL FRAMEWORKS

Currently, there is no comprehensive theoretical framework that contributes to a full understanding of the development of children and adolescents within adoptive families. Consequently, the conceptualization of this research project has been guided by several theories, each of which has generated substantive predictions about the consequences of adoption for the child and the family. In this section, these theories will be summarized.

Psychoanalytic Theory

Psychoanalytic theory suggests that the circumstances surrounding the child's birth, including adoptive parents' unresolved concerns about infertility and the adoptees' concerns about having two sets of parents, can set the stage for emotional disorders in adopted children (Brodzinsky et al., 1984). Several psychoanalytic hypotheses have been advanced. Emotional disorders among adopted children may result from the unconscious and unresolved aversion toward parenthood in one or more of the adoptive parents, particularly the mother (Tousseing, 1962). The child's efforts to determine the reasons for being relinquished for adoption may generate an identity problem, especially in adolescence as he or she might come to identify with perceived "bad" birthparents (Simon and Senturia, 1966). Emotional problems can result from adoptive mothers' guilt about taking children that did not belong to them, a guilt that presumably arises from unresolved anger and rivalry toward their own mothers (Dukette, 1962; Walsh and Lewis, 1969). Relationships between adopted children and their parents may be vulnerable to "splitting," in which adopted children attribute all the bad qualities to their adoptive parents and all the good qualities to their unknown but idealized birthparents (Freud, 1986).

Genetic Theory

A genetic account of the etiology of disturbance among adopted children would begin with the assumption that the backgrounds of adopted and non-adopted children are different on both genetic and environmental grounds. Parents who relinquish children for adoption are likely to be younger than married parents at time of birth (thus placing the child at higher risk during gestation), to be more ambivalent about the pregnancy (thus creating the possibility that they will take health risks during the pregnancy), and to be less likely to obtain adequate prenatal care. It is also likely that some birthmothers relinquish their children for adoption because they are unable to care for them due to their own emotional disturbance. There is clear evidence that psychiatric disorders such as schizophrenia and depression have genetic contributions, thus placing children of these birthmothers at higher risk for future psychopathology than their non-adopted peers (Scarr and Kidd, 1983).

Few studies have documented differences between birthparents who place children for adoption and parents who keep their children. However, using the National Survey of Family Growth, Cycle III, conducted by the National Center for Health Statistics in 1982, Bachrach (1986) found that women who placed their babies for adoption were similar with respect to income, welfare dependency, and educational attainment at the time of the survey to women who married before giving birth or women who had abortions. Compared with unmarried women who chose to raise their babies, the women who placed their children for adoption were less likely to be poor, less likely to have received some form of public assistance in the past year, and more likely to have finished high school. These indicators, however, do not adequately address the emotional or intellectual status of these birthmothers.

In other studies comparing personalities of unwed birthmothers who keep their babies with those who place them for adoption (e.g., Horn and Turner, 1976; Vincent, 1961), the birthmothers who place are usually considered healthier than unwed birthmothers who choose to keep and raise their infants. Horn and Turner (1976), however, found substantial variability within both groups, suggesting that no blanket generalizations are warranted. Further research is needed in order to determine definitively if birthmothers who relinquish their babies for adoption constitute a significantly different gene pool from married women who have their own children or from adoptive mothers.

Genetic theory would also acknowledge the contribution of heredity to individual differences in both intellectual ability and personality. Because adoptive parents are typically of middle to upper-middle class, they tend to have high expectations for their children in terms of education and achievement. If their adopted children fail to meet those expectations, issues of "goodness-of-fit" (see below) between the children and their respective adoptive families may arise. Similar issues may emerge concerning personality differences. In biologically related families, inheritance acts in such a way as to maximize the possibility that there will be some similarity between parents and their children. In adoptive families, there is no guarantee of similarity. It is possible that a lower degree of perceived similarity (Scarr, Scarf, and Weinberg, 1980) and/or actual similarity may be associated with distancing between adoptive parents and their children when behavioral problems begin to occur.

Attachment Theory

Attachment theory has its roots in ethological theory (Ainsworth, 1973; Bowlby, 1969) and holds that the primary function of the attachment relationship is to ensure the proximity of the immature infant to its caregiver for provision of safety and food. The infant's behaviors, such as crying, cooing, babbling, and smiling serve to bring the infant into close contact with the caregiver. Recent versions of attachment theory emphasize not only the goal of proximity maintenance but also the goal of achieving "felt security" through the relationship (Sroufe and Waters, 1977).

When placed in an assessment situation that involves multiple episodes of the caregiver's entering and leaving a room (the "Strange Situation," Ainsworth, 1979), securely attached infants explored a novel environment freely in their mother's presence. They did not necessarily cry when their mothers left the room, but they did greet her return with pleasure. In contrast, avoidant babies avoided contact with their mothers upon reunion, sometimes actively looking away and averting their gaze. Distress was as easily comforted by a stranger as by the mother. Resistant or ambivalent babies were quite distressed when their mothers left, but were difficult to console upon reunion. They often resisted contact with their mothers while at the same time signaling that they wanted to be comforted.

Focused attachment relationships such as those described above develop gradually over the first six to eight months of life. According to Ainsworth and colleagues, the roots of secure attachment lie in the caregiver's responsiveness to the needs of the infant. In a feeding situation, mothers of securely attached infants have been found to be more sensitive, accepting, and psychologically accessible than mothers of anxiously attached infants (Ainsworth et al., 1978). Mothers of avoidant infants seemed to be especially rejecting and had an aversion to physical contact. Recent evidence (Egeland and Farber, 1984) suggests that some resistant babies are more difficult to care for early in life (e.g., are less alert or active than other babies). When coupled with caregivers who were not unusually sensitive, the attachment relationships have taken this distinctive turn.

A sizable body of evidence has accrued to indicate that attachment relationships in infancy have long-term consequences for the psychological and relational functioning of the individual child. For example, toddlers who were more securely attached as infants have been shown to be more willing to explore a novel physical environment than toddlers who were anxiously attached infants (Hazen and Durrett, 1982). In addition, securely attached infants showed better problem-solving ability and sociability at age two (Matas, Arend, and Sroufe, 1978; Pastor, 1981) and more curiosity and flexibility during the preschool years (Arend, Gove, and Sroufe, 1979). These and other studies suggest a great deal of continuity in behavior from infancy through early childhood in terms of the legacy of attachment.

The implications of attachment theory for the study of adoption are profound, especially for infants who were adopted when they were older. Since the literature strongly suggests that the attachment relationship develops gradually over the first six to eight months, it seems plausible that any child placed after that age would be at risk for developmental difficulties to the extent that disruptions or variations in parental responsiveness occurred. Similarly, to the degree that early placements are associated with continuous and responsive caregiving, it seems reasonable that the earlier the placement, the better the outcome. An important mediating variable in the situation for later-adopted children would be the quality of the foster home or preadoption placement(s). Because children can develop multiple attachments, attachment to a birthmother or foster mother should not preclude later relationships with adoptive parents. However, abuse or neglect during the first year could have strongly negative consequences in terms of the child's ability to establish a sense of "basic trust" (Erikson, 1950).

Recent research on attachment in adopted children (Singer et al., 1985) has tested some of these theoretically based predictions. One aspect of the study compared attachment relations of twenty-seven non-adopted infants and their mothers with those of twenty-seven intraracially adopted infants and their mothers. The infants had been placed very early in life (mean age of placement was 1.3 months). No differences were found between the frequencies of adopted and non-adopted children in the "Strange Situation" attachment classifications. The authors concluded that "lack of early contact per se does not place middle-class adoptive families at risk for the development of anxious mother-infant attachment relationships" (p. 1547) and therefore "it is unlikely that the higher incidence of psychological and academic problems among adoptees in middle childhood and adolescence . . . can be explained in terms of insecure family attachment patterns in the infancy years" (p. 1547). However, most of these infants were placed quite early. Furthermore, the insecurely attached adopted infants had experienced an average of 0.63 foster placements prior to adoption in contrast to the 0.16 foster placements experienced by securely attached infants. These data do not preclude the possible impact of adoption history on attachment. Further research with a more heterogeneous sample will be necessary in order to test these predictions adequately.

In another study of infants placed with adoptive mothers at approximately five to seven months of age, after being institutionalized, maternal behavior suggestive of overstimulation was noted (Kennell et al., 1986). Adoptive mothers varied in their ability to adapt their stimulating behavior to the needs of the infant; perhaps it is these cases in which problematic relationships developed over time.

Goodness-of-fit Theory

Goodness-of-fit theories hold that an individual's development is optimized in those situations in which there is a "match," or compatibility between characteristics of the individual and characteristics or demands of the salient environment. Examples of this model include Hunt's (1961) notion of the match in intellectual development; Holland's (1973, 1985) concept of person-environment congruency in the occupational world; and Lerner's (1985) goodness-of-fit model of infant temperament and environmental responsiveness. Consistent with attachment theory, goodness-of-fit theory states that when infants are raised by parents who understand them and are sensitive to their needs, development will be optimized. When parents are not able to accommodate the needs of their children, mismatch problems can occur. Although parental sensitivity is a key determinant, compatibility is viewed as a joint product of the characteristics of the child, the characteristics of the parents, and the family's social situation (Lamb and Gilbride, 1985). The characteristics of parents or children are not static; both change in dynamic responsiveness to one another. Goodness-of-fit, then, involves both the family members' ability to attain this state and their ability to retain it through dynamic interaction over time (Lamb and Gilbride, 1985).

Compatibility problems can occur with greater frequency in adoptive than in biological families, since adoptive parents usually are less similar to their children. Data from studies of family similarities (e.g., Horn, 1983; Scarr and Weinberg, 1983) suggest that the average parent-child IQ correlation in biological families is approximately .40; in adoptive families the correlation averages .14, even though the adopted child has lived in that home since early infancy. Average correlations on personality traits are .15 for biological parent-child pairs and .07 for adoptive parent-child pairs. In addition, adoptive parents typically are more highly educated, are more often in middle to upper-middle socioeconomic status, and are married longer when they first become parents (through adoption) than are biological parents and children living together (e.g., Zill, 1985).

From results such as these, it could be predicted that the degree of actual and perceived similarity would be less in adoptive than in biological families. Mismatches can occur between intellectual levels or personalities of parents and children, between characteristics of adopted siblings, or between adopted children and biological children within the same family. When major mismatches occur, there is a potential for conflict or for parental disappointment. The impact of such mismatches can be profound when adoptive parents attempt to diminish the importance of the child's biological heritage and behave as if he or she were just like their own birthchild (see discussion of Kirk's adoptive kinship theory below).

Other factors that can reduce adoptive parents' ability to be optimally responsive to their infant include unresolved parental ambivalence concerning infertility; parental tentativeness in interacting fully with the infant in order to protect against loss, should the agency or birthparents not permit the adoption to be finalized; lack of support typically available to biological parents, such as childbirth preparation classes and hospital-based programs; and attributions that the child is "different" and therefore "not ours."

Cognitive-Developmental Theory

In recent research, Brodzinsky, Singer, and Braff (1984) documented developmental changes in children's understanding of the meaning of adoption. In keeping with the cognitive-developmental tradition, they suggested that the child's understanding of adoption is a constructive process that does not reach a mature level until adolescence.

Although adoptive parents might begin talking with their child about adoption at an early age, it will be necessary for ongoing discussion to take place in order to help the child develop a mature concept of the meaning of adoption. In terms of cognitive-developmental theory, then, the timing and content of adoption revelation will have a major impact on the child's emerging concept of adoption as well as on the child's concept of self-as-adopted-child.

Brodzinsky, Singer, and Braff (1984) suggested that many adoptive parents overestimate their child's understanding of adoption and might stop talking about it before the child has a mature concept. Their results imply that information about adoption must be developmentally matched to the child's ability to understand it and that repeated discussions of the meaning of adoption must take place over time, especially into early adolescence.

Kirk's Adoptive Kinship Theory

Kirk (1964, 1981) has applied social-role theory to adoptive family relationships, noting that biological and adoptive parenthood are inherently different experiences in a number of ways. For example, adoptive parents must deal with the feelings associated with their infertility. They have no other adoptive family experiences to serve as models, and they have no physical pregnancy to serve as emotional preparation. They are subjected to intensive screening and must endure a probationary period following placement that creates insecurity. Their parents or family members may not be supportive, and they must undertake the difficult task of revealing the adoption to their child. Kirk believes that these situational discrepancies create stressful experiences for adoptive parents and result in their being handicapped in their role performance.

Kirk contends that the adoptive family situation is different from biological parenthood at the interpersonal level. To ensure family cohesiveness, this difference must be acknowledged. Adoptive parents suffering from role handicap might cope by rejecting rather than acknowledging the differences between adoptive and biological parenting. This rejection-of-difference coping mechanism can lead to poor communication between parent and child and can adversely affect adoptive family relationships. The acknowledgment-of-difference coping mechanism is considered by Kirk to be conducive to good communication between parent and child and can contribute to the dynamic stability of adoptive families.

Attribution Theory

Attribution theory refers to a family of theories (e.g., Heider, 1958; Jones and Davis, 1965; Kelley, 1971, 1972) that are concerned with how individuals ascribe meaning to their observations about responsibility for the behavior of others and themselves. The attribution process includes three steps: observation of an action (either of another person or of oneself), judgment of presence or absence of intention, and formation of a causal attribution of responsibility (Shaver, 1975). The goal of the attribution process is to be able to explain current and past behavior and to predict future behavior. The focus of the theory, then, is on the processes impinging on perceivers that affect their explanation and prediction of events. Most theories are concerned with such phenomena as attributions about success or failure, intentionality, and how people cope with uncontrollable situations.

In a recent application of attribution theory to the study of parent-child relations, Dix (1984; Dix and Grusec, 1986) has outlined sources of potential bias in attributions parents make about their children. Attribution theorists note that behaviors perceived to harm or benefit the perceiver in an impactful way (i.e., are *hedonically relevant* to the observer) are likely to motivate the perceiver to search for a cause of the behavior. In the case of the aversive behavior demonstrated by the adopted children in this study, the principle of hedonic relevance implies that parents will attempt to assign responsibility for the behavior.

Several attributional errors can influence the process of inferring responsibility. First, the parent may be making the *fundamental attribution error*, preferring to attribute the behavior to a disposition of the child ("because he's adopted") rather than to situational factors influencing behavior (e.g., the family dynamics). This error may be further reinforced by the attributions made by friends and relatives. Second, parents may be affected by the *self-serving bias* (Heider, 1958), which holds that in an intimate relationship, members have an investment in one another and parents are motivated to perceive their children's behavior in ways that make both the parents and the child feel and look good. Parents can make themselves feel good by disclaiming responsibility for the child's behavior. ("I know I'm a good parent — the adoption agency approved me, didn't it? Therefore, it must be my child's fault.") They might also make themselves feel good about their children by taking away the child's responsibility for his or her behavior ("He can't help it — it's in his genes.") Once this line of reasoning has begun, subsequent attributions can be affected by the *confirmation bias*, in which incoming data are fit into well-entrenched views. Attributions of these adolescents can be accentuated because of the *feature-positive bias*, which holds that attributions are more strongly influenced by the commission of behaviors (e.g., acting-out behaviors) than by their omission.

Complex motivational and affective factors are involved in adoptive parents' attributions about their children, as illustrated by Heider (1958, pp. 120–21): "Since one's idea includes what ought to be as well as what is, attributions and cognitions are influenced by the mere subjective forces of needs and wishes as well as by the more objective evidence presented in the raw material."

A FRAMEWORK FOR UNDERSTANDING ADOPTIVE FAMILY RELATIONSHIPS

We have drawn upon the pertinent theories summarized above to develop a new, integrative, more comprehensive framework for understanding the familial and contextual factors associated with the placement of emotionally troubled adopted adolescents in residential treatment. The framework is divided into three major sections representing 1) parent and child background factors, 2) the child and family's developmental history, and 3) the outcome for the child (see Figure 1.1). Factors pertaining to parents in both the adoptive and control groups are enclosed by solid lines; additional factors that apply to adoptive parents and children are enclosed by broken lines.

The framework reflects our belief that behavior is multiply determined and that no single causal factor leads directly to emotional disturbance. In addition, a developmental perspective on psychopathology is taken, assuming that emotional disorders develop over a period of time as a function of the interaction between the developing child and his or her changing environment (e.g., Sroufe and Rutter, 1984).

Parent and Child Background Factors

This component of the framework concerns the attitudes and characteristics that predate the adoption or birth of a child. For parents in both the adoptive and control groups, this factor includes their attitudes toward becoming a parent, their expectations for the child, their individual personality characteristics, and the quality of their marital relationship before the child's birth or adoption. Additional factors concerning adoptive parents include their motivation for

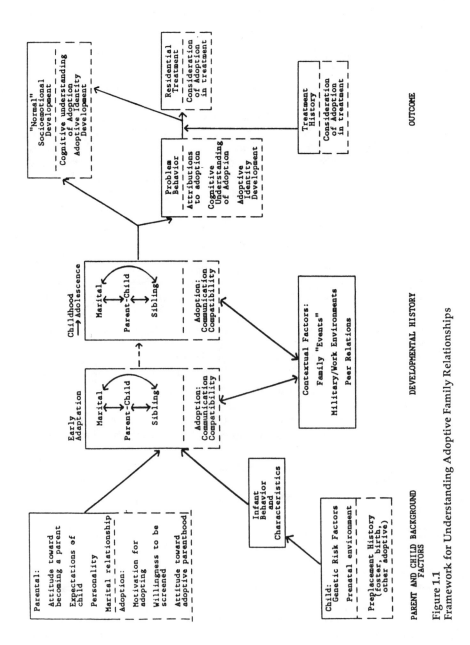

PARENT AND CHILD BACKGROUND
FACTORS

DEVELOPMENTAL HISTORY

OUTCOME

Figure 1.1
Framework for Understanding Adoptive Family Relationships

adopting, their willingness to submit to the screening process involved in adoption, and their attitudes toward adoptive parenthood.

Child background factors include genetic risk factors, such as a family history of schizophrenia or alcoholism, and the quality of the child's prenatal environment. For adopted children, other pertinent background factors include the child's history prior to adoption — specifically, the quality of care received in the child's experience with birthparents, foster parents, or other adoptive parents.

Developmental History

In this component of the framework, we will consider the development of the child within the family and the family within a broader social context over time. The adaptation of the family during the child's early years will be given special attention because of the foundational role that early attitudes and expectations play in later relationships. The birth or adoption of a first child creates major changes in the family, modifying it from a two-person relationship to a more-complex triadic system (Belsky, 1981). Not only must the child be considered as an individual, but the family must also be considered in terms of the reciprocal impact of the new child on the marital relationship (and vice versa) and the creation of two new parent-child subsystems. If siblings are already present in the family, the picture becomes more complex. Specific patterns of child behavior such as hyperactivity, physical disabilities of children, and avoidant attachment relationships with parents will be considered.

In addition to the significant changes experienced in biological families, adoptive families must also develop a method for communicating with one another and with outsiders about the adoption. As mentioned earlier, Kirk (1964, 1981) has discussed the impact of acknowledgment or rejection of the differences between adoptive and biological parenthood on the family's adjustment. Adopted children typically are different from their adoptive parents in appearance, temperament, or talents. The assessment of the perceived compatibility of the child with the family will be considered in terms of its role in the child's development.

As indicated in Figure 1.1, development within the family will be considered with respect to the ongoing, reciprocal relations between marital, parent-child, and sibling interaction. Marital relationships will be considered for their quality as well as for histories of divorce and remarriage. Parent-child relationships will be examined with a dual focus on parenting skills and parental mental health or pathology. Sibling relationships will be examined for contributions to the child's difficulties.

Development of the child within the family takes place within a broader social context. Important contextual factors that will be considered in this framework include traumatic family events, such as the death of a parent or significant other, a severe physical injury, or an untimely family move that may have longstanding impact on the child and family. Other contextual factors under consideration include military or work environments that involve prolonged parental separation, frequent moves, and discontinuities in school and peer experiences. Finally, peer relations will be examined in terms of their contribution to emotional disturbance as well as the consequences of the disturbance for the quality of subsequent peer and family relationships.

Outcomes

For both the adopted and control children in this study, the common outcome is placement outside the family into residential treatment. Our framework considers the child's pathway to residential treatment in terms of the child's early expression of problematic behavior and the response of the family and helping professionals to it.

As indicated in the framework, adoption is assumed to play a key role in the family's interpretation of the child's problem behavior and the action they take concerning it. For example, parents might assign responsibility for the problem behavior to the fact that the child was adopted by attributing the problem to the child's poor genetic heritage or difficult preplacement experiences. The child's cognitive understanding of adoption in general (Brodzinsky, Singer, and Braff, 1984) as well as the child's identity as an adopted child (Stein and Hoopes, 1985) can motivate the child to behave in provocative ways toward his or her parents.

The child's treatment history and the degree to which adoption was considered in the child's treatment will also be considered. Attempted interventions have the potential to determine whether the behavior can be rerouted into more normal developmental paths, or whether the behavior will become progressively so unacceptable that treatment outside the family becomes necessary.

ORGANIZATION OF THIS BOOK

Information about the methodology followed in this study, including details about the samples and procedures, is presented in Chapter 2. Succeeding chapters focus on specific aspects of the framework discussed above. Chapter 3 discusses factors predating the child's birth or adoption. Chapter 4 focuses on the early adaptation of the child within the family. Chapter 5 examines family relationships:

marital, parent-child, and sibling; and Chapter 6 focuses on the contexts of family relationships. In Chapter 7 peer relations are discussed. Chapter 8 presents information pertaining to the clinical issues involved in the study, including data on symptoms, diagnoses, prognosis, and treatment history of the children in the study. Chapters 9 through 11 focus on the adoption issues encountered by the children in the adoptive sample and in the Minnesota sample. Finally, Chapters 12 and 13 present conclusions, highlighting theoretical issues (Chapter 12) and practice issues (Chapter 13).

Although the various problems encountered by the families in this study are discussed in different primary chapters, it is important to note that all families in the study were faced with multiple problems and that the outcome for any particular family is the product of the interaction of the factors facing them. Throughout the book, whenever possible we have attempted to address the interactive nature of those factors.

2
Method

Three samples of families are represented in the analyses reported in this book. Data from a sample of adoptive families who had an adolescent in residential treatment and a sample of non-adoptive families with an adolescent in treatment were collected by the authors for this study. For comparison purposes, archival data from a sample of non-clinical adoptive families with adolescents were also used. Each of the samples is described below in detail.

ADOLESCENTS IN TREATMENT SAMPLES

Two availability samples of families with adolescents in residential treatment in Texas and Minnesota participated in this study. One sample consisted of fifty adopted adolescents and their families. In addition, in order to separate relational issues specific to adoptive families from relational issues that may lead to institutionalization in all types of families, a comparison group of fifty institutionalized non-adopted children and their families were selected from these same facilities.

Subject Recruitment

In the fall of 1983, residential treatment centers in Texas and Minnesota were contacted about participating in the study. Staff from each of these facilities were asked to identify institutionalized children who had been adopted before the age of two and non-adopted children who were currently between the ages of eleven and eighteen as potential participants in the study. Criteria for participation were as follows: 1) at least one parent must provide written consent for participation of self and child, 2) the child's caseworker or therapist must agree that the interview would not be psychologically harmful to the child at his or her stage of treatment, 3) the child must provide written consent for his or her participation and for the audiotaping of the interview, and 4) a professional staff member of each of the centers who is familiar with the child must be present during the interview.

Since the sample selection process was totally dependent on the willingness of staff and administrators to contact families to request participation, delays were encountered in gaining access to some treatment centers. Although all of the centers concurred about the necessity of research on adoptive family relationships, staff turnover, time limitations, and concerns about confidentiality were among the reasons given by several centers for declining to participate. Fourteen treatment centers (see Appendix A for list) ultimately agreed to participate by identifying children and their families and cooperating in the research process.

Sample

Every effort was made to interview the adoptive father, adoptive mother, adopted adolescent, and the caseworker or therapist for each adoptive family. Interviews in this sample of fifty families were ultimately completed with thirty-six adoptive fathers, forty-four adoptive mothers, forty-seven adopted adolescents, and forty-nine caseworkers. When complete data were not available from all four data sources in each family (father, mother, child, caseworker), analyses were conducted using the available information rather than eliminating the entire family from consideration in the study. The nonparticipating parents were unavailable because they were deceased (three fathers), they could not be contacted (seven fathers and five mothers), parental rights had been terminated (one father), or they refused to be interviewed (three fathers and one mother). The nonparticipating children were unavailable because they refused (two) or because they were in treatment out-of-state (one). One caseworker did not participate because she was in private practice and could not be reached.

The availability sample of adopted children included twenty-six males and twenty-four females ranging in age from eleven to seventeen (mean age = 14.96). The majority of the children (72 percent) had been placed in their adoptive homes by the age of six months; 86 percent had been placed by the age of one year. The median age of placement was three months. The adoptive parents mostly were middle class, with a median annual income approximating $45,000. Mothers had an average of 14.3 years of education; fathers, 15.7 years. Mothers averaged 43.6 years of age at the time of the study; fathers, 46.8 years. Additional descriptive statistics for the adoptive-family sample can be found in Table 2.1.

The second availability sample (the control sample) consisted of fifty non-adopted adolescents in residential treatment and their

Table 2.1
Sample Description

	Category	Adoptive Sample (N=50)		Non-Adoptive Control Sample (N=50)	
		Freq.	Percent	Freq.	Percent
Sex of Child:	Male	26	52.0	31	62.0
	Female	24	48.0	19	38.0
Race of Child:	Black	6	12.0	2	4.0
	White	37	74.0	41	82.0
	Mex. Am	1	2.0	6	12.0
	Nat. Am	4	8.0	0	
	Other	2	4.0	1	2.0
Age of Child:	11	1	2.0	1	2.0
	12	2	4.0	3	6.0
	13	6	12.0	2	4.0
	14	6	12.0	12	24.0
	15	14	28.0	15	30.0
	16	16	32.0	11	22.0
	17	5	10.0	5	10.0
	18	0		1	2.0
	(mean age=14.96)			(mean age=14.90)	

Age at Placement into Adoptive Family:

	Freq.	Percent	
< 1 month	16	32.0	N/A
1-3 months	13	26.0	
4-6 months	7	14.0	
7-9 months	2	4.0	
10-12 months	5	10.0	
13-24 months	4	8.0	
25-36 months	3	6.0	
(median age=approx. 3 months)			

Type of Adoption:

	Freq.	Percent	
Non-Relative, Inracial	41	82.0	N/A
Transracial	6	12.0	
Relative	3	6.0	

Child's Parents Currently Married to Each Other?

	Freq.	Percent	Freq.	Percent
Yes	30	60.0	12	24.0
No	20	40.0	38	76.0

Birth Siblings in the Home?

	Freq.	Percent	Freq.	Percent
Yes	26	52.0	28	56.0
No	24	48.0	22	44.0

Table 2.1 continued

Category	Freq.	Percent	Freq.	Percent
Family Income Range:				
10,000-19,000	5	10.0	2	4.0
20,000-29,000	7	14.0	3	6.0
30,000-39,000	6	12.0	7	14.0
40,000-49,000	4	8.0	1	2.0
50,000 +	18	36.0	8	16.0
Unknown	10	20.0	29	58.0
(median income approx. $45,000)			(med. income app. $35,000)	
Parental Education:				
Mothers	14.3 years		13.5 years	
Fathers	15.7 years		15.4 years	
Parental Age: (at time of study)				
Mothers	43.6 years		39.5 years	
Fathers	46.8 years		42.5 years	

families. Again, every effort was made to interview the father, mother, adolescent, and caseworker for each family. As with the adoptive families, when complete data were not available, analyses were performed using the information that had been collected. Interviews were ultimately completed with twenty-two fathers (four of whom were stepfathers) and twenty-six mothers (including one stepmother), forty-nine adolescents, and forty-eight caseworkers. Reasons for nonparticipation included the following: parental rights had been terminated (ten fathers and ten mothers), parents could not be contacted (twelve fathers and eight mothers), parents refused (two fathers and three mothers), parent was deceased (one father), and equipment failure (three fathers and three mothers). One adolescent did not participate because he ran away from the center and was discharged before an interview could be arranged. Two caseworkers were not interviewed, one who worked with the adolescent who ran away and one because of tape recorder failure.

The control adolescents included thirty-one males and nineteen females, ranging in age from eleven to eighteen (mean age = 14.90). The parents of these adolescents had a median family income of approximately $35,000 per year. Mothers had an average of 13.5 years of education; fathers, 15.4 years. Mothers averaged 39.5 years of age at the time of the study; fathers, 42.5 years. The demographic data on the control families must be considered with caution because of the missing data from parents. It is likely that the income and education figures are high estimates of those attributes in the full sample, since no data were available for the parents whose rights had been terminated by the state. In addition, many control families were only represented by one income resulting from the high incidence of divorce. Additional demographic information on the control families is included in Table 2.1.

Procedure

After receiving written parental consent for participation in the study, staff from each facility scheduled separate interviews with the child, the father, the mother, and the caseworker for each family. All of the children and their caseworkers were interviewed at the treatment facility. Although the majority of interviews with the parents were held during their regular visits to the residential treatment facility, a few families were interviewed by telephone because they lived out-of-state and infrequently visited the center. All interviews were tape recorded and were later transcribed verbatim. Interviews with parents lasted from one to two hours; interviews with children and caseworkers lasted approximately thirty minutes to one hour.

Because of the need for sensitivity in interviewing a clinical population of children and their families, the three co-principal investigators and the two research associates with extensive interview training conducted the interviews (the interviewers had graduate degrees in such fields as child development, psychology, sociology, and social work).

Instruments administered to parents included the interview; the Quality of Marriage Index (Norton, 1983); the Acknowledgment of Differences, Empathy, and Communication scales concerning adoption (Kirk, 1981) (for adoptive parents only); and a demographic questionnaire. Instruments administered to the children included the interview and the Kirk adoption scales (for adopted children only). The caseworkers were also administered an interview.

Instruments

Parent interview. The semi-structured interview, administered separately to mothers and fathers, consisted of questions focusing on the parents' marital history and relationship (including any divorces or remarriages), the family's history, the child's social adjustment in the family and with peers, circumstances leading to the child's institutionalization, parental perceptions of the problems leading to treatment, and recommendations to other parents. In addition, adoptive parents were asked questions concerning the child's birthparents, previous adoptive or foster placements, and how the family has dealt with adoption. A copy of the parent interview schedule can be found in Appendix B.

Child interview. The child interview schedule included items concerning the child's perception of the family history, the circumstances leading to the child's institutionalization, the child's school performance, and the child's relationships with parents, siblings, and peers. In addition, adopted children were asked questions concerning their understanding of adoption, their knowledge of their birthparents, and their reflections about being an adopted child. A copy of the child interview schedule is presented in Appendix C.

Caseworker interview. The caseworker interview schedule included questions about the adolescent's presenting problems, course of treatment, diagnosis, and prognosis. In addition, caseworkers were asked to discuss the adolescent's relationships with his or her parents and peers and how they would assess the role of adoption in the adolescent's disturbance (if applicable). Approximately six weeks after the adolescent's interview, the caseworker was recontacted to assess the impact (if any) that participation in the study had had on the adolescent. A copy of the caseworker interview schedule can be found in Appendix D.

Quality of Marriage Index. The Quality of Marriage Index (QMI) (Norton, 1983) was administered to mothers and fathers separately. The QMI consists of six questions, each of which assesses a global, unidimensional evaluation of the marriage. Five of the items are scored on a 7-point Likert scale (from "very strong disagreement" to "very strong agreement"), and one of the items is scored on a 10-point scale (from "very unhappy" to "very happy"). Thus, total scores can range from a low of 6 to a high of 45. In a factor analysis of a larger scale from which these items were drawn, Norton (1983) reported that all six items that comprise the QMI loaded strongly on the first factor, thus supporting the claim that the scale is unidimensional. The scale was adapted for this project by asking spouses to respond to the items in terms of four time frames: the time they decided to adopt (or have a baby), the time of adoption (or birth), the time when the child started having problems, and now.

Adoption scales. Three scales were adapted from the work of Kirk (1981) in order to assess attitudes of adoptive parents and their children concerning adoption: Acknowledgment of Differences, Empathy, and Communication. The Acknowledgment of Differences (AOD) scale consists of six Kirk items. Two modifications were made in administration of the items. First, responses to the items were elicited on a 4-point Likert scale ("never," "infrequently," "sometimes," "often") rather than the 2-point yes-or-no scale used by Kirk. Second, two sets of responses were requested: as the parents recalled the child's early years and now. Scores on the scale could range from 0 to 18. The Empathy scale included four items drawn from Kirk's work. Finally, a four-item Communication scale from Kirk was administered. As with the AOD scale, the Empathy and Communication scales both used 4-point response options at two points in time. Scores on these two scales ranged from 0 to 12.

Symptom identification. To collect systematic information on the symptoms exhibited by the adolescents in treatment, Klein's (1982) Adolescent Behavior Checklist (ABC) was completed for each adolescent. This instrument consists of eighty-six items designed to differentiate internalizing and externalizing symptom patterns (Klein, 1982). Items included on the scale were derived from factor-analytic studies of symptom checklists (Achenbach, 1966; Achenbach and Edelbrock, 1978). As a result of factor analysis, thirty-three items were found to be indicative of externalization and thirty-three of internalization.

Ideally, the ABC would have been administered to each adolescent's caseworker. However, because of the turnover in employment among caseworkers and other methodological constraints, an alternative approach was used. The behavior problems reported on all interviews for each case (i.e., from the father, mother, adolescent, and caseworker) were listed by a research associate with clinical expertise and coded onto the ABC. These items were then scored according to Klein's procedure in order to determine the number of internalizing and externalizing symptoms. In order to determine the validity of recording behaviors from the interviews, a procedure was used in which the ABC itself was completed by caseworkers for five of the adolescents. The reported behaviors on the ABC were compared with the behaviors that were listed from the interviews. Correlations between the direct ABC reports and the ABC protocols that were completed from the interviews were .83 for externalizing behaviors and .61 for internalizing behaviors. On the basis of these results, and given the methodological constraints noted above, it was decided that the ABC would be completed for each case by scanning all interviews for symptoms and noting them on the form. Interrater reliability for coding the behavior problems in this manner for a subsample of ten cases was .94.

Data Analysis Approach

All the audiotaped interviews were transcribed verbatim, and the text files were stored in a computer for subsequent analysis. Four complementary approaches to analysis of the interview data were used.

First, content analysis of the interviews was undertaken, using the family as the unit of analysis. In this analysis, all pertinent information for each family was reviewed by the research team. Qualitative analysis was undertaken according to the data-management plan outlined by Miles and Huberman (1984). The research team examined family data in order to develop a pattern code. Such pattern codes for qualitative data are difficult to develop in detail ahead of time, as they depend on the emergence of patterns, themes, or constructs from the coded data. Miles and Huberman describe this level of coding as "the analogue to the cluster-analytic and factor-analytic devices used in statistical analysis" (1984, p. 68). Pattern codes were developed through strategies involving frequency counts of cases, clustering of cases in which similar effects appeared or failed to appear, and consideration of further reduction of variables. For example, the data from each family were examined concerning whether difficulties in the parents' marital relationship appeared to play a role in the child's emotional disturbance. The subset of cases in which such problems were found was then further examined for information regarding the specific dynamics of the marital relationships and interactions with other factors, such as parental pathology. Although it is perilously easy to develop a pattern code from a small number of cases, it is the application of the code to succeeding cases and the cross-validation of conclusions with other analytic methods that test the significance and validity of the proposed patterns.

Second, codebooks were developed for the parent, child, and caseworker interviews. Quantitative scales (usually at the ordinal or quasi-interval levels) were developed for most questions on each interview schedule, and interviews were coded independently. Before coding, raters worked together to achieve reliability. Before actual coding began, reliability assessments were made. The average percent agreement achieved across items on the parent interviews was 74.4 percent for adoptive parents and 83.4 percent for control parents. The average percent agreement achieved in the child interviews was 96.0 percent for adopted children and 92.0 percent for control children. The average percent agreement achieved on the caseworker interviews was 82.5 percent for caseworkers of adopted children and 94.9 percent for caseworkers of control adolescents. When discrepancies in coding were noted, agreement was reached through discussion among the members of the research team. Reliability checks and discussions were held throughout the coding process.

Third, a computer software program designed for qualitative analysis was used to search interview protocols for key words, phrases, and combinations of words. This approach was used as an adjunct to the two approaches discussed above. For example, in order to verify that alcoholism was involved in a certain number of cases, the program was asked to search all interviews for the occurrence of related words, such as alcohol, alcoholic, and alcoholism. This approach was also used to explore new hypotheses and to search for specific cases in which certain issues were present. Finally, since up to four interviews were conducted with each family, the perceptions of the different family members were compared in order to examine the degree to which they viewed the family's problems in a similar way.

The data presented in this report are supplemented by case illustrations developed from family members' interviews. In all cases, names and certain characteristics of the families were changed or composite descriptions were used in order to safeguard confidentiality. Quotations appearing in this report have been taken directly from transcripts, with the exception that names were changed.

Limitations

The data from these samples are limited in that they rely on the retrospective recall of children and their parents. Therefore, the account of the child's developing emotional disturbance is subject to the parents' current recall and interpretation of what actually happened. In addition, since many of the parents and children have received mental health services of various kinds over an extended period of time, their accounts are subject to the additional filtering and interpretations of the various professionals with whom they have interacted. In order to counteract this bias, the four participants for each family were individually interviewed. In the report, differences in perceptions of mothers, fathers, adolescents, and caseworkers will be discussed.

The data in this study are also limited in that they are all self-report in nature, relying on interviews and questionnaires. No systematic observations of interaction were made; however, all four participants in each family discussed interactions that had occurred within the family.

This study was exploratory in nature and was not designed to test a representative sample of emotionally disturbed adolescents. Our approach is similar to that recently adopted by Marks (1986), who noted that "the inductive, qualitative, exploratory purpose of this book makes the question of generalizability irrelevant. Exploratory studies are designed to show how a process or pattern of development works, not to indicate its frequency in a given population. The aim is to clarify and illuminate phenomena about which too little is known" (p. 251). Because this study is the first to examine emotional disturbance in adopted adolescents within a broad framework of familial and contextual factors, its primary contribution is to identify important issues so that future research can devote more focused attention to particular factors.

MINNESOTA ADOPTION SAMPLE

Subjects

For purposes of comparison, this study included a third group (the Minnesota sample) of 115 "normal," Anglo, adoptive families whose adolescents were not in treatment. These families had participated in Scarr and Weinberg's study of individual differences in cognitive and personality functioning in both adoptive and biological families (Grotevant, Scarr, and Weinberg, 1977; Scarr and Weinberg, 1978, 1983). All families were interviewed and tested by graduate research assistants between 1974 and 1976. All but eight of the adoptive families included both parents and at least one adopted child. Ten of the adoptive families also had biological children, but none of those children was included in the study. All adopted children were genetically unrelated to their adoptive parents and to each other.

Most of the families were recruited through a mailing sent out by the Minnesota Department of Public Welfare to all families in Minnesota who adopted children between 1953 and 1959. The other third of the sample volunteered for participation after hearing about it through the media or from other participating families.

The mean age of placement of these children into their adoptive homes was 2.6 months. All but six of the children for whom placement data were available were placed by the age of nine months. The children ranged in age from 14.1 to 24.8 (mean age = 18.2). Their adoptive parents had completed some college (on average, 14.9 years of education for fathers and 13.9 years for mothers). Average family income was approximately $25,000 per year (in 1974–76 dollars).

Adoptive families participated in a large battery of cognitive and personality measures. The only data being considered in the present study were from interviews individually administered to each parent and adolescent. Of interest in this study were questions pertaining to the family's experience with adoption. Questions were asked concerning how adoption was typically discussed in the family, what information the adolescent had or wanted to know about his or her birthparents, what kinds of services the family had received or sought for their child or family, and what kinds of problems or difficulties the child had as he or she was growing up.

Each interview was coded from a codebook developed specifically for the present project. Coders were trained before beginning to work with the actual interviews, and reliability was checked and maintained throughout the coding process. Average percent agreement among coders was 90.7 percent for parent interviews and 90.3 percent for child interviews.

Because the Minnesota study had been conducted primarily for the purpose of assessing genetic and environmental sources of variance in intelligence and personality, data were not collected concerning all issues that are included in the framework outlined in Figure 1.1. The material that is most relevant to the present study pertains to the adoption issues. Therefore, a comparison of the findings from the Minnesota sample of normal adoptive families and the two samples of adolescents in treatment will be discussed in terms of adoption issues in Chapter 11.

3

Child Background Factors: Genetic Risk, Prenatal, and Preplacement Factors

Eighteen adopted children (approximately one-third of the sample) were considered at risk before coming into the adoptive family because of genetic, prenatal or preplacement factors. These included such factors as birthparent characteristics that constitute a genetic risk to the offspring, such as schizophrenia; poor prenatal care; drug and alcohol use by the birthmother; and poor and/or multiple preplacement experiences. Five of the control children were considered at risk at birth due to parental schizophrenia or drug usage.

This chapter will provide a review of some of the theoretical issues associated with these genetic and preplacement influences on behavior and will give examples of factors that were identified as having affected the behavior of the children in this study.

GENETIC INFLUENCES

Schizophrenia

Conclusions about the etiology of schizophrenia vary along a continuum of opinions as to whether the disorder can be attributed more directly to genetic or environmental factors. Although few definitive conclusions can be reached about the specific mode of genetic transmission, it is clear that genetics do make an important contribution to schizophrenia (Gottesman and Shields, 1976).

Twin data, adoption data and biochemical data all suggest a genetic component to schizophrenia. The probandwise concordance rates in monozygotic (MZ) twins are almost always higher than those in dizygotic (DZ) twins, and both rates are higher than the population prevalence of schizophrenia. Adoption studies of the biological relatives of schizophrenic individuals (e.g., Heston, 1966; Kety et al., 1968; Kety et al., 1975) and of a small number of MZ twins reared apart show that cultural or social transmission among relatives is inadequate as the sole explanation for the increased frequency of the disorder in biological relatives of schizophrenics. Therefore, some genetic transmission is strongly indicated.

Non-genetic events have also been found to have some influence on the development of schizophrenia. For instance, only about 10 percent of the offspring of schizophrenics can be expected to become schizophrenic; only about 10 percent of schizophrenics are born to a schizophrenic parent (Rutter and Garmezy, 1983); and not all identical co-twins of schizophrenics are both schizophrenic. Thus, identical genotypes do not always lead to identical phenotypes.

The research evidence cited above suggests that genetic and environmental components interact in the development of schizophrenia. Therefore, it is important to consider the possible genetic risk for schizophrenia among the subjects of this study.

In three, possibly four, of the adopted cases there was genetic risk due to schizophrenia in the family background. This was specifically reported in the biological families of three of the adopted children in residential treatment. Two children had birthmothers who were described as being schizophrenic and one child's maternal grandmother was labeled paranoid schizophrenic. The fourth child's birthmother was described as having "mental problems," which may or may not have a hereditary basis. Two of the three children with schizophrenic family members had also been diagnosed schizophrenic, and the third one had been seen by several psychiatrists prior to placement in residential treatment. Schizophrenia was not reported in the adoptive families of any of these subjects. Both parents of one child in the control sample were described as schizophrenic and the child has been diagnosed as schizophrenic, paranoid type.

Caution should be used in labeling birthparents in the adopted sample as schizophrenic because of the ambiguous nature of the diagnosis and the nondefinitive information possessed by the adoptive parents. Three adoptive parents reported the schizophrenia in birthparent families and a caseworker reported that one control child's parents were schizophrenic, but there was no confirmed diagnosis in the data. The adoptive parents' information may have come from the adoption agency report on the birthparents that they received at the time of the child's adoption.

Alcohol Risk Factors

Geneticists have found that there appears to be a high prevalence of alcohol problems among the relatives of alcoholics. In fact, children from alcoholic families are twice as likely to develop alcohol problems as children from non-alcoholic families. Studies have shown that even children with one alcoholic birthparent who were adopted at infancy and raised by non-alcoholic adoptive parents are found to be at high risk for alcoholism (McClearn, 1973). Other research data indicate that some children of alcoholic families can be delinquent and hyperactive and can suffer from an array of psychosomatic complaints. They can be predisposed toward alcoholism either as a result of environmental or hereditary factors or both.

One of the adopted children in the study had an alcoholic birthrelative. The child was described as hyperactive and an alcohol abuser. Six children had adoptive parents who were chemically dependent and five of the six children also have had problems with alcohol or drugs. Of the nineteen control children who had alcoholic or substance-abusing biological parents, seven were identified as substance abusers. Of these seven, three were also described as hyperactive. Of the fifteen control children who were hyperactive, six had substance-abusing parents.

The potential contribution of genetic factors should not be underestimated, especially given the high level of parental pathology in the control group (see Chapter 5 for further discussion). In the adoptive group, genetic contributions to intelligence and personality (Scarr and Kidd, 1983) set the stage for the goodness-of-fit between adoptive parents and child.

As one adoptive father stated,

> I really believe it's genetic. It's kind of like you get a roughed-out marble statue that, if it's a statue of a bird, you're not going to make it a ship. You've got a bird here, now we need a little work on getting the wings honed down. And I believe that how you can channel those traits can be impacted by environment and discipline. . . . I think in her case, she came from the womb with some medical traits, and it just made it danged difficult to hone those wings. It's like you could never get your file on them because she wouldn't let you.

PRENATAL AND BIRTH FACTORS

Fetal Alcohol Syndrome

One of the children in the adopted sample was described as being born with fetal alcohol syndrome, another prenatal environmental risk that may influence later behavior. The syndrome, which occurs only in cases of heavy maternal drinking, is characterized by prenatal and postnatal growth deficiency and an altered pattern of morphogenesis, including craniofacial abnormalities, frequent joint and limb anomalies, and possible cardiac defect. These physical symptoms are also accompanied by delayed development and mental deficiency (Little, 1979). Maternal alcohol consumption may cause various disorders associated with the mental development of the children, ranging from cerebral palsy to attention-deficit syndromes in children with normal intelligence (Gal and Sharpless, 1984).

The adopted child in the study suspected of having fetal alcohol syndrome never wanted to be held as a baby and has now been diagnosed as hyperactive. She has severe auditory processing problems and borderline personality. Her parents attribute her poor behavioral control to fetal alcohol syndrome. Although her current behavior is consistent with the sequelae of fetal alcohol syndrome, the etiology of her problem most likely involves a complex interaction of variables over time, one of which is fetal alcohol syndrome.

Any chemical that crosses the placenta can affect the fetus. Many drugs cross the placenta and have much more powerful effects on the fetus than on the mother because of the fetus's immature development and because its small size and blood supply allow a drug to attain higher concentrations than in the mother. Chronic drug usage during pregnancy increases the chances that the fetus will become physically dependent. Mothers who are drug dependent may have babies that exhibit nervous-system disorganization (Dinges, Davis, and Glass, 1980; Newman and Newman, 1984).

According to a control mother, "I was using drugs during my pregnancy and my doctor feared that he [her child] would be addicted at birth. However, although he weighed only about six pounds when he was born, he seemed normal." The child's caseworker too confirms this assessment. According to him, "The problems which led to his placement in residential treatment are more related to adolescent and family adjustment issues than to drug use by the birthmother."

Data on birthmothers are based solely on the adoptive parents' recall of information that adoption workers may have provided at least thirteen years ago. Therefore, it is impossible to know for certain how many children in the adopted sample might have been affected by maternal drug usage. Similarly, it is also unlikely that birthmothers in general would necessarily be totally honest with agency personnel about drug usage.

Poor Prenatal Care

There are many ways in which the emotional state of a pregnant woman can physically affect the development of her fetus. Strong emotions can cause cortisone, adrenaline, and other hormones to be released into the mother's blood stream. These can, in turn, pass through the placenta and affect the fetus (Thompson, 1957). Several studies have focused on the behavioral consequences of prenatal stress (e.g., Huttenen and Niskanen, 1978; Sontag, 1966; Turner, 1956). These studies demonstrate a relationship between increased maternal emotionality during pregnancy and the increased incidence of irritability, hyperactivity, and other behavioral problems among offspring.

The mother's emotional state is also likely to affect the mechanical aspects of the birth process itself. It has been found that pregnant women who scored high on various measures of anxiety later experienced more complications of delivery and had more children with congenital abnormalities than did women who scored low in anxiety (Davids and DeVault, 1962; Davids, DeVault, and Talmadge, 1961). An adoptive mother in the sample suggested that her child's problems were attributed to "womb rejection." She felt that the birthmother was so troubled about her pregnancy that she somehow transmitted her negative feelings toward the child while still in the womb. Although it is impossible to measure or validate this phenomenon, it is feasible that a mother contemplating relinquishment is under a great deal of stress and may try to resolve her ambivalence by denying positive feelings for the baby. Moreover, the mother under stress can be more inclined to engage in one or more behaviors that are pathogenic to a developing fetus, such as smoking, alcohol consumption, and improper attention to nutrition and medical appointments.

Adoptive parents of one of the children in the sample suggested that their child's problems were most likely caused by the birthmother having received poor prenatal care. This is not surprising, as many of the birthmothers may have tried to hide the pregnancy as long as they could, and economic constraints of single birthmothers may have caused them to fail to seek adequate prenatal care.

Maternal malnutrition has been found to have an impact on fetal development and is most likely to be evidenced by low birth weight. These babies have a higher rate of infant mortality, more postnatal complications, and a higher risk of mental or motor impairment than do babies who are of average weight for their gestational age (Winick, 1974). Malnutrition can cause a child to be born with fewer brain cells than normal, a deficit that can never be made up. However, research reports suggest that some of the effects of malnutrition can be offset after birth depending on the array of resources and opportunities available to the child (Newman and Newman, 1984). Moreover, although not specifically mentioned in reference to a child in this study, adolescent birthmothers are often less likely to receive adequate medical and nutritional supervision during pregnancy and are more likely to experience complications during pregnancy. According to reports of the adoptive parents, the majority of birthmothers in this study had received average to good prenatal care, had no pregnancy and delivery problems, and their babies were over six pounds at birth.

Despite the presence of these genetic and prenatal risk factors, it is unlikely that disturbance in adolescence could be traced to them in any linear or straightforward way (Sameroff and Chandler, 1975; Sameroff and Seifert, 1983). All adolescents in this study were exposed to multiple risk factors at various times in childhood, and a key purpose of this book is to explicate the many potential interacting factors that affected their development.

PREPLACEMENT FACTORS

Twelve of the adopted children in the study had experienced preplacement problems, including multiple and poor placements prior to the adoption, neglect, malnutrition, abuse, and feelings of instability within the foster-home situation. In considering how these early experiences may have influenced the children's later development, insight is probably best garnered from the literature on the long-term consequences of early experiences in general. One of the most compelling issues in the field of developmental psychology relates to the supposition of enduring influences of early experience. The assumption is that the accumulation of early life experiences, beginning in infancy, is critical for and determinative of later development. The effect of stress events on the developmental process and on subsequent functioning is of central interest here. It is also one of the most difficult phenomena to investigate rigorously, if only because of the problems of separating the effects of early events from those of later events (Rutter, 1980).

There is a paucity of data concerning the effects of stress events in general or more specifically neglect/abuse on either the developmental process or later functioning (Rutter, 1983). Traditionally, attention has been focused on the direct effects of adverse experiences in leading to overt disorder; however, the indirect effects of stressors are equally important. Thus, early events may operate indirectly through their action in altering sensitivities to stress or in modifying styles of coping (Rutter, 1983).

Several studies have shown that adverse experiences of various kinds can substantially increase the risk of psychiatric disorder in childhood (Rutter, 1981b). However, most of these studies refer to rather chronic and long-lasting adversities involved in prolonged family discord, such as the long-term parental rejection, neglect, or abuse experienced by the other two groups of subjects mentioned above. Increasing attention is given now to the subtly interacting conditions that work in combination, either to attenuate the effects of otherwise powerful antecedents or to turn a minor developmental crisis into a life catastrophe (Sameroff, 1975). Many midstream events take place in a child's life that alter the effects of early experiences; therefore, clear prediction of antecedent-consequence relationships is difficult at best.

Impact of Multiple Placements

Rutter's (1979, 1981a) reassessment of maternal deprivation suggests some consistent findings with regard to stressful early life experiences that are associated with separation from significant caregivers. One of those consistent findings is that multiple foster-home and institutional placements in early childhood can contribute significantly to the development of later psychopathic and antisocial behavior. The source of privations to which children may be subjected in poor institutions and poor placements requires study in order to learn about the specific effects of specific early life experiences on development.

In the recent studies of the stressors that affect children, greater emphasis is being placed on contextual situational factors. Outcomes are seen as dependent upon the interactions the child has with significant adults in the environment (Garmezy, 1983).

Bretherton (1980) has hypothesized that a young child who must continually reorganize his or her security-regulating system may become unwilling to engage in this task yet again, leading to the inability to form a loving relationship with anyone. Infants remaining at an Athens home for infants and children waiting for adoption placement beyond one year of age typically developed problems in relationships with adults (Dontas et al., 1985). Changes in staff and therefore in principal attachment figures are inevitable, and some children may eventually become unable or reluctant to enter into new attachment relationships.

There has been no systematic study of transitions from one attachment figure to another. Also, there are no data relating the quality of an infant's attachment to a foster parent to the ease with which an attachment to an adoptive parent is made or to the type of relationship that develops between infant and adoptive parent (Dontas et al., 1985).

Five children in the study had been in multiple placements before being adopted. Two of the five had been moved repeatedly back and forth between birthparents and foster parents before finally being placed in an adoptive setting. Children who had been in several preplacement environments often exhibited very rejecting distrusting behavior when finally placed for adoption. They were reluctant to become close to anyone and seemed to expect rejection. A caseworker described one of the children as follows:

> Mary, now 18 years old, was placed into her adoptive home at the age of four months. Her birthparents were unmarried and in their early 20's. She was relinquished for adoption at birth, but was placed in three foster homes before finally being adopted. Her adoption had been delayed because she cried all the time due to a milk allergy. She was a very difficult baby to care for, and after about a month her foster parents would ask to have her removed and she would have to be replaced in another home. The quality of physical care in these homes is presumed to have been acceptable. However, the frequent moves are thought to have contributed to her difficult temperament. Her adoptive parents found her to be a very active, non-cuddly baby who cried a lot. When she was older, she wouldn't do her school work. She ran away several times. She never ever really learned to love and trust anyone.

As the child's resolution of this early trust-mistrust conflict is an interactional phenomenon, the relationship between the infant and the caregiver is paramount. A mutual matching of needs and responses in repeated interactions determines whether trust or mistrust develops. Constant, reliable care promotes the baby's sense of trust, enabling the infant to learn to tolerate frustrations and to delay immediate gratification. If a baby's needs are not consistently met, he or she can develop a sense of mistrust and will react to frustration with anxiety and upset.

If a baby does not receive an appropriate response to his or her needs, or if the caregiver is unusually harsh in responding to the infant's needs, he or she may become doubtful about the trustworthiness of the environment. Also babies tend to feel the power of their own anger and may doubt their own lovableness as they "encounter the violence of their own capacity for anger" (Newman and Newman, 1984, p. 113). Babies whose physical and emotional needs are not met or who perceive their environment as inconsistent, painful, or threatening may develop a sense of mistrust and may exhibit symptoms of depression and grief. Babies who are abused can begin to feel unworthy or unloved.

Adaptation and Attachment Issues

The transactional view that mother and baby are reciprocal actors in the process of development has made an important and necessary contribution to the study of attachment relationships. It is clear that infant characteristics such as temperament play an important role in the quality of attachment that takes place (Rutter, 1979). The importance of this relationship has been affirmed by Crockenberg (1981) in an evaluation of the complex relationships among 1) temperament ratings of infant irritability in the first weeks of life; 2) maternal responsiveness to infant distress signals at three months of age; 3) infant attachment to mother as adduced from the strange situation at one year of age; and 4) the magnitude of stress upon the mother and her availability of support from the spouse, older children, and others at that one-year mark. Results indicate that lack of social support for mothers is associated with unresponsiveness to irritable infants' distress signals at three months and to anxious attachment in these infants at one year.

The complexity of the interactions among infant temperament, maternal responsiveness, maternal stress, and available social supports offers important clues regarding both risks and protective factors that can interact to influence the subsequent adaptation of the infant. Although not specifically studied in this research, the father's presence and the degree of support and intimacy he can provide point to another potentially protective factor that requires research. The father's behavior too can markedly modify, enhance, or disrupt the child's adaptation to mother and others (Lamb, 1981).

Adaptation, as used in Ainsworth's (1984) "developmental mental health" model, focuses on how well or how poorly development equips individuals to cope with the impact of their environments. Waters and Sroufe (1983) suggest that from a developmental perspective the notion of a good outcome needs both proximate and ultimate criteria. For instance, avoidance of an attachment figure in infancy may be adaptive in the short term because it may be the best the child can do under the circumstances, and it helps the infant cope with the anxiety and conflict resulting from parental rejection. However, it may be deleterious in the long term, since it is likely that an anxious avoidant attachment to a parent will operate against the formation of affectional bonds in later relationships.

Attachment issues of children in the study are exemplified in the following quotation from a caseworker:

> He was malnourished when he came into the adoptive family. He had been with caretakers for twenty-two months. Although this was not the best arrangement, he had made an attachment. He suffered a loss when he was removed and he was too young to talk about it. He's never been able to reattach to this other family. He's been battling them. We theorize that when he begins to attach, his body sends him messages and he has feelings that aren't describable in terms of words and then he gets back into fighting the enemy. His family is the enemy. His adoptive family had to put him in a foster home. He couldn't make it there so he was sent to another foster family — then to a hospital and later to two different treatment centers.

Recent theoretical work has tended to focus on the optimal resolution of the salient task of developing an attachment relationship with the caregiver and has described the secure pattern as that which promotes competence. However, the examination of maltreated infants illuminates the variability and range of behavioral outcomes that may emerge. The maltreated infant may develop certain organized modes of responding to the caregiver that would serve to reduce the likelihood of subsequent abuse and/or neglect. Similarly, the maltreating caregiver may adopt certain caregiving styles that minimize the degree of contact with the child and/or serve to fulfill basic obligatory functions without incorporating any emotional or affectionate involvement. The adaptive significance of the patterning of attachment behaviors adopted by the avoidant infant, for example, needs to be considered independently of the expectations for what may be the optimal or most-competent solution (i.e., achieving a secure attachment relationship) to this developmental task. It therefore becomes important to distinguish between a behavioral outcome that is typically defined as competent (i.e., secure attachment) and an outcome that may be adaptive for the maltreated infant (i.e., avoidance of the caregiver). A central question for developmental theory then becomes whether the use of alternative pathways for resolving stage-salient tasks predisposes the infant to current or subsequent adaptation or maladaptation across behavioral domains (i.e., cognitive, social, emotional) (Schneider-Rosen et al., 1985).

The results of Schneider-Rosen and colleagues (1985) suggest that the adaptive resolution of the attachment relationship for the maltreated child (i.e., anxious/avoidant) does not necessarily promote concurrent adaptive resolution of other developmental issues. The child may use alternative pathways in later tasks and make himself or herself more vulnerable to difficulties in accomplishing these subsequent tasks (Schneider-Rosen, et al., 1985). For example, children who must adapt to many different and possibly aversive environments (foster homes, abusive families etc.) may have problems in handling later developmental tasks.

In this study, the twelve children who were at risk before coming to the adoptive home because of preplacement factors ranged in age from 2.5 months to thirty-six months at the time of adoptive placement. Eight had been neglected and four had been abused by either their birthparents and/or their foster parents. One of the abused-before-adoption children was identified by his adoptive parents as hyperactive, and three were referred to as "elbow babies" because they pushed away from their parents and did not want to be held or cuddled (see Chapter 4 for discussion). One of these children was subsequently abused by the adoptive family. This discontinuity of experience places the early maltreatment in a different light than that experienced by either the adopted subjects maltreated by their adoptive parents or the control group children. In the control families, there were twenty-five cases of abuse and neglect: fifteen cases of abuse without neglect, six of neglect without abuse, and four more cases combining abuse and neglect.

The following case illustrates some of the adjustment problems experienced by an adopted child who was neglected prior to the adoption:

> Robert, now 15, was adopted at the age of 13 months. The son of a fifteen year old birthmother, Robert weighed about five pounds at birth. He stayed with his fifteen year old birthmother for the first few days of his life. Robert's maternal grandparents pressured his birthmother into relinquishing him for adoption so that she might complete her education. He was placed in a foster home for thirteen months while the agency worker searched for a family that would be willing to send him to college. However, during this time, he was malnourished and neglected by this foster family. He was anemic at the time of his adoptive placement. Problems first arose when

Robert was two years old. He was extremely destructive and rebellious, and would not respond to discipline. His parents put him in a therapeutic program when he was five. He used to break out windows, and knock holes in walls at home and away from home. He also ran away repeatedly.

Adopted children in the study who had been in several preplacement environments often exhibited very rejecting distrusting behavior when finally placed in adoptive homes. They were reluctant to become close to anyone and seemed to expect rejection. A caseworker described one of the children as follows:

James, age 17, lived with his 18 year old unemployed birthmother during the first eleven months of his life. His mother was abusive to him and on two occasions fractured his skull. She suffered a mental breakdown. James was taken away from his mother and placed in foster care for three weeks where he was presumably neglected. At the age of one year, James was adopted. He was unable to crawl or walk. The adoptive parents described him as being very aggressive and very difficult to handle. At the age of four, James attacked another child. At seven, he was sent to see a psychologist because he cursed out the teachers at school. Once he even tore the door down to his brother's room. The parents had to change all the locks on the bedrooms in their house to keep him out. His parents and the school staff tried all kinds of discipline from spanking to psychological rewards, nothing worked.

CONCLUSION

Although it is impossible to make a definitive statement that the genetic, prenatal, or preplacement issues identified in this section were responsible for the later emotional problems that eighteen children in the sample experienced, we can suggest that these factors placed the children at high risk for eventual problems. Since children with schizophrenic and alcoholic parents are at greater risk for developing these same problems, adoption agencies should prepare families for these possibilities and to be able to detect early signs so that appropriate treatment can be sought. Moreover, as the information that agencies provide adoptive parents on their child's genetic history is generally dependent solely on the honesty of birthparents' revelations about their family history and their own behavior, agencies must select adoptive families who are flexible enough to accept unanticipated problems that may have been genetically transmitted.

The emotional state of the birthmother during pregnancy might also influence the physical development of the fetus and can determine the likelihood of her seeking appropriate prenatal care. Limited economic resources, immaturity, and stress associated with the pregnancy can influence the type of prenatal care as well as the quality of nutrition the mother receives during her pregnancy. Although the majority of birthmothers in this study were reported to have received good prenatal care, each of these factors should be carefully assessed during the birthmother counseling process. Birthmothers should be advised about the relationship between maternal emotional and physical health and that of the developing fetus.

Stressful life experiences associated with multiple placements also can influence the child's early adaptation and attachment to the adoptive family. It is essential that adoption and foster-care agencies minimize the possibility of children being repeatedly moved while awaiting a permanent home. Also, adoptive parents must be prepared to handle the rejecting, distrusting behaviors often exhibited by children who have experienced early maternal deprivation or maltreatment. These children may be struggling with their experiences of the past, a new family situation, and feelings of loss, which may result in developmental delays and an inability to conform to the expectations of adoptive parents. Mental health professionals must also become aware of these sources of potential conflict and strain in the family situation and address these issues in treatment.

4

Early Childhood Factors and the Development of Parent-Child Compatibility

This chapter focuses on the development of compatibility, or goodness-of-fit, within the parent-child relationship from infancy into adolescence. Lamb and Gilbride (1985) have defined a compatible parent-child relationship as one in which the behaviors of the partners are well meshed, such that communication between them is efficient and accurate. Although parent-infant interaction is a reciprocal process involving the contributions of both parent and infant, a key determinant of the success of the early parent-infant relationship is the sensitivity of the parent to the infant's signals and needs (Lamb and Gilbride, 1985).

A number of the children in both the adoptive and control samples were described by their parents as having had problematic behavioral styles involving either hyperactivity or avoidance of contact since early childhood. In addition, several children were identified by their parents as having physical problems that contributed to their subsequent difficulties. Presumably, such problems could set the stage for interactional difficulties within the family that, without intervention, might grow into major problems over a period of years.

HYPERACTIVITY

Hyperactivity, currently classified in the *Diagnostic and Statistical Manual of Mental Disorders* (DSM-III) (American Psychiatric Association, 1980) as Attention Deficit Disorder (ADD) with hyperactivity, is generally defined as a developmental disorder characterized by inattention, impulsivity, and excessive activity level. It arises in infancy or early childhood, has pervasive influence across a number of domains of functioning, and is not the direct result of general intellectual retardation, severe language delay, or emotional disturbance (Barkley, 1982). The disorder is ten times more common in boys than in girls and is estimated to affect at least 3 to 5 percent of the population.

Although many theories concerning the etiology of hyperactivity have been proposed, it is generally agreed that hyperactivity is a heterogeneous disorder with multiple developmental pathways (Paternite and Loney, 1980; Sroufe and Jacobvitz, 1987). Regardless of etiology, hyperactivity greatly affects many domains of the child's functioning and presents serious challenges for family adaptation.

Several studies suggest that the presence of an ADD child in a family is associated with other aspects of family stress and dysfunction; however, the direction of effects is not clear. For instance, Delameter, Lahey, and Drake (1981) found that learning-disabled ADD children came from families characterized by a significant amount of psychosocial stress including marital separation, illness, alcoholism, and child abuse. Other studies (Ackerman, Elardo, and Dykman, 1979; Cohen and Minde, 1983) have similarly noted associations between family disorganization and hyperactivity. Child characteristics may contribute to these family stressors, and these family problems may in turn exacerbate symptoms in hyperactive children. The parents of ADD children also report less confidence in their parenting knowledge, and mothers report more social isolation and more stress associated with the mother-child relationship (Mash and Johnston, 1983). The causal network of these family patterns appears to be quite complex, and the contribution of genetics is suspected yet unknown.

In an attempt to circumvent the difficulties inherent in drawing causal inferences from correlational and retrospective studies, Jacobvitz and Sroufe (in press) conducted a prospective longitudinal study examining the early caregiver-child relationship in thirty-four children who were considered hyperactive by kindergarten age and thirty-four matched controls. They predicted that ADD may stem, in part, from the child's difficulty in modulating or regulating his or her own arousal level to meet situational demands (Douglas and Peters, 1979) and that early parental behavior with the child may exacerbate this problem. Consistent with their prediction, caregivers of hyperactive kindergartners (in comparison with controls) scored significantly higher on the scale of Maternal Interference when the child was six months of age and scored higher on the scale of Overstimulating Care in a teaching task administered when the child was forty-two months of age. Although these data do not rule out other contributing factors, they do point to the potential importance of the early parent-child relationship in the development of hyperactivity.

Although the primary symptoms of hyperactivity may decrease as the child gets older, many secondary problems develop or worsen during adolescence. For example, hyperactive adolescents appear to be at risk for serious academic difficulties, as well as for legal encounters resulting from their antisocial, aggressive acts. They also appear to have frequent feelings of sadness, low self-esteem, and lower expectations of future success (Milich and Loney, 1979).

Findings are beginning to emerge that suggest that variables related to the child's aggressiveness predict, to varying degrees, outcomes in adolescence for hyperactive youngsters. For example, Weiss, Minde, Werry, Douglas, and Nemeth (1971) found that ratings of aggression and family pathology (poor mother-child relationships, poor mental health of parents, and punitive child-rearing practices) at referral were significantly related to overt antisocial behaviors at follow-up. Parenting variables, including parental consistency, firmness, and respect for the child, also differentiated the improved from unimproved learning disabled/hyperactive children in the Kauai longitudinal study (Werner and Smith, 1977). Milich and Loney (1979) also concluded that aggression and concomitant parenting and environ-mental variables appear to be much more powerful predictors of adolescent outcomes than is the degree of hyperactivity itself. Thus, the child's hyperactivity is seen as taxing the family's adaptive resources, and the developmental sequelae of this behavior in adolescence will depend on the manner in which the child's family and other socializing agents have responded (Sroufe and Jacobvitz, 1987).

In order for a child to be coded as hyperactive in the present study, at least one person interviewed about the child must have used the word *hyperactive* in describing the child, stated that the child was labeled or diagnosed as hyperactive by a professional, or indicated that the child had been placed on Ritalin or other medication for treatment of hyperactivity. Almost equal numbers of cases of hyperactivity were reported in the adoptive (sixteen cases) and control (fifteen cases) families ($\chi^2(1) = 0.05$, ns).

The presence of hyperactivity covaried with several other early childhood factors in the adoptive sample. Hyperactivity tended to occur more frequently than expected by chance in combination with physical problems ($\chi^2(1) = 14.49$, p < .001), incompatibility ($\chi^2(1) = 4.07$, p < .05), and learning problems ($\chi^2(1) = 5.65$, p < .05). It occurred less frequently than expected in combination with preplacement history problems. The positive covariation with physical and learning problems suggests that, in these cases, the hyperactivity may have been part of a larger syndrome of problematic behavior. The covariation with incompatibility highlights the difficulty that some adoptive parents had adapting to the child's behavior (see below). The negative covariation with problematic preplacement history suggests that early experiences of abuse or neglect did not seem to play a role in the subsequent development of hyperactivity.

The frustration of trying to adapt to the child's hyperactive behavior was noted by several adoptive parents. For example, one adoptive mother noted, "She can't sit still long. Once upon a time, she was on medication, the early part of her life. She always demands attention."

Another adoptive mother stated,

> He was a colicky baby and I knew all the stories about colic, but I think I caused it by being so nervous. Because I would hold him out here. I was scared I was going to crush him. I couldn't cuddle him like a mother ought to be able to do. . . . That's when I started noticing [his hyperactivity], when he was about two he was very hyper. . . . [When he started kindergarten,] he was put on medication. He went through the ritalins and the dexadrines and the testing and the special classes and the whole route. Some of them helped . . . but then after awhile they all fell through for one reason or another.

An adoptive father stated,

> Ever since we first got her, she's been hyperactive. . . . That was our biggest problem. She was just the one to be constantly, whenever you turned around she was always into something and that was, she's always been pretty much that way. Just nervous, wanting to be doing something no matter what you were doing. She'd want to be doing it faster or doing it more.

"ELBOW BABIES"

A second adaptational challenge is faced by families when the emotional and behavioral responsiveness of their infant is deficient. We have called such infants "elbow babies" because of the description given about the mother of one of the adopted children in the study. The child's caseworker stated, "She's just a mother who has wanted to be a mother to this boy from the very beginning. She feels real strongly that he never let her. She describes him as an 'elbow baby' — one who pushed away from infancy." The most typical behavior associated with this pattern involved the child's actively pushing away from contact beginning at an early age.

For children who were placed in their adoptive homes in later infancy, attachment theory provides a useful framework in which the "elbow baby" pattern can be considered (see Chapter 1). Evidence from maternal-deprivation research suggests that when the environment of infancy includes no caregivers sufficiently available to respond to an infant's proximity-promoting behavior, the infant fails to become attached to anyone. And, if this state of affairs endures long enough (eighteen to twenty-four months can be sufficient), it is subsequently difficult for a child to become attached even when a responsive caregiver is available (Ainsworth, 1984). Current research evidence suggests a substantial degree of continuity of infant attachment patterns into early childhood, with the implication that anxious patterns once established tend to persist unless there is some major change in the environment that brings about a major shift in the organization of the attachment system (Waters, 1978).

The maltreated infant may develop certain organized modes of responding to the caregiver (such as disengagement or avoidance) that would serve to reduce the likelihood of subsequent abuse and/or neglect. Similarly, the maltreating caregiver may adopt certain caregiving styles that minimize the degree of contact with the child and/or serve to fulfill the basic obligatory functions without incorporating any emotional or affectionate involvement.

Thus, several possible pathways may lead to the "elbow baby" pattern. For children adopted in early infancy, the child's temperament and the adoptive parents' responsiveness may play a key role. For later-adopted children, their preplacement history and its effect on their primary attachments must be considered.

The "elbow baby" pattern was noted in ten of the adoptive cases in the present study, and, interestingly, in none of the control cases ($\chi^2(1)$ = 11.11, p < .001). One adoptive mother recalled,

> My feelings about him? I felt a little bit unglued because he didn't seem to want to be held. Even coming from the hospital home, he wanted always to be in the bed or left alone. All my other babies have been cuddled and wanted it. He never seemed to want it. . . . He did not like to be picked up. [How did that make you feel?] Made me feel rejected. Like I was doing something wrong. [What was your relationship like during those early years?] Well, I think I must have pushed him aside a little bit because he pushed me aside. I feel in my heart that the little mother that had him must not have wanted him very badly, and I feel that the child even as a fetus must have felt that. I feel that's why he rejected love and attention from us, because he felt so rejected from birth.

Half of the ten adopted children described as "elbow babies" were placed in their adoptive homes before six weeks of age, several of them directly from the hospital to the adoptive family. Thus, possible confounding factors involving poor-quality foster homes or rejecting birthparents can most likely be ruled out in these cases. Parents reported that the child hated being cuddled from the beginning, never liked to be held, or was always headstrong.

This pattern of child behavior might be a reflection of genetically based temperamental styles. In defining temperament, Campos, Barrett, Lamb, Goldsmith, and Stenberg (1983) stated that the construct "refers to individual differences in the intensive and temporal parameters of behavioral expressions of emotionality and arousal, especially as these differences influence the organization of intrapersonal and interpersonal processes" (p. 832). Implicit in this definition is the notion that such behavioral differences have important consequences for interaction and the development of relationships. An alternative hypothesis is that this child behavior may reflect effects of the prenatal care of the birthmother or the developing child's prenatal environment (e.g., prenatal exposure to alcohol or drugs, high doses of obstetrical medication, etc.).

In the other five cases, the child was placed later in the adoptive home, between 2.5 and twenty-two months of age. In four of these five cases, information was given concerning abuse or neglect that the child had experienced in a foster home or, in one case, poor prenatal care by the birthmother. Thus, although the behavioral manifestations of the "elbow baby" pattern appeared similar, the etiology of the pattern appears to have varied across these ten adopted children as a function of their placement history. In the cases of the early-adopted children, the pattern may reflect a temperamental tendency or style on the part of the child. In the cases of the later-adopted children, it is likely that the behavioral pattern evolved in response to poor quality interactional environments (which may, of course, have been elicited by temperamental characteristics of the infant). The behavior of some of these children resembles the "anxious-avoidant" attachment styles described by Ainsworth and colleagues (Ainsworth, Blehar, Waters, and Wall, 1978). Rather than apply this label to the early relationship on the basis of the information available, however, we prefer instead to use the "elbow baby" characterization to be descriptive of the child's behavior.

The fact that none of the control families reported behaviors resembling the "elbow baby" pattern suggests one of four possible explanations: adoptive parents as a group may have different expectations of their babies than do biological parents. Adoptive parents are well aware that their babies are different from them genetically, and they might be very sensitive to perceiving behavioral differences as they begin interacting with the child. When differences are noted, especially troublesome differences such as pushing away from contact, adoptive parents might attribute the cause of such behavior to the child's background or to the child himself rather than take any responsibility for the behavior. Biological parents, on the other hand, know that the child is theirs genetically and are not so easily able to attribute blame for the problems outside the family.

Second, parents in the control group were also more highly stressed with personal and marital problems (e.g., mental illness, alcoholism, divorce) than were the adoptive parents. Focus on their own problems could have deflected their attention from their children's problems and resulted in reduced reporting of atypical child behavior.

A third possible explanation was offered by Klein (1982), who also noted the "elbow baby" phenomenon in his sample of adopted and non-adopted children in psychiatric treatment.

Many adoptive mothers have commented on their difficulty in comforting and snuggling their child. The infant has been characterized as stiff and rigid, as well as hungry and difficult to satisfy. These reactions appear more common in women who have later born their own children and look back from that perspective. Such reactions may betray feelings of inadequacy. They may also reflect the absence of pregnancy and the birth experience and the attunement and sense of ownership which may arise from them. [P. 85]

In order to test his hypothesis that the elbow baby phenomenon is because of mothers' comparisons with their own biological children, the frequencies of children noted as elbow babies were compared for families in which the adoptive parents did or did not have biological children as well (see Table 4.1). Contrary to Klein's observation, no association was found ($\chi^2 = 0.41$, ns).

A fourth possible explanation that could account for these data is that the "elbow baby" behaviors may have simply been underreported in the control group. Since a number of the control parents were not available for interview because parental rights had been terminated, we might not have had access to information concerning this pattern.

PHYSICAL PROBLEMS

Other characteristics of children can affect the development of compatibility within the parent-child relationship. Six of the adopted children and four of the control children in the sample showed evidence of serious and/or prolonged physical illnesses that appeared to tax the coping resources of the family system. Research concerning handicapping conditions of children has shown that physical

Table 4.1

Frequencies of Adopted Children Noted as "Elbow Babies" in Families in Which Parents Do or Do Not Have Biological Children

		Presence of Biological Children		
		No	Yes	Total
"Elbow Baby"	Yes	3	7	10
	No	19	21	40
	Total	22	28	50

$\chi^2 = 0.41$, ns.

disabilities can result in hostility and poor self-concept on the part of the child and anxiety and troubled marriages within the broader family system (Miller, 1978).

In two of the adoptive families affected by children's physical problems, children were described as having been sickly as babies. Joan's mother said that "she came down with Salmonella when she was six months old and had water faucet diarrhea for two years. Whenever she had any illness, it was not just an illness, it was major." She had to be hospitalized several times as a baby because of dehydration following illness. Her parents later divorced, and then her father died.

Ronnie, another adopted child, was described by his mother in this way:

> Ronnie was a very sick baby, sick all the time. I spent a good share of my nights and days holding him because if he was warm and against me he was all right. All through there, there was a lot of conflict and trouble and Ronnie didn't talk at all. He didn't hear, which I later on felt very guilty about, because I figured I should have picked up on it and didn't. It was because of all the ear infections; he didn't speak until three.

At the entrance to kindergarten, Ronnie had an 80 percent hearing loss in both ears. His mother holds herself responsible for not being sufficiently aware and attentive to his problems.

Four families in the control group were faced with physical problems of their children. For example, Fred's family has had to deal with his diabetes since he was very young. Fred himself stated that he would "get fed up with it and sneak out of my room in the middle of the night and take sugar stuff." When his sugar levels were off, his father noted that behavioral changes would follow. "Whenever he had a day where his sugar levels were extremely high, you could predict that we were going to run a series of three or four days where he was going to humiliate kids. He was going to get them so mad that they wanted to kill him. And he would spend several days in detention or get expelled. . . . His sister has always been the child you can count on." (However, the sister is now acting out since the brother is in residential treatment.) Fred's mother stated, "He was stealing from me and buying candy and had put himself in a coma a couple of times." He tried to falsify the results of his sugar tests in order to be able to eat more sugar.

In another family, the child had had thirteen or fourteen operations before he was thirteen years old. He missed a great deal of school because of illness and repeated hospitalizations. Although he was diagnosed as borderline dyslexic and borderline hyperactive, the conditions were not considered serious enough by school authorities to warrant special services.

The examples illustrate major additional stresses with which some of the families in the sample have had to cope over extended periods of time. Research on handicapped children (e.g., Kazak, 1986) has shown that the adequate care of the child demands restructuring of role demands for all family members.

It is very likely that handicaps or chronic illnesses of children would tax the adaptive powers of even the most flexible and understanding of families. The divorce rate among married couples with handicapped children has been estimated to be as high as twice the rate in the general population (Tew, Payne, and Laurence, 1974). There appears to be a positive, linear relation between the severity of the handicap and the degree of marital stress (Tew and Laurence, 1975). However, the degree to which the handicap is experienced as stressful depends on the family's support network, which may serve as a buffering resource (e.g., Cochran and Brassard, 1979).

PARENT-CHILD COMPATIBILITY

As discussed in Chapter 1, Goodness-of-Fit theory predicts that development is optimized when there is a good match or fit between the characteristics of the developing child and the child's physical and social environment. Consistent with attachment theory, goodness-of-fit theory states that when infants are raised by parents who understand them and are sensitive to their needs, development will be optimized. When parents are not able to accommodate the needs of their children, mismatch problems can occur.

Lamb and Gilbride (1985) have defined a compatible parent-child relationship as one in which the behaviors of the partners are well meshed, such that communication between them is efficient and accurate. Although parental sensitivity is a key determinant, compatibility is viewed as a joint product of the characteristics of the child, the characteristics of the parents, and the family's social situation (Lamb and Gilbride, 1985). The characteristics of parents and children are not static; both change in dynamic responsiveness to one another. Goodness-of-fit, then, involves both the family members' ability to attain this state and their ability to retain it through dynamic interaction over time (Lamb and Gilbride, 1985).

Compatibility develops as a joint function of the characteristics of the parent, of the infant, and of their social situation. Contributions of parents include personality styles, expectations, attitudes about children and about adoption, histories of interaction with infants, and role models. Contributions made by the infant include variations in behavior used to elicit behavior from adults, the infant's temperament, and any special physical or social needs of the infant. The social situation in which the early parent-infant relationship develops is critical. Even potentially well-functioning parent-infant dyads can be made ineffective by a nonsupportive physical or social environment. In addition, compatibility problems can occur with greater frequency in adoptive than in biological families, since adoptive parents usually are less similar to their children.

From results such as these, it could be predicted that the degree of actual and perceived similarity would be less in adoptive than in biological families. Mismatches can occur between intellectual levels or personalities of parents and children, between characteristics of adopted siblings, or between adopted children and biological children within the same family. When major mismatches occur, there is a potential for conflict or for parental disappointment.

In eight of the adoptive families and one of the control families in the present study there appeared to be a lack of compatibility between the behavioral style of the child and that of his or her family ($\chi^2(1) = 5.98$, $p < .05$). One striking example of the development of incompatibility over time was noted by an adoptive father whose own style contrasted sharply with the hyperactivity and difficult behavior of his son.

> I strongly believe that behavior is inherited. I wish somebody had counseled me on that before we got into this. There needs to be a good match-up between the personality traits with the family traits. But how do you do that with an 18-month-old kid? Outside of that, the characteristics you'd look for in an adoptive parent is flexibility. My wife and I come from "walk the straight and narrow path" kinds of backgrounds. Our tolerance range is pretty narrow! If you had somebody whose tolerance range was out to here, it would make them more receptive to a wider range of kids. . . . The advice I'd give is don't feel obligated to follow through if there is any trait in that kid's personality that seems totally incongruent with your own. Don't feel weird about taking them back and trying somebody else. . . . The blackest part of my whole life is having that kid and everything that it's done to our family. There are times it's come within a hair's breadth of tearing the whole family apart.

In another family, the adoptive mother described herself as sedentary and her child as hyperactive. Another set of parents described themselves as industrious and very affectionate people, whereas their adopted son was both lazy and distant. In another case, the parents described themselves as introverted and perfectionistic and their daughter as an extrovert, a thrill seeker, and a slob. In each of these cases, the perception of differences in behavioral style appears to have set the stage for dissatisfaction with the parent-child relationship. Without intervention or reframing of family attitudes, it is not surprising that some of these families developed strongly entrenched convictions that their adopted child simply did not belong in their family. Some families commented that they felt that the child had been placed with the wrong family.

All but one of the eight adoptive families had either another adopted child or a birthchild. The parents' perception of the adopted child as "different" may be a reflection of the "good-bad" split often observed between siblings within clinic families (Schachter, 1985). (Sibling issues will be discussed more fully in Chapter 5.)

Incompatibility problems appeared to emerge in families in which adoptive parents either diminished or accentuated the importance of the adopted child's heredity to an extreme degree. When the importance of heredity was diminished, parents appeared to deny the difference between adoptive and biological parenting and opened the door for problematic communication about adoption (Kirk, 1981). When the importance of heredity was accentuated, parents attributed the problem to biology and abdicated any responsibility for their role in creating or ameliorating the problem. A more adaptive position appears to be one that acknowledges the potential role that the child's heredity might play while still taking at least partial responsibility for the child's socialization.

The large difference between the incidence of compatibility problems among adoptive and nonadoptive families may be due to the number of interviews that were conducted. As noted in Chapter 2, a larger number of the control than the adoptive-family parents were not available for interview. Thus, the difference may be because of differences in reporting rather than differences in compatibility. It is also possible that control parents do not report compatibility problems because they do not make that attribution of the situation.

PARENTAL EXPECTATIONS

Another issue involving lack of fit between parent and child centered around the child's violations of the parents' expectations or aspirations for him or her. This was typically evidenced in the discrepancy between the parents' aspirations and the child's actual accomplishments. Problems in this area were noted in eleven of the fifty adoptive families and four of the fifty control families.

Examples include a mother who expected her adopted daughter to be both successful and conforming, whereas the daughter was wild. In another case, the adoptive mother wanted a "doll" to play with and found instead that she had responsibility for an infant girl with many needs of her own. One adoptive father always wanted his son to be a great athlete; it took him a long time to accept his son as an artist. In another case, the adoptive father was highly achievement oriented and appeared to base his expectations for his son on his own achievement needs rather than his son's capabilities.

One boy in a non-adoptive family noted that he was an only child and had a hard time living up to his father's expectations. "He didn't give a whole lot of room for mistakes." In another non-adoptive family, the daughter stated, "I have problems because I couldn't meet up to my parents' little statue of me, how they wanted me to be."

In all of the cases discussed in this chapter, then, an underlying discrepancy between the child's actual or perceived behavior and the parents' willingness to work with or tolerate such behavior appears to have developed over time. In some cases, the mismatch was apparent from the very beginning; in others, the discrepancy gradually developed over time as parent and child styles became more and more discrepant.

Interviews completed with the adoptive families support our hypothesis of an attributional process occurring in which the parents attribute the child's unacceptable behavior to the fact that he or she was adopted (i.e., "not ours") in order to reduce the cognitive dissonance they may be experiencing concerning their skills as parents. Adoptive parents may be especially at risk for such an attitude, because the screening they have already undergone through the adoption agency is likely to have convinced them that they should be excellent parents. Attribution of the problem to the child and increasing lack of ownership of the problem on the part of the parents is likely then to lead to increased tension between parents and child. When the behavior becomes so out of control that the family system cannot tolerate it, treatment outside of the family context may then be sought.

CONCLUSION

This chapter has examined the development of compatibility, or goodness-of-fit, between the child and family from infancy into adolescence. Interview data from the parents suggested that the early expression of hyperactivity or of chronic illness on the part of the child contributed to problematic interactional patterns in both the adoptive and control families.

In only the adoptive families, a second behavioral style, the "elbow baby" pattern, appeared to contribute to problematic outcomes in 20 percent of the families. Although factors ranging from temperament to poor interactional environments in preadoption settings may have accounted for this style, adoptive parents reported its inhibiting effect on the development of a close relationship with the child.

Goodness-of-fit theory provided a conceptual framework for understanding the impact on development of the match between the child's characteristics and his or her environment. Significant problems were noted in two areas: lack of compatibility between the child's temperament or behavioral style and what the parents were able to tolerate, and the lack of fit between parents' expectations for their children and the children's actual accomplishments.

5

Family Relationships

In preceding chapters the focus has been on the unique early childhood and genetic factors that the child brings into the family. However, the child's characteristics interact with the characteristics of other family members and the relationships among them. The conceptual framework presented in Figure 1.1 highlights the consequences of the dynamic interactions among the marital, parent-child, and sibling relationships in the family over time for adolescent psychosocial development. Therefore, in order to understand the development of the child, it will be essential to consider his or her family as a context for development. Discussion in this chapter will center around the marital, parent-child, and sibling relationships in the adolescents' families.

MARITAL RELATIONSHIPS

Marriages are generally considered to serve as a parental support network and to provide both emotional and instrumental assistance to the parents. Moreover, the quality of the marital relationship can influence the general psychological well-being and level of functioning of the parents (Belsky and Vondra, 1985).

According to family systems theory, the family is an interactional system in which each family member's behavior affects another's. Marital interactions can influence and can be influenced by parent-child interactions as well as by parental problems such as alcoholism and drug abuse. In cases in which the parents have divorced, economic and social adjustments associated with single parenthood, cohabitation, remarriage, and postdivorce family relationships can all affect the child's social-emotional development.

Marital Status

Several significant differences were noted in the marital situations of the adoptive and control families. Although the majority (thirty) of the adoptive families were married at the time of the study, the majority (thirty-eight) of the control families were not (see Table 5.1). This difference may be attributed to the careful screening process that adoption agencies routinely undertake as part of the adoption home-study procedure. Adoption agencies strive to select prospective adoptive parents who have been married for several years and appear to have stable marriages at the time of the adoption. This study indicates that the agencies have been somewhat successful.

Moreover, adoptive parents may feel that since they have been certified by an adoption agency as competent parents who are presumed to have good marital and family relationships, they are more likely to fulfill this image by being more committed to the relationship than biological parents in the control families. Because twenty-two of the fifty adoptive parents had tried unsuccessfully to have birthchildren prior to the adoption, they were probably more likely to work to keep their marriages stable and to keep their families together in order to raise a child that they had, in many cases, waited for years to have.

Marital Quality

The adoptive and control parents in this study completed the Quality of Marriage Index (Norton, 1983) to assess their perceptions of their marital relationship at four points in time: at the time when they decided to adopt (or have the child), at the time of the adoption (or

Table 5.1
Marital Status at Time of Study

	Adopted	Control
Parents' Marital Status		
Married	30 (60%)	12 (24%)
Not Married	20 (40%)	38 (76%)
TOTAL	50	50
	$\chi^2 = 13.3005$	$p < .01$

birth), at the time when the child's trouble began, and at the time of their participation in the study. Although these data represent retrospective perceptions and varying sample sizes between the two groups, they nevertheless provide some insight into the marital relationships. No significant mother-father differences were found within each time period (see Table 5.2). The lowest ratings for the marital relationship occurred at the time when the trouble began.

The only significant difference between adoptive and control parents was that the control fathers tended to rate their marriages significantly higher than the adoptive fathers at the time of their participation in the study. Several possible interpretations can be made of this finding. Since the incidence of divorce and remarriage was higher in control families, it is likely that the control fathers may have been rating their new marriages. It is also possible that the control fathers who rated their marriages high may have been so relieved that the child was out of the home and receiving help that they felt more positively about their marital relationship. The adoptive fathers, although relieved that the child was receiving help, might have felt some guilt or feelings of failure as a "chosen" adoptive parent and therefore rated the marital relationship lower than the control fathers.

Reasons for Divorce

Adoptive families. The adoptive families indicated a variety of causes for their divorces. In two cases the parents believed that their marriage failed because they married for the wrong reasons. These couples married either to get out of the house, to satisfy dependency needs, or as a facade for homosexuality. In eight cases the marriages appeared to start off strong, but the couples grew apart. In one case the differences in the parents' styles of interacting and parenting led to the divorce. In five cases either the father or mother became an alcoholic, and in two cases physical violence between the parents was the cause of the divorce. Below are some case vignettes describing problems experienced in the adoptive sample.

One adoptive mother stated,

> Our divorce was a shock to all our family, friends and the community. Although we had been married for seven years, no one really realized the extent of our problems. Richard was my first and only boyfriend. I wasn't in love with him but my mother thought that he could give me the world. She pushed me into marrying him. Things just didn't work out. For a while we thought that having a child would bring us closer. But since I was infertile, we had to adopt. About four years after we got Sally, I filed for divorce.

The child's caseworker described the mother in this family as being immature and superficial. The father was characterized as being confused, unable to parent, and extremely immature.

Table 5.2

Descriptive Statistics: Marital Scale Scores for Mothers and Fathers at Four Points in Time

	At Time When Decided to Adopt	At Time of Adoption	At Time When Trouble Began	Now
ADOPTIVE MOTHERS				
Mean	38.3	38.7	32.0	37.1
Std. Dev.	6.6	5.7	12.1	11.0
Range	18-45	24-45	6-45	6-45
N	34	34	31	27
ADOPTIVE FATHERS				
Mean	39.3	39.3	36.3	38.2
Std. Dev.	5.9	6.0	8.0	7.3
Range	20-45	20-45	14-45	14-45
N	30	30	28	29

	At Time When Decided to Have Child	At Time When Child Born	At Time When Trouble Began	Now
CONTROL MOTHERS				
Mean	34.8	34.0	28.0	36.5
Std. Dev.	12.3	11.9	13.2	9.5
Range	6-45	6-45	6-45	13-45
N	12	12	13	11
CONTROL FATHERS				
Mean	32.3	30.5	30.4	41.7
Std. Dev.	13.7	16.5	15.0	2.4
Range	11-45	6-45	6-44	38-45
N	11	11	13	11

Note: Possible range on Marital Scale: 6 - 45

Another adoptive mother stated,

> Our relationship was always strained. It was based on dependency. My husband used to hit me all the time although he denies it. We argued constantly. When Tony was little, we moved around a lot because of his father's job. I hated it and so did Tony. There was so much resentment, we couldn't stand each other any longer so we divorced. Tony sees his father once a year or so. It's better this way because when we were together, he had started playing us against one another. He knew how to get us to arguing and he would end up getting his way.

Seven of the adoptive parents who divorced have since remarried other spouses. Two of these couples have remarried several times. In all but one case, the children appear to have accepted the stepparent.

According to the adolescents' caseworkers, seven (22 percent) of the adoptive families who are still married have troubled marital relationships. The issues experienced in these families include alcoholism, cold or distant fathers, lack of communication, physical violence, and emotional abuse between parents. There were six cases of physical neglect and/or abuse and one case of sexual abuse of an adopted child in the sample. The remaining intact families described their relationships as nonproblematic.

Control families. Thirty-eight of the control children in residential treatment came from divorced families. Because many of the children and residential treatment center staff had no contact with many of these families of origin, much of the data on marital relationships were gleaned from the caseworker interviews.

A closer examination of the adoptive and control samples reveals that nineteen of the divorces in the control families occurred before the child reached six years of age. Equal numbers of adopted and control families divorced during the period of time in which the child was between six and ten years of age. Only three divorces among the adoptive families and one in the control families occurred after the child was eleven years of age (see Table 5.3).

The most prevalent problems noted among these families were alcoholism in and/or drug abuse by parents, parental neglect or abuse of the child, and physical violence between parents. Twenty-seven of the control families frequently experienced these problems in contrast with twenty of the adoptive families (χ^2 = 1.9671; p = .1581). Living in these often violent home environments, many of these children also experienced lack of consistent nurturance and indicated that they felt rejected by their parents.

Responses from caseworkers as well as family members suggested that in six of the control families, the parents used the children to express anger toward one another or scapegoated the child. For example, in several instances, when the mother was angry at her

Table 5.3
Child's Age When Parents Divorced

Child's Age at time of Divorce	Adopted	Control
less than 6 yrs.	5	19
between 6 and 10	8	8
11 or more	3	1
TOTAL *	16	28

$$\chi^2 = 7.33 \quad p < .05$$

*Information on 44 known responses.

husband she would vent her hostility on the child. In another case, the father discontinued communication with the child after his divorce because the mother had been awarded custody.

In other families, the child or a parent became triangulated (Bowen, 1978). Although triangles occur in all families, they become dysfunctional when one person becomes scapegoated or blamed for all of the family's problems. In this study, troubled parents frequently told the child negative things about each other. Also, some couples dealt with their own problematic relationship by focusing their attention on the negative behavior of the child and thus avoiding their troubled marriages (e.g., Napier and Whitaker, 1978). The child therefore became fixed in the outside position and was blamed for everything that went wrong in the family.

There was a lack of cohesiveness in the family structure of many of these families. The father was described as being peripheral or uninvolved in thirteen of the control families and the mother was considered uninvolved in three of these families. Two families were characterized as having one childlike or fragile parent. In six families the father was dead, and in two of these cases the child witnessed the parent's death.

Since nineteen control families divorced before the child was six years old, several postdivorce family adaptation patterns emerged. Six of the families moved at least twice after the divorce. Some moved back to their family of origin in another state or community, whereas others moved in with friends. The children found these moves to be quite traumatic, as they had to learn to adjust to new environments frequently and reestablish peer relationships.

In thirteen families, the father remained largely uninvolved after the divorce and the mother kept the children. In three families the mother was peripheral and uninvolved. Two families had a joint custody arrangement but did not actually share parenting because the father was viewed as living too far away or did not discipline the child as the mother prescribed. However, within this subgroup of families, the mothers eventually gave up active parenting, when the child's behavior problems escalated, and sent the child to live with the father. If the father could not handle the problem, the child was sent back and forth until a residential placement could be found.

Within the divorced families in the control sample, eight children had parents who remarried several times or had a series of live-in mates. In several families in which there was an early divorce, the child became enmeshed with the mother and resented the intrusion of a stepfather.

Dynamics of Divorced Families

From the preceding discussion of the marital relationships among adopted and control families in this study, it seems as if troubled marital relationships may have contributed to some of the problems that the institutionalized children experienced. As mentioned earlier, twenty-seven of the control parents were unstable and abusive or alcoholic. They frequently used the children to express anger toward each other. It is also very likely that the exposure to multiple parental figures that characterized many of the remarried families may have been stressful to the children. The financial and emotional stress of single parenthood might also have contributed to the parents' unstable behavior. Almost all of the divorced control mothers indicated that their long work hours prevented them from spending time with their children, and these mothers indicated that they overcompensated by not disciplining their children. The enmeshment found in some of these family situations may also have led to some of the trauma that the children experienced.

Conversely, in the abusive cases the child might have been much less traumatized if the divorce had taken place much earlier, thereby denying access of abusing parents to the young child. Children from conflict-free divorced families are less likely to have problems than children in intact families that exhibit continuing parental conflict (Emery, 1982).

Although marital problems were less prevalent and less serious in adoptive than in control families, there were conflictual marital and family relationships that may have had an impact on the adopted children. Unlike the control families, most divorced adoptive parents had not remarried repeatedly, had live-in mates, or moved several times since the divorce. The major marital problems in the adoptive group seemed to stem from pathological behavior of the parents that developed some years after the adoption.

The high divorce rate in this sample is not surprising given the increasing incidence of divorce among all couples in the United States. In 1950, one in five marriages ended in divorce, and in 1980 one in two marriages ended in divorce. The social acceptability of divorce and the availability of "no fault" divorce are two factors that are generally viewed as contributing to the nation's increase in marital dissolutions (Coleman, 1984).

Family systems theory (e.g., Minuchin, 1974; Napier and Whitaker, 1978) highlights the potential interaction between marital discord and childhood problems. The association between marital and childhood problems can be expressed in at least two directions: marital problems can influence childhood problems and childhood problems can influence marital problems. In a study of a non-clinical population, the probability of having a discordant marriage, given a child with psychological problems, was less than the probability of having a child with psychological problems, given a discordant marriage (Emery and O'Leary, 1983).

Rutter (1970) assessed the relationship between marital discord and childhood psychopathology in a sample of 250 families. There was a greater likelihood of a male child being judged antisocial if the parents had poor marriages than if the parents had good marriages. No association was found for girls. The clinical characteristics of parent disorder were largely unrelated to the child's problems, except in the case of boys where antisocial personality types tended to have children with emotional problems. Similarly, Block, Block, and Gjerde (1986) found that boys especially are consistently affected by predivorce family stress.

The family boundaries can become more permeable as extended family members and friends assume more responsibility for child rearing. Also, the boundaries can become more rigid in some families, and an enmeshed relationship might develop between the custodial parent and children. If the single parent later chooses to enter another relationship, the family system must accommodate. In cases in which there are numerous live-in mates and remarriages, the child might be very resentful of the constant adjustments and life-style changes. The child might become very oppositional and hostile toward his or her parent and the spouse or companion.

Although remarriage and reconstituting a family can have positive effects on children, some of these systems are characterized by stress, ambivalence, and low cohesiveness (Pino, 1980). Children in blended families can feel that to show affection toward or acceptance of the stepparent would be disloyal to their birthparent. The child can fear losing his or her special place in the family. Also, children who have suffered numerous losses in the past may refuse to develop an attachment to another new family member and instead withdraw. Others can have high expectations of the stepparent and expect him or her to make up for previous losses. Remarried family restructuring may take a minimum of three years (Dahl, Cowgill, and Asmundsson, 1987), and families who are not prepared for the inevitable problems might find themselves in a very troubled, chaotic relationship. Although the association between child disturbance and family disturbance is strong, interpretations regarding directionality of influence are difficult to make. Although previous research has emphasized the etiological role of the family as an antecedent for child psychopathology, current findings strongly suggest many disturbed-child effects on the family (e.g., Bell and Harper, 1977).

Nineteen control and six adopted children were in family environments in which one parent was an alcoholic. According to Freeman (1985), such families can be characterized by financial problems, abuse, and children prematurely assuming adult roles. The impact on the child can include feelings of rejection and low self-esteem, lack of involvement in school activities, and poor school performance.

Since almost all of the pathological family systems eventually dissolved, the children then had to adjust to a new life-style. According to Hetherington (1979), the first year after separation is often very chaotic as role definitions and the emotional climate change. The family must adjust to economic loss by relocating as well as the custodial parent becoming employed or taking on a second job.

PARENT-CHILD RELATIONSHIPS

Belsky's (1984) model of parenting suggests that parental functioning is influenced by a variety of forces, including three major determinants: 1) the personality and psychological well-being of the parents, 2) the characteristics of the child, and 3) contextual sources of stress and support. Data from this study will be explored briefly in terms of the three components of Belsky's model. Characteristics of the relationships among the parents and children will be discussed in this chapter; influences of the family context on functioning will be explored in Chapter 6.

An extensive literature on socialization suggests that certain kinds of parenting appear to promote optimal child functioning. In the infancy period, studies reveal that cognitive-motivational competence and healthy socioemotional development are promoted by attentive, warm, stimulating, responsive, and nonrestrictive caregiving (e.g., Ainsworth, 1979). The work of Baumrind (1967, 1971) has demonstrated that during the preschool years high levels of nurturance and control foster the ability to engage peers and adults in a friendly and cooperative manner, as well as the capacity to be instrumentally resourceful and achievement oriented. As children grow older, parental use of induction or reasoning, consistent discipline, and expression of warmth have been found to relate positively to self-esteem, internalized controls, prosocial orientation, and intellectual achievement during the school-age years (e.g., Coopersmith, 1967; Hoffman, 1970; McCall, Applebaum, and Hogarty, 1973).

Consideration of these findings and others suggest that, across childhood, parenting that is sensitively attuned to children's capabilities and to the developmental tasks they face promotes a variety of highly valued developmental outcomes, including emotional security, behavioral independence, social competence, and intellectual achievement.

It seems reasonable to speculate that the people most able to provide the sensitively attuned parenting noted above would be mature, psychologically healthy adults. Although the literature linking personality and parenting is not as rich as one might like, there are data to support the notion that personal maturity, psychological well-being, and growth-facilitating parenting covary with each other (Belsky, 1984). There were a variety of parent factors that may have contributed to the ineffective parenting skills noted in this sample. For example, several parents were very immature, and several had unrealistic expectations for either themselves or their children. Some families for whom poor parenting skill was an issue also demonstrated evidence of parental pathology, such as child abuse or neglect, spouse abuse, alcohol or drug abuse, or mental illness.

In addition to parental pathology, another factor potentially affecting the ability to parent involved whether or not the parents really wanted the child to begin with. In four of the control and in five of the adoptive families, the institutionalized child was either rejected or unwanted by the parents. Within the control sample, the unwanted children were often unplanned and/or were abandoned or rejected by one of the parents. One of the rejecting adoptive couples adopted only as a result of pressure from extended family members to adopt a child from a relative. Two of the adoptive fathers in this group agreed to the adoption to make their wives happy but never really wanted the child themselves. Another adoptive parent rejected the child after determining at a very early age that the child was "a bad seed." This family wished to return the child to the agency.

Characteristics of Parents

Parent pathology. Twenty of the adopted children and twenty-seven of the control children had parents who exhibited clear signs of pathology. Fifteen of the adopted children and twenty-five of the control children experienced some sort of abuse and/or neglect by at least one of their parents ($\chi^2 = 4.1667$; $p < .04$), and six adopted and nineteen control children lived in families with alcoholic or drug-dependent parents. The mother of two of the control children not only drank and neglected her daughters but also made no secret that she supported herself through prostitution. Drawing conclusions about mental illness among parents was difficult because of the lack of information about actual diagnoses in most cases; however, several parents were described as manic-depressive, suicidal, paranoid, schizophrenic, or schizotypical. One control mother was considered mentally retarded and another had spent time in a state mental hospital. One adoptive father abused his wife, was accused by her of attempting to kill her and their son, and later suffered a "nervous breakdown." Another adoptive father attempted to kill himself by crashing the family car, with the rest of the family in it; he later succeeded in killing himself. In several cases both parents in the family exhibited some variety of pathology.

In terms of Belsky's model of parenting, the personality and psychological well-being of parents is a major determinant of parental functioning. Fifty-two percent of the children in the entire sample, however, had parents who exhibited some sort of pathology. These parents tended to exhibit poor parenting skills in the form of inconsistency in discipline between mother and father or ineffective and punitive discipline. These parents were not functioning well themselves and were not able to provide the kind of care their children needed. In addition, they probably failed to provide an example of effective coping for their children. This conclusion is consistent with the report of Smith and Hanson (1975), who found that abusive parents in particular hold extreme and unrealistic attitudes toward their children. They may expect the children to exhibit behaviors that are age-inappropriate and punish them severely when the expectations are not met.

Sexual abuse by a parent was reported in four adoptive and four control families. In the broader population, it is estimated that two-thirds of the children who are sexually abused appear to suffer emotional difficulties. A child's immediate response may be guilt, anxiety, fear, or anger. A family's response to sexual abuse is highly influential in the child's later emotional development. Many aspects of family life are already disrupted by the time sexual abuse occurs. Marital conflict is quite likely. Parent-child boundaries may be ill defined, causing family members to take on inappropriate roles (Slager-Jorne, 1978). The issue of sexual abuse in the adoptive family may be similar to that found in stepfamilies. The incest taboo may not be as strong in these families because of the lack of biological ties.

Effects of parenting styles. A number of studies have suggested that parents differ from one another in two major dimensions (Maccoby, 1980). The permissiveness-restrictiveness dimension concerns the level of control and restriction of children's behavior. The warmth-hostility dimension concerns how parents vary in the openness or frequency with which they express affection and in the degree to which affection is mixed with feelings of rejection or hostility.

When parents consistently enforce their rules and demands and do not let their children's noncompliance or resistance divert them, their children have been found to be able to control aggressive impulses and not be coercive toward parents (Patterson, 1976), to approach new situations with confidence, to take initiative and persist, and to be generally positive in mood and not withdrawn (Baumrind, 1967, 1971). An important element in enforcement of demands and rules is parental vigilance to notice whether children have complied. The effort required to monitor their parenting may have exceeded the capabilities of many of the parents in this study.

Becker (1964) stressed that the effect of restrictiveness depends on certain other parental attitudes. Restrictiveness, in an overall context of parental warmth, was associated with politeness, neatness, obedience, and nonaggressiveness. But restrictiveness, when imposed by hostile parents, was associated with a variety of neurotic symptoms, including withdrawal from social interaction with peers.

The authoritarian parent is highly controlling and establishes rules, restrictions, and requirements by fiat. Power is frequently asserted arbitrarily by these parents, in which case children have been found to be weak in establishing positive relationships with peers; frequently sad and somewhat withdrawn (Baumrind, 1967, 1971); and aggressive-impulsive and coercive, especially boys (Patterson, 1976). Many studies of juvenile delinquents reveal that parents of these children used discipline arbitrarily, with little explanation and sometimes considerable violence.

Becker (1964) similarly reported that the effects of permissiveness also depended on parental warmth. Children whose parents were both warm and permissive tended to be socially outgoing, independent, active, and creative, while children whose parents were hostile and permissive (a combination that is close to neglect) tended to be aggressive or delinquent and noncompliant with adult demands.

In general, the relationships among parental practices and children's characteristics are statistically significant but are seldom very strong (Maccoby, 1980; Maccoby and Martin, 1983). The more important predictor is the parents' ability to use discipline and guidance appropriate to the needs of the individual child.

Parenting skills. Ineffective and inadequate parenting skills presented problems in forty-eight of the adoptive families and forty-nine of the control families. The pervasiveness of these problems suggests a potential link with the children's disturbances.

Table 5.4 provides breakdowns of the major areas of problem parenting found in the adoptive and control families. The category "Ineffective discipline" refers to the parents' ineffective attempts to deal with the child's behaviors. This was the most frequently occurring adoptive parenting problem and was second only to "abuse/neglect" among the control families. The typical parent in this category reported that they had "tried everything" to control the child's behavior and/or that "nothing worked." A frequently occurring category among both the adoptive and control families was "inconsistent discipline." This category refers to inconsistency either between the parents or within one or both parents over time. Most often the discipline between the

Table 5.4
Frequency of Parenting Problems in Adoptive and Control Families

Problem	Adoptive	Control
Ineffective discipline	31	23
Punitive discipline	11	9
Inconsistent discipline	17	10
Marital problems inflicted on child	7	6
Not willing to let child grow up/ overprotective	4	3
Abuse/neglect by parent	15	25
Drug dependence or alcohol abuse of parent	6	19
Parents insecure about parenting adolescent	6	6
No discipline/overly permissive	5	7
Child expected to fill adult role	0	5
Natural parent never present	N/A	12

parents was inconsistent, with one parent (often the mother) being lenient and the other (often the father) being strict. "Punitive discipline" refers to the use of unusually harsh or physical punishment. "Marital problems inflicted on child" refers to a child being caught in the problems between the husband and the wife. These cases typically involved immature parents or a child feeling guilty about the parents' divorce.

"Abuse/neglect" was more frequently noted in the control group than in the adoptive sample. This category refers to instances of neglect and physical, emotional, or sexual abuse. "Drug dependence/alcohol abuse" also occurred more frequently in the control families.

In the control group, the category "natural parent never present" involved the total absence of one of the natural parents from the time of the birth of the child. The category "child expected to fill adult role" included families in which the child was given a great deal of responsibility, often inappropriately, and was expected to take care of the parent(s).

These parenting problems seldom occurred singly within a family; there was a great deal of overlap. For instance, in both groups, alcoholic, drug-abusing, or mentally ill parents were also likely to be abusive; and abusive or alcoholic parents tended to use ineffective or inconsistent discipline.

Parenting takes place within a context that includes the marital relationship of the parents. During the elementary school and adolescent years, high interspousal hostility has been linked to the frequent use of punishment and the infrequent use of induction or reasoning as a disciplinary strategy (Dielman, Barton, and Cattell, 1977). Parental stress can influence parenting behavior. For instance, Hetherington, Cox, and Cox (1976, 1979) studied the effects of divorce on parents' interaction with their children. During the first year following divorce, both divorced parents made fewer demands on their children, showed them less affection, communicated with them less well, and were notably inconsistent in their discipline. Mothers imposed more punishment and more often refused to give in to the child's demands; fathers tried hard to keep the children's affection, so most were highly permissive and indulgent. Hetherington, as well as Wallerstein and Kelly (1976), found that, following divorce, changes in parenting were closely related to the children's becoming more resistive, aggressive, and manipulative and less affectionate.

Almost without exception, the parenting-skills problems of both the adoptive and control families in this study co-occurred with marital problems. In seven of the adoptive families and in six of the control families, it appeared that the marital problems of the parents were being inflicted on the child.

Characteristics of Children

The characteristic of the child that has received the most attention in terms of influencing parental functioning is temperament, especially those behavioral styles that make parenting more or less difficult (Bates, 1980). Some evidence suggests that difficult temperament, especially in infancy, can undermine parental functioning. For example, Campbell (1979) reported that when mothers rated their infants as having difficult temperaments at three months, they interacted with them less and were less responsive to their cries at three and eight months.

As has been previously noted, many of the children in the adopted group exhibited early childhood characteristics that may have placed them at risk for later problems; these characteristics typically had to do either with hyperactivity or some other dimension of temperament, such as the "elbow baby" phenomenon. Poor parenting skills were present in twenty-eight of the thirty adoptive families for whom early-childhood characteristics were an issue.

Recently, it has been recognized that within the family, abused children must be considered as potential contributors to their own maltreatment. The child may be a causative, though unintentional, agent in the abuse process. The evidence reviewed by Frodi (1981) strongly suggests that atypical infants and children are at risk for child abuse. She proposed an explanatory model whose fundamental assumption is that certain characteristics are perceived as aversive, either because of their objectively aversive features or because of the idiosyncrasies of the perceiver. In addition to the atypical child, Friedrich and Boriskin (1976) also provide evidence that the parents' perception of the child as "different" can be a critical factor in contributing to child abuse.

Many of these children may exhibit characteristics that are particularly aversive to the parents, which in turn put the child at greater risk for abuse. This observation seems particularly relevant in terms of one adopted adolescent who was described as having "learned the victim role."

Any evaluation of the role of child characteristics in abuse must of course take into account the match between parent and child. Characteristics of a child make sense as elicitors of abuse only when considered vis-à-vis the caregiver's attributes (Belsky, 1978; Parke and Collmer, 1975; Sameroff and Chandler, 1975). The child characteristics are part of an interactive process, and it is doubtful that temperament or any other child characteristics alone shape parenting. Rather, the goodness-of-fit between parent and child determines the development of parent-child relations (Lerner and Lerner, 1983). (See Chapter 4 for further discussion.)

Parenting methods may be a response to the child's temperament as well as a cause of it. Thomas, Chess, and Birch (1968) followed children from birth and found that it was not children with difficult temperaments or children whose parents had maladaptive parenting styles who needed psychiatric help but children whose temperaments did not match their parents' styles. Disturbances arose when parental demands were in conflict with children's temperamental characteristics, placing the children under heavy stress. Research has been able to establish associations between patterns of parental behavior and child characteristics; however, cause-effect relationships are much more difficult to establish.

SIBLING RELATIONSHIPS

The emotional problems of the adolescents in this study were reflected in their behavior with siblings as well as with other family members. Qualitative analysis of the adoptive and control sample interviews revealed that problematic sibling relationships were evident in eleven of the fifty adoptive families and five of the fifty control families. Discussion in this section first explores differences in sibling problems as a function of sibling position and then examines the role of three aspects of family dynamics in sibling problems: perception of favoritism, fear of displacement, and deidentification.

SIBLING POSITION

The distribution of adolescents in the samples by sibling status is reported in Table 5.5. In both the adoptive and control samples, over

Table 5.5
Distribution of Target Adolescents by Sibling Status

	Adoptive	Control
Only Children	7	3
First Borns	16	18
Later Borns	27	29
Total	50	50

half of the children were later-borns (i.e., had at least one older sibling), while most of those remaining were firstborns and a few (seven adopted and three control children) were only children.

Among those adolescents for whom sibling relationships were problematic, there was no difference (p = .41) between the adoptive and control groups in the proportion of adolescents who were later-borns (seven, or 63.6 percent in the adoptive sample and three, or 60 percent in the control sample) or firstborns (four, or 36.4 percent in the adoptive and two, or 40 percent in the control sample). It is not surprising that more later-borns than firstborns were affected, since later-borns include those that were born second, third, fourth, or later.

When sex of sibling was examined in the group for whom sibling relationships were problematic, it was found that in the adoptive group, 27.2 percent (three) had only same-sex sibling(s), 36.3 percent (four) had only opposite-sex sibling(s), and 36.3 percent (four) had siblings of both sexes. In contrast, all five adolescents in the control sample had only same-sex siblings (see Table 5.6). It is likely that this difference was simply because of sampling.

In general, sibling relationships did not appear to contribute to the initial appearance of the emotional problems of the adolescents. The problems between siblings typically began after the onset of the target adolescent's problem behavior. In one case, however, the sibling relationship may have contributed to the child's difficulties, as one adopted male had been repeatedly sexually molested by an older adopted brother over the period of a year when he was nine years old.

Table 5.6
Distribution of Siblings by Sex for Cases in Which Sibling
Relationships Were Identified as Problematic

	Adoptive	Control
Same Sex	3 (27.2%)	5 (100%)
Opposite Sex	4 (36.3%)	0
Both Sexes	4 (36.3%)	0
Total	11	5

One hypothesis tested in this study is that problems in sibling relationships are most likely to occur in the case in which parents adopt a child and subsequently have a biological child. This hypothesis was tested in three ways. First, all adolescents in the adoptive sample who had problematic sibling relationships were identified. No differences were found between the frequencies of adoptive versus biological siblings of these adolescents (nine adopted versus ten biological). In a second approach, sibling compositions within the eleven adoptive families demonstrating problematic sibling relationships were examined. In four of the families, all of the siblings were adopted; in six of the families, all of the siblings were biological; and in one family, both types of siblings were present. Again, there appeared to be no difference in sibling composition among families. Third, all families were identified in which the first child was adopted and one or more subsequent children were born to the parents. Of those nine families, only three were also in the group for whom sibling relationships were problematic ($\chi^2 = 0.21$, ns). Thus, the specific mix of adoptive and biological siblings did not appear to be associated with problematic sibling relationships in a strong or uniform manner across adoptive families.

Favoritism

When sibling relationships were noted as problems, the adolescents typically complained of favoritism that had been shown to siblings by their parents or relatives. For example, Frank, an adolescent in the control sample, complained about his younger brother, "I've felt for a long time, well, why is he the little angel and I'm the one who gets blamed for everything?" Frank's mother noted that he resented any time they spent money on his younger brother. "He would write it down on a piece of paper. He would remember every cent and want that same amount spent on him. However, I never agreed with the thought that you need to spend the same amount on each one. Their needs are different at different times."

Interestingly, parents of adolescents who complained of favoritism often acknowledged that the siblings were treated differently. However, the children tended to attribute the favoritism to the fact that the sibling was the parents' biological child or favorite child, whereas the parents noted that additional privileges were granted because the sibling was older or more responsible. In several families, the adolescent's perception of favoritism increased over time, as the adolescent's behavior became more and more aversive and the parents became less willing to trust or grant privileges to the adolescent. Thus, a cycle of adolescent and parental behavior made the perception of favoritism an entrenched reality.

Fear of Displacement

Adopted children often appeared jealous of their siblings and expressed this through anger or direct hostility toward their siblings. Interviews with the adolescents suggested that this jealousy resulted from the adopted adolescent's fear of being displaced in the family.

Martin, a thirteen-year-old adopted boy, commented that he didn't get along at all with his younger brother — he was angry with him for being born. "I thought I wasn't getting as much attention." His father disagreed, explaining that "he got all those rights that the oldest child got, but then we got to the point where he didn't trust us and we didn't trust him. We also got to a point where we did not trust him with the other children." Martin's mother added,

> He would ask me little questions from time to time, and then when his younger brother was born I guess they confirmed that there was something different about him. It used to put me on edge because I didn't know how to let him know that, hey, it's OK, I love you. OK, so we have another child born into the family and you are adopted. But that's OK with Mom, I love you. I feel as though the distance that was between us was because of something he didn't believe. Maybe we were unsuccessful in trying to show him that it didn't matter to us that he was adopted.

Deidentification

A striking contrast effect was noted in a number of cases in which the child would develop his or her identity around the fact that he or she was "different" from either parents or siblings. In some cases, this perception was based on fact, because the adopted child looked different from siblings or had different talents than they did. This phenomenon of "sibling deidentification" (Schachter et al., 1978; Schachter, et al., 1976) has been noted in normal families and has been hypothesized to function in order to reduce sibling rivalry.

In normal families, this process is thought to be benign and even beneficial, providing each sibling with his or her own "turf" (Schachter, 1985). However, in clinical cases, the contrast effect may take an extreme stance, such that the child views himself or herself as the "devil," or "bad one," and the sibling as the "angel," or "good one" (Schachter, 1985).

Schachter's work with both normal and dysfunctional families suggests that in dysfunctional families, the process of conflict resolution concerning identity is hindered. Instead of proceeding through the cycles of conflict and reconciliation that siblings in normal families experience, the sibling roles become fixed, with the "bad" or "devil" sibling constantly harassing the innocent victim, the "angel." The consequence of such a pattern is that angel siblings do not learn how to defend themselves or assert their rights, and devil siblings never learn how to negotiate or accommodate to the rights of others.

As the bad child's behavior becomes more unacceptable within the family, this attribution may be confirmed by the parents' actions or verbalizations and may thus reinforce the child's identification as the bad one. Placement in residential treatment outside the family setting is a logical outcome for children whose behavior becomes locked into such roles.

Martha, an adopted girl, was twenty months older than her parents' biological son, Roland. Her father recalled, "She said Roland was goody-two-shoes and that we treated him differently. And I think she's right." Her mother agreed: "She felt that we were much more fair with him and that she was always the one getting in trouble. Actually she didn't like him because he was a goody-two-shoes. . . . I think she was treated differently. What I did was protect her to a great deal and my husband was very hard on her."

It is clear that sibling relationships do not exist in isolation from other relationships within the family. Tsukada (1979) reviewed a number of studies finding that prolongation of sibling rivalry was generally attributable to parental exacerbation of the conflict. Furthermore, inconsistency in parental discipline was cited as the outstanding cause of sibling rivalry, and parental inconsistency was noted in a number of families in this sample. Clinical studies that she reviewed concluded that when the marital relationship in the family was weak, one child was more likely to become involved in a triangulated relationship with the parents. The intense involvement of one child with the parents may effectively close other siblings out of such involvement, setting the stage for stereotyping of the children as the good and bad siblings.

CONCLUSION

This chapter has highlighted the network of family relationships in which the child's development is embedded and has illustrated the multiple risk factors to which children in the study had been exposed. In terms of marital relationships, the adoptive parents had been married longer than control parents on the average and tended to have more solid marriages. When marital problems developed, divorce seemed to be a much more common solution among the control than the adoptive families. In remarried family situations, the control parents seemed to be more willing to place the child in treatment than risk the marital disruption often found in stepparenting or newly blended families. On the other hand, adoptive parents tended to be much more committed to keeping the family intact and were less likely to resort to divorce to solve problems.

The parent-child relationships in the adoptive and control families were strikingly different, although common themes were present. Virtually all parents in the study felt ineffective in accomplishing their goals as parents, despite the best of intentions. The ineffectiveness could have been because of problems on the part of the parents (such as inconsistency) or the children (such as uncontrollable behavior). In most cases, it is likely that both the parents and children contributed to the problematic parent-child relationships, which deteriorated over time to the degree that the adolescent could not remain at home. Almost half of both the adoptive and control families were characterized by parental pathology of some sort. Although the incidence of parental pathology was high in both samples, the parental problems appeared to be more severe among the control parents.

With regard to the role of problematic sibling relationships in the adolescents' emotional disturbance, no systematic link was found between the child's sibling position within the family (either in terms of birth order, sex, or mix of adopted and biological children) and sibling relationship problems. However, the interviews concerning sibling relationships did reveal that three patterns of family dynamics appeared related to sibling problems: the perception that a sibling was favored by the parents, the fear of displacement by a sibling, and deidentification within the family. In interpreting these data, it is important to note the differences in perceptions of children and their parents. For example, some parents stated that their children were treated differently from their sibling(s) because they were bad and did not take responsibility; however, their children stated that they became bad because they were treated differently. Future research could profitably address how this attributional cycle could begin and escalate.

Understanding development in families presenting multiple risks is extremely challenging. Although individual risk factors may be potent enough to lead to disturbed development, the interactions among variables must also be considered (Sameroff and Seifer, 1983). "Where the mutual regulation of individual and context succeeds, a healthy, happy child develops; where the system regulation fails, deviance appears. It is the identification of the sources of failure in system-regulatory functions that will provide the clearest path to understanding how to insure optimal outcomes for children at risk" (p. 1265).

6

Context of Family
Relationships

As noted in the preceding chapter, parent-child, marital, and sibling relationships have an influence on the adjustment of a child in the family. However, the functioning of these subsystems is affected by contextual factors such as family relocations, parental absence, loss of a family member, or family violence. This chapter will include a review of the literature and discussion of the influence of stressful family events and circumstances of parental work environments that may have placed children in this sample at risk for the development of emotional disturbance.

STRESSFUL FAMILY EVENTS

One observation readily made about the members of this sample is that they have experienced a number of negative and stressful circumstances (i.e., divorce of parents, death of parent, abuse, etc.). In addition, for fourteen of the adopted children and eighteen of the control children specific stresses seemed to be particularly salient, precipitating factors for their problem behaviors. We called these stresses that served as precipitating factors "family events." This section is an attempt to explore the relationship between family events and the development of psychopathology or deviance among the adolescents in the sample.

One of the most commonly addressed concerns in stress research is the question of whether there is an association between stressful events and subsequent development of psychiatric disorders. There is reasonably strong evidence that, in adults, stressful events play a significant .role in provoking the onset of suicide, depressive conditions, neurotic disorders, and to a lesser extent schizophrenia (Andrews and Tennant, 1978; Lloyd, 1980; Paykel, 1978). There is, however, a paucity of evidence on the possible importance of stressful life events in the genesis of psychiatric disorders in children and adolescents.

Research in this area typically involves measuring the occurrence of discrete life events during some specified period of time and correlating these life-event scores with measures of psychological functioning. Much of this literature shows that, as with adults, life stress is significantly related to emotional maladjustment (e.g., Gersten, Langner, Eisenberg, and Simcha-Fagan, 1977; Johnson and McCutcheon, 1980; Newcomb, Huba, and Bentler, 1981).

Under the general heading of "maternal deprivation" there have been studies indicating that various kinds of adverse experiences can substantially increase the risk of psychiatric disorder in childhood (Rutter, 1981a). Most of these studies refer to chronic and prolonged adversities, such as long-term family discord, parental rejection and neglect, or an institutional upbringing.

Less is known about the effects of relatively acute stressful events on children and adolescents. However, Hudgens (1974) noted a relationship between severe personal stressors and depression in a group of adolescents with medical disorders, and Heisel, Ream, Raite, Rappaport, and Coddington (1973) found that a high number of stressors was more common in children with psychiatric disorders than in general population controls.

Gender is a pertinent variable in consideration of consequences of stressful events. There is considerable evidence that boys are more vulnerable to stress events than are girls (Rutter, 1970, 1983). Young boys tend to show more adverse effects in response to hospital admission (Rutter, 1981a), change in day care (Rutter, 1981b), and the birth of a sibling (Dunn, Kendrick, and MacNamee, 1981), and, in response to divorce, disturbance tends to be more severe and more prolonged in boys (Wallerstein and Kelly, 1980). Additionally, there is a tendency for boys to show more aggressive behavior in response to parental discord and disharmony (Rutter, 1983).

Four of the fourteen adopted and eight of the eighteen control children who appear to have been affected by family events are male. In addition to the more aggressive and externalizing behaviors of these males, depression, feelings of worthlessness, withdrawal, and suicidal ideation are among the symptoms exhibited by ten of these twelve males.

The prospective study by Gersten and colleagues (1977), however, casts doubt on the etiologic role of negative events alone in the maladjustment of children and adolescents. They found that negative life events did not predict subsequent maladjustment, once social and familial variables (e.g., mother's mental health, stability of marriage), categorized as "stressful processes," and initial maladjustment were statistically controlled. They concluded that the significant relationship between negative events and psychological disorder was due to both variables' significant relationship with "stressful processes."

In a similar study, Swearingen and Cohen (1985) found that stress events not only fail to predict the level of subsequent psychological distress but are themselves partly determined by previous distress. The authors' explanation for this relationship is again the existence of a third variable that engenders both psychological distress and the occurrence of life events.

LOSS AS A FAMILY EVENT

A theme that appears to run through these family-events cases is one of loss. Paykel, Myers, and Dienelt (1969) and Paykel and Tanner (1976) have stressed the importance of undesirable "exit" events (loss of an important person). Paykel (1974) has found that "exits" are more strongly associated with psychiatric disorder in children than are "entrances."

Of the fourteen adopted children for whom a life event was particularly salient, six were related to the death of someone close to them and five to the loss of a parent through divorce or separation. Of the eighteen control children with a family event, seven were related to a death, two to the loss of contact with someone close, and one to abuse. For instance, fourteen-year-old Paula perceived her problems as beginning with the death of her grandfather. "When I was 13 my grandpa . . . I was real, real close to him, he passed away. Thirteen, that's when all my problems started." And sixteen-year-old Robert attributed his problems to his mother's death. "I was about seven years old (when) my mom died. Well, she was my adopted mother. I think that was when I started messing up a whole lot."

Five of the adopted children and six of the control children who experienced the loss of a close relative through death or separation exhibited some signs of depression, withdrawal, feelings of worthlessness, and suicidal thoughts as measured on the Adolescent Behavior Checklist (see Chapter 8 for further discussion).

Although research on bereavement in childhood remains a relatively neglected area, several consistent results have emerged. Maternal loss (but not paternal loss) in childhood tends to be associated with depressive states in adult female offspring. When vulnerability is studied with respect to age at time of loss, the age bracket of five to ten years old seems to be the most vulnerable age of all (Tennant, Bebbington, and Hurry, 1982). The strong impact of the family events on the children in the present study is consistent with this finding, since most of the family event losses occurred for this sample between the ages of three and thirteen.

The separation or divorce of parents is another important source of loss for children. Parental divorce and/or separation generally take place following a rather prolonged period of discord and disharmony.

Numerous studies indicate that much of the disturbance in the children stems from this discord, rather than from the separation per se (Rutter, 1971). In a recently published study, Block, Block, and Gjerde (1986) showed that the preseparation environment of a couple who would subsequently divorce had a major impact on the development of the children in the family. The behavior of boys in this situation tended to be impulsive, aggressive, and inappropriately energetic. The effect on girls was less extreme and less easily characterized than that of boys. Nonetheless, the recent longitudinal studies by Hetherington, Cox, and Cox (e.g., 1979) and by Wallerstein and Kelly (1980) clearly show that in many children emotional disturbance tends to worsen immediately following a divorce. It would appear that the circumstances associated with the divorce itself may also constitute an additional stressor that may aggravate or precipitate emotional difficulties.

Many of the children in both the adopted and control groups experienced parental divorce, which may have added to their stress. However, for some the parental divorce or separation appeared either to play a precipitating role in the child's problems or to set up a situation that prompted problems. For instance, the parents of one adopted child, Carla, separated when she was three and divorced when she was four. Her father had several subsequent marriages, all of which seemed to be particularly upsetting to Carla. She spent a summer with her adoptive father when she was seven. "She came home a different person," according to her mother, and her problem behaviors began. She had been sexually molested by a friend of her brother's while she was away, and her relationship with her father's newest wife was very tense and hostile.

The outcomes of stressful events cannot be viewed solely in terms of the properties of the event. Rather, they must be considered in terms of developmental history, individual characteristics and resources, and the social and physical context. For instance, evidence suggests that most children can cope and adapt to the short-term crisis of divorce within a few years; however, if the crisis is compounded by multiple stressors and continued adversity, developmental disruptions may occur (Hetherington, 1984). The postdivorce family relationships — between the parents and between each parent and the child — play a major role in determining the consequences of divorce for the children.

Other factors also influence the impact of bereavement on children, including family closeness preceding the loss, the prior relationship between the affected child and the deceased parent, whether the parent is of the same or opposite sex as the child, the religious beliefs and social-class background of the family, and the suddenness (as opposed to gradual onset) of the event. In general, the risk of psychiatric disorder in adults in relation to parental loss in childhood appears to be relatively low but tends to be heightened by accumulated stressors, whether these occur in childhood or in adulthood (Garmezy, 1986).

The response to stress will also be modified by the characteristics of the child and family and the resources available in the family for the management of the stress. These include personal resources such as financial, educational, health, and psychological resources and individual characteristics such as personality, temperament, intelligence, age, and sex. In addition, family resources such as cohesion, adaptability, and communication and problem-solving skills (McCubbin et al., 1980) and social supports (Hess and Camara, 1979; Hetherington, Cox, and Cox, 1982) such as neighbor, kin, and friendship networks and self-help groups are important in coping with stressful life events.

Although we have no information on the majority of these resources for our sample, it is likely that the adoptive parents had the financial, educational, and perhaps health resources or they would not have been chosen as adoptive parents. The family resources, however, may be particularly at risk in the families we have sampled, in which case the families may not be well equipped to manage stress as it occurs.

Although one event may seem to have precipitated symptoms in these children, in no instance in our sample did either these family events or other negative life stress events occur in isolation. These children experienced multiple stressors in their families, as may be seen in the following examples:

> Jonathan, now age 16, suffered a major illness as an infant, his parents separated when he was five and a half, and he went to live with his alcoholic father in an impoverished environment at nine. He subsequently experienced not only the death of his father, but was told thereafter that he "had broke daddy's heart" and that's why he had died. His older brother committed suicide sometime after his father's death.

> Agnes, now age 16, experienced a series of losses due to illness and death. Her mother was near death and experienced multiple hospitalizations, then her aunt, uncle, grandmother, and pet kitten died within a short period of time. After her mother's hospitalizations she had to be literally dragged out of her home by a social worker to attend school. She was so frightened that something would happen to her mother and felt that she should stay home to take care of her.

In many cases, these family events occurred in combination with parental issues such as child abuse or alcoholism or child issues such as difficult temperament. Jonathan (above) had an alcoholic father. Five other children experienced abuse and/or neglect in their homes in addition to the reported family event. Frank was abused by his mother, who was involved in both alcohol and drug use. She made their home a shelter for teenage runaway boys and one day, in a fit of anger, threw Frank's dog over a brick wall and killed it.

These multiple stressors put the families at risk for providing the necessary support and resources that the children need for successful coping. The complex of variables that consistently emerge as discriminating between children whose outcomes are either positive or negative is related to the quality of family functioning. Families under stress do not tend to function very well, and families that do not function very well tend to have a great deal of distress.

In many of these cases the salient event was different depending upon who was providing the information. There was often a discrepancy between what the child saw as a major event in his or her life and what the parents or caseworker saw. For instance in the case of Frank (above), he saw his parents' divorce as a major upsetting event, his mother saw the father's remarriages as particularly upsetting to Frank, and his father saw the mother's life-style subsequent to the divorce and the death of Frank's dog as a major source of his problem.

Stressful family events are important in the lives of these children; however, they must be considered in terms of how they were dealt with at the time (Rutter, 1983) and in what familial context they occurred. The resources of the child and the family influence how a stress is dealt with when it occurs, and how the stress is dealt with influences how subsequent stresses are handled.

WORK-RELATED ISSUES

The Military Family

For five of the adopted children and six of the control children, being a member of a military family seems to have contributed to their problems. Several special circumstances appear to be operating in the military family that may influence the child's development. Frequent moves, father absence (Privitera, 1978), and child abuse (Hunter and Nice, 1978) are common concerns in the study of these families.

The structure of the armed forces may create stressful family circumstances. Life on a military base is predictable, orderly and rigid. Military children are expected to conform to a strict code of behavior, and military homes tend to have strict rules.

When asked what problems led to his residential placement, one child in the control sample replied,

> Mishandling anger, and that's when I finally started realizing I wasn't as close to my Dad as he — or he wasn't as close to me as he'd led me to believe. I got in trouble with the [military] police for indecent exposure, because we

were on a military base and nothing would happen if that happened. He [father] was getting in trouble for it. He was threatened with an Article 15.

In a recent paper about military families, Long (1986) cited several professionals who specialize in the problems of the military family. According to West Palm Beach psychologist Florence Kaslow, most of our present-day military personnel are technicians and bureaucrats and, contrary to stereotypes of professional soldiers, are not necessarily more belligerent than anyone else, nor is their profession particularly violent. Of course, some men are highly trained for combat readiness and may have difficulty leaving their soldier mentality behind when they leave work. According to psychiatrist Alex Rodriguez, former medical director of the military health-insurance plan, there is a small group of aggressive men who joined the armed forces to live the warrior myth. Researchers do not know what, if any, effects these fathers may have on the development of their children's behavior.

The military life-style can isolate its members from outside supports such as friends, grandparents, church, and community groups. When family difficulties arise, support may be scarce, and problems may escalate if the family lacks essential communication or problem-solving skills. Many military families are reluctant to seek professional counseling, either because of their "can do" philosophy or their fear of tarnishing their records. Even when families want and seek such counseling, it may be difficult to find (Long, 1986). The military families in this study cited frequent problems in getting appropriate treatment for their children. This included refusals for humanitarian reassignments to cities where residential treatment was available and being constrained to seeking psychiatric help from military sources, which did not have programs designed for young children.

Frequent moves. The frequent relocations and special assignments experienced by military personnel are often stressful for their families. However, as was true for the stressful family events discussed above, the impact of the military family events on the child depends in part upon the child's age and developmental level.

According to Privitera (1978), the frequent moves inherent in the military life do not appear to be intrinsically disruptive to the preschool child. Parental attitudes about the moves and the ability of the family to provide a supportive emotional framework for the child seem to be of paramount importance (Pedersen and Sullivan, 1964). It appears that the social stresses of military life, which disrupt the continuity and emotional stability of the family, are most disruptive for the preschool child.

Very young school children, who are just beginning to feel secure away from their parents, are particularly vulnerable to the effects of moving. However, relocation can also upset older school-aged children by disrupting their friendships. Three adopted and three control children experienced a high degree of difficulty with school because of their families' constant moving. One control father described his son's pain at losing friends time after time: "After talking with Clint, I hadn't realized the effect that the Army was having on him. But every time he would get situated and make friends in one location, we'd have to move, and he'd go off and lose those friends. Or if we didn't move, the friend's family would move because of the Army. And he never had any lasting friendships."

After having to leave close friends repeatedly, these children become adept at making superficial friendships. An adoptive father said of his daughter: "She uses people; she runs through friends like water through a sieve."

Caseworkers commented on the superficial friendships of two adopted adolescents as follows: "He presents himself as a beautiful boy — talented, skilled, athletic, etc. When it comes down to real friendship, I'm not sure Chuck can return it," and, "He's detached; it's superficial, he doesn't share very much of himself."

In three adoptive and three control cases the disruption of friendships was believed to play a role in the adolescents' current problems. Current friendship problems were described by caseworkers as the following: not getting along well with the other children; being picked on and called names; being a loner; having detached, superficial, and poor relationships with peers; having no skills for making friends; and making friendships with children who are much less skilled. For adolescents, moving in the junior or senior year of high school is most difficult (Long, 1986).

In a large study of more than 2,000 Air Force children, Orthner (cited in Long, 1986) found that the longer the adolescents remained in the same community, the better adjusted they were. He found that civilian youth enrolled in schools near military communities had more close friends and a larger network of peer supports, whereas military adolescents spent more time with their parents. Although both groups showed the normal adolescent break from parents, it came somewhat later for the military youth.

An additional problem that can accompany the mobile family who is experiencing difficulty is that resources for help and treatment may differ from place to place. A child who is having difficulty and receiving treatment in one location is uprooted from this treatment, must start over again, and may receive entirely different treatment at the new location. This seemed especially problematic in two of the adoptive military families. One mother related different types of treatments being recommended at each of their moves: behavior modification, which only led the child to wanting bigger and better things; family therapy, which seemed to help the parents but never changed the child's behavior; medication for the diagnosis of hyperactivity, which actually made her condition worse; and eventually residential placement for the diagnosis of autism. In the other case the child had been diagnosed as learning disabled (LD) and was in a small classroom especially designed for children with these problems. According to the mother, "They were equipped to make sure there were no tidal waves." After their move to another state where there was no special-education program, the best the teacher could offer was the following, "I don't think he's going to be public school material, but since you're retiring I'll do what I can."

Parental absence. Many children must cope with extended and/or frequent absences of one parent, usually the father. Long separations of six to ten months are common in the Navy and Marine Corps when the parent "ships out." Infants and toddlers were often raised in what is virtually a single-parent family. Often, the child does not remember or recognize the parent upon return from the tour of duty. One control adolescent, describing the relationship between him and his father:

> *Interviewer:* What about your father from your earliest memory, when you were real little?
> *Adolescent:* I didn't know him. I still don't know him.
> *Interviewer:* And now you still don't know him?
> *Adolescent:* Well, I am trying to get to know him, but I still don't know him.

For adolescents, an absent parent's return can be an unwelcome intrusion. A departing father may proclaim the oldest son as the "man of the family" in his absence. The adolescent can be confused by being thrust into an adult role, but the confusion can be even worse after the family adjusts to the absence and then the father returns.

Parent absence may influence the child's development in indirect as well as direct ways. The child's responses to the parent's absence itself can have consequences for development, but the change in the remaining parent and in the family structure as a result of the absence can also have consequences for development. This sample of military families had one adopted and three control adolescents who had failed to develop close relationships with their fathers because of his repeated absences when they were young children.

Most of the research concerned with the adaptation of military families to separation in general, and the coping patterns of military wives in particular, deals with families undergoing extended or unusual separations (one-year or longer wartime separation, prisoner-of-war and missing-in-action families, etc.). Few studies have been conducted that are concerned with the regular and frequent family separations necessitated by the father's choice of a military career. The absence of the father places stress on the mother, who must assume his role as well as her own. This alteration of roles may have functional and/or dysfunctional effects on the family. Adjustment to separation may be viewed as a developmental task for all members of the family with problems occurring before, during, and after the actual separation (Rienerth, 1978).

An ex-wife of a military career man discussed the reasons for her decision to divorce:

> A lot of it was his job, but my inability to cope in that he is military and we moved a lot and he was gone a lot. And I didn't like moving around. So, I couldn't cope in that situation. It's just that once I became a mother then my expectations of the family life changed. A father that's absent is not my image of what a father should be. And I didn't want to move around; I wanted the kids to be in a school and stay someplace. We did real well as two separate people married, but as a family, it just . . . didn't work out.

In a widely cited study of Norwegian sailor families, Lynn and Sawrey (1959) demonstrated that boys in the father-absent families were more dependent and immature, had less-adequate peer relationships, and showed more compensatory overaggressiveness than controls. However, the authors attribute the reported differences not to the absence of the male model but rather to the effects of husband-absence on the mother. Many of the wives in the families were more isolated from social contacts, overprotective, and more concerned with obedience than controls.

Pedersen (1966) compared the extent of father-absence in the histories of a group of emotionally disturbed and a comparable group of normal male children in military families. While the extent of father-absence did not differ between the groups, within the disturbed group only the degree of father-absence was highly correlated with emotional disturbance. In addition, the mothers of the disturbed children were significantly more disturbed than the mothers of the normal adolescents. This finding led the researcher to hypothesize that in some instances the effects of father-absence may be a function of his ability to mediate between the children and the disturbed mother.

A caseworker described one such relationship between a child and his adoptive mother and father:

> There are some subtle hints that the mother was abusive at times when she became very frustrated with him, when he wasn't able to follow her directives. And there's several indications from him that he was choked on a couple of occasions, slapped really when she was at her wits end. His father was gone quite a bit. He was an air force man. That to Brian was very difficult in that it left him with this mother who could not tolerate him very well, so there would be some feelings towards his father of being left by his father, and yet when the father was around, they got along real well.

In other cases, the father's mediation between the mother and child was needed because the mothers were extremely childlike in their behavior. Many children tended to become the "parentified child": "I kind of felt like what I had to do was take care of my mother a lot." A caseworker described another control mother as "an inadequate, child-like Mom with no parenting skills." This adolescent was described as having pent-up rage and hostility toward all women at this point in time.

Child abuse and family violence. There were two cases of child abuse and/or neglect reported in the adoptive military families and one case in the control families. Little research has dealt systematically with child abuse in the military community (Schnall, 1978). It is frequently assumed that military parents are more abusive than other parents. However, there are no valid data to support the contention that the military life-style tends to make military parents more abusive than their non-military counterparts (Lanier, 1978). The military consists largely of younger, less financially secure families, who are the very types most likely to resort to physical abuse. Lanier (1978) found that military parents abuse and neglect their children for the same reasons as civilian parents.

Lanier also found that 40 percent of the abusing military families had been in the area less than a full year. In a non-military sample, Gil (1970) found that nearly one-half of the families had lived in the home one year or less at the time of the incident. Lanier (1978) cited a study by Maden in which it was reported that child-abusing families were considerably more nomadic than the national average; thus, the evidence strongly suggests that abusing families are unusually mobile. Despite the high mobility rate of the military family, this does not appear to be a distinguishing characteristic of the military child abuser. The child-abusing family in the military is very much like its civilian counterpart on the factor of mobility.

Child outcomes. The consequences of being raised in a military family are not clear. Much of the available research is quite old and was conducted during wartime in an era when family roles and values were quite different from today's. Most of the more recent studies on peacetime military families have been criticized for their poor methodology. Expert opinion is enormously varied; it runs the gamut from saying that military children are worse off than their civilian peers to asserting that they are no different or even better off (Long, 1986).

The experts do agree, however, that the mental health of any given child depends in part on the well-being of the family and on the supports the child receives. Psychologist Edna Jo Hunter, director of the Family Research Center at the U.S. International University in San Diego, claims that many children in career military families are better adjusted and more adaptable than other children. She admits, however, that behavioral problems are more common when military families are separated from one parent for long periods of time or when both parents work and the children become "latchkey kids" (Long, 1986).

In one of the few studies that has investigated the relationships among developmental phases and the responses of children to the social stresses inherent in military life, Darnauer (1976) examined the adolescent experience in career army families. Sixty adolescents and their parents were interviewed independently. The majority of the adolescents indicated that they believed the major negative factor in military life was the frequent family moves. Of those teenagers, 67 percent had experienced at least one family move since the ninth grade. A negative influence of much less concern to the teenagers was the requirement for their compliance with army policy regarding personal behavior. They felt that their freedom of self-expression and experimentation was severely curtailed by their obligation to stay out of trouble and avoid any negative impact on their fathers' careers. Although 75 percent of the teens had experienced a period of father-absence during adolescence, they rarely mentioned it as a factor.

Darnauer concluded from his data that in general neither youths nor parents appeared to view adolescence in the army family as dissimilar from adolescent life in the civilian world. The major difference was the adolescent's vulnerability to relocation. The capacity for intimacy involving sustained interpersonal relationships was the factor that appeared to be most vulnerable to the geographic mobility of the family.

This study tends to support these findings. Father absence in and of itself was cited as a causative factor in the current problems for only four adolescents in the military families. Furthermore, these absences were traumatic when the adolescent was a young child. What appears to be most problematic is when father absence occurs in combination with other circumstances. For example, what happened in the family when the father was gone? In two adoptive families and one control family, when the fathers left home the children were left alone with abusing or rejecting mothers. In the less extreme cases, three adoptive mothers and two control mothers simply could not manage their children by themselves (most of the children were described by these mothers as difficult or hyperactive). On the other hand, how did these fathers relate to their children when they returned home? Two adoptive fathers and three control fathers were described as being cold and distant in their emotional interactions with their families. Three control fathers were described as childlike and immature in their relationships with their families. The key to understanding is in the quality of the family's ongoing relationships.

Non-Military Families

It is important to note that issues relating to parental work in the non-military families appeared to contribute to adolescents' disturbance in eight adoptive families and four control families. Some of the same issues affecting the military families emerged: physical or emotional absence of the father, frequent moves, inability of either parent to buffer a dysfunctional relationship of the child with the other parent, low social support, and difficult children. Further research is underway to clarify these patterns.

CONCLUSION

Many of the children in this sample experienced multiple stressors, which may have placed them at greater risk for the development of emotional disturbance. Frequent parental absence; relocations; abuse; and loss of a relationship with a parent due to separation, divorce, or death were among the contextual factors that may have affected their adjustment in the family. It is impossible to determine the potential impact of any one of these stressors; many of the children in this study had experienced more than one of these significant family events. Moreover, the impact of these factors may be determined by such factors as the family's resources (economic, educational, personal, health, and psychological), age of the child and developmental level, family cohesiveness, and adaptability.

As there were frequent discrepancies noted between the child's perception of the impact of a particular event and that of the parents, it is important for mental health professionals to obtain a record of significant occurrences from each family member. Their individual accounts of the impact of the event on themselves and others in the family will provide much-needed contextual data to facilitate an understanding of the etiology of disturbances. It is also important to note mediating factors operating in some families that can buffer the development of later disturbance.

Since many of the family events in this study occurred in combination with parental pathology, adoption agency staff must develop more effective assessment tools to assess prospective adoptive families. Adoption agency staff can educate prospective adoptive parents about the impact of contextual stressors on children, assist families with the development of problem-solving skills, and encourage the formation of strong social-support networks that can be useful in coping with stressful life events.

7

Peer Relationships

Peer-group activities and friendships are particularly important in the lives of children and adolescents (Hartup, 1984). Caring about and sharing experiences with another are both enjoyable and rewarding undertakings and serve to increase overall positive feelings about oneself. Positive peer relationships are considered to be an important social achievement and a sign of healthy adjustment (Millon, 1981). Moreover, research evidence suggests that well-adjusted adults generally had positive peer relationships during their childhood and adolescence (Hartup, 1978; Janes et al., 1979).

The dynamics of normal children's friendship patterns are related to the cognitive developmental level of the child (Selman and Selman, 1979). Young children between the ages of three and seven, who are limited in the way in which they take another's point of view, judge friendships in terms of what they want. For example, friendships can be based on how close another child lives or what kinds of toys the other child has. Until approximately the age of nine, a good friend is considered to be "someone who does what you want him to do." These relationships typically are shallow and fleeting. They are heavily dependent on situational characteristics such as proximity within the neighborhood or classroom. For example, children who live across the street from each other or are in the same class at school may become friends.

At approximately the ages of nine or ten, "chumships" develop generally among children of the same age and sex who spend considerable time together (Sullivan, 1953). During this stage the child is much less self-centered and more emotionally mature (Selman and Selman, 1979). Friendships have the potential to be characterized by reciprocal understanding and support. Another unique characteristic of school-aged children is that they have on the average five best friends, more than preschool children and adolescents generally acknowledge (Hallinan, 1980).

During adolescence, friendships become important and intimate. At this stage, adolescents have much in common to share with one another and often feel more comfortable talking with a trusted peer who has the same concerns and experiences than with parents and family. Because of their level of cognitive maturation, adolescents are better able to handle social interactions and to understand the motives and actions of others (Kimmel and Weiner, 1985).

Children who have problematic peer relationships are generally considered to be at risk for later emotional and behavioral disturbance. Difficulties with peers often lead to feelings of rejection, alienation, and negative self-concepts. The most consistently reported presenting problem of children referred for mental health services is poor peer relationships (Achenbach and Edelbrock, 1981).

In this study, almost all of the adopted and control children had experienced some problems with peer relationships. Their relationships were characterized in many negative ways including "shallow," "warm but not trusting," "guarded," "blaming," "abusive to others," "a wall flower," "a loner," "rejected by others," "self-centered" and "unable to share feelings."

A caseworker described one child as follows:

> Tony (age 14) comes to the peer group with a lot of self-defeating behaviors. He doesn't really know how to establish himself with peers. He pokes, aggravates, teases, name calls. Those are the issues we have been working on in his therapy. To the extent that he's well supervised, he will lessen the frequency, but the moment the adult leaves the room, there's some kind of a problem, usually involving Tony. He typically doesn't do well in game situations. If he doesn't understand the game, then his goal is to disrupt it.

Another child was described as follows:

> Steven (age 15) has friends for a few days then he begins to bully them or manipulate them. As a result, they have nothing else to do with him. He is out for himself. He can't relate to others and has no trust in anyone else. When he was at home he tried to buy friendships. He would steal things and give them to kids at school to try to get them to like him. That would only last for a few days or so though. The kids would get tired of him. He always wanted them to do what he wanted to do.

These vignettes exemplify the troubled friendship patterns of many adolescents in this study. Although the peer relationships were not the primary presenting problem that necessitated the child's institutionalization, they probably contributed to and/or resulted from some of the other emotional problems the children were experiencing.

PATTERNS OF PEER RELATIONSHIPS

In the study, the child, the caseworker, the mother, and the father were separately asked to respond to questions regarding the child's peer relationships. Varying and often conflicting remarks were noted among the responses of the four parties. For example, the child might say that he had no friends, the parents might indicate that he had several, while the caseworker might say that he had many friends. These differences might be attributed to varying definitions of the term *friend*, or perhaps the parents were referring to the number of friends the child had when he was at home while the caseworkers were referring to the number of friends at the treatment center. In order to analyze more closely the peer dynamics, caseworker and child responses were used as they reflected the child's current friendship patterns. After a comprehensive review of all the interview responses to questions pertaining to peer relationships, several clusters or patterns of relationships emerged. Although there was some overlap in categories (i.e., some children had both superficial and hostile relationships at varying times during their treatment), an attempt was made to categorize cases depending on the most-current evaluation of peer interactions. These patterns were based upon the level of involvement or degree of mutually shared relationships.

Peer relationships among the adopted and control children could be assigned to four categories: 1) no involvement with peers; 2) hostile/negative interactions; 3) superficial, short-lived, or one-way relationships; and 4) close positive attachments (see Table 7.1). Although forty-eight of the adopted and forty-three of the control adolescents did have some involvement with peers, thirty-eight of the adopted and thirty of the control children who indicated they had friends exhibited either hostile/negative interactions with peers or superficial, short-lived relationships. No statistically significant differences were found between the adopted and control groups on peer relationships. This is not surprising, as most children in residential treatment tend to have problematic peer relationships.

No Involvement with Peers

Most of the children who had no friends were verbally and physically abusive to other children, were unable to relate to peers, and found it hard to fit in. Their family histories indicated that they generally had moved frequently as a result of a divorce or some other family problem and seemed afraid to make friends or did not possess the necessary skills to do so.

As noted in Table 7.1, seven control and two adopted children were identified as having no friends. This may be attributed to the high

Table 7.1

Frequencies of Adopted and Control Adolescents Experiencing Four
Styles of Peer Relationships

	No Involvement with Peers	Hostile/ Negative Interaction	Superficial Short-Lived	Close Positive Interaction
Adopted	2	15	23	10
Control	7	10	20	13
Total	9	25	43	23

Note: $\chi^2 = 4.3784$, ns.

incidence of family disruption and the abuse experienced by many of
the children in the control sample. Perhaps these children did not form
secure attachments with their caretakers during early childhood, and
therefore they were unable and fearful of attachment to others. These
children were typically described by caseworkers as "not allowing
themselves friends." Others exhibited infantile behavior that precluded
interaction with others, and some saw themselves as "unable to fit in
with peers."

Sroufe and Fleeson (1986) hypothesized that young children carry
from their attachment relationships in early childhood the
expectations and skills for future ones. In essence, they reconstruct the
patterns of early experiences in subsequent ones. Evidence suggests that
these same links occur or persist into adolescence.

Hostile/Negative Interactions

The fifteen adopted and ten control adolescents who had
hostile/negative interactions generally knew many other children but
would not risk revealing too much about themselves. According to the
caseworkers, these children were often very hostile and had
manipulative, nontrusting relationships with others. They tended to
have a difficult time dealing with emotions, so in peer situations they
remained very controlled. A caseworker, in describing one of the
adolescents who fell into this category, stated that "he presents a very

self-assured individual, who is, in fact, lonely and isolated. A lot of his peers don't like the way he approaches them, with the intellectual logic games." Other children who fell into this category were described as "negative leaders," "domineering," "rejected by others," "critical," and "alienating of others."

Although not statistically significant, more adopted than control children were found to have hostile/negative interactions. This might have occurred because most of the adopted children in this subgroup had been in several different foster homes before coming into the adoptive home. It is likely that they could form relationships with others but remained very untrusting of others. They may have learned to expect rejection and now relate in a very hostile manner toward others in order to protect themselves from further rejection.

The adopted children in this category seemed to expect rejection because they believed that they had initially been rejected by their birthmothers. By acting hostile, aloof, and distant, they may have consciously or unconsciously created situations with peers so that they would be rejected, thus recreating past patterns (Wilson, 1985).

Moreover, studies of children with healthy peer relationships suggest that their parents are emotionally supportive, infrequently frustrating and punitive, and encouraging of prosocial behavior (Winder and Rau, 1962). Factors such as unemployment, terminal illness, family conflict, and divorce have been found to have an effect on friendship patterns (Hartup, 1978). As mentioned in Chapter 5, the control sample in this study had a high incidence of family conflict, divorce, and pathology. This may partially explain some of their hostile/negative peer interactions.

Superficial/Short-Lived Peer Relationships

Twenty-three adopted and twenty control children experienced superficial peer relationships. Unlike the hostile/negative pattern, children who had superficial peer relationships tended not to be cold, distant, or harshly rejecting. These short-lived friendships often met the dependency needs of these children. They maintained friendships only in order to have someone with whom to associate or to participate in an activity. When asked for a definition of a friend, a typical response was "a person that you do things with for a week or so."

This friendship pattern seems identical to that of much younger children. As mentioned earlier, children between the ages of four and nine think mainly about what they want from the relationship. They often only think about the present and select friends based upon who can participate in an activity with them at a particular moment.

Children in this category tended to play with younger children, saw friends as a means to an end, and would back off when it appeared as if the friendship was growing. Others believed that friends are not to be trusted and found it hard to form attachments. Five children in this group described their peers as "a means to an end." Several came from very enmeshed families, and their superficial peer relationships may have stemmed from their inability to differentiate and relate to others within their families.

Close Attachments

Ten adopted and thirteen control children seemed to have very close reciprocal relationships with peers. For example, one adolescent was described as having "lots of close friends, excellent peer relationships, easy to get to know, and very involved in athletic and other activities." In comparison with children who had problematic friendship patterns, this group of children was considered popular and had sustained social relationships. Although it is possible that many children had improved their interactional skills as a result of treatment or may never have had difficulties in this area, further investigation is needed to explore what other qualities these children may have had that enabled them to have positive peer interactions.

Peer Influence

Four adoptive and three control families of children in the study blamed peers for the bad behavior of their institutionalized children. They reported that their children's drinking, drug usage, and sexual acting out were because of the influence of their peers. However, studies of adolescent peer influences reveal that psychologically mature adolescents are more likely to have had family experiences that have encouraged them to individuate rather than to use their peer groups as models for behavior. These higher-maturity males and females are more likely to have close friends with whom they have explored their sense of self-definition and differentiation in a context of mutuality (Josselson, Greenberger, and McConochie, 1977). Because of their maturity, they are able to sustain a distinctive point of view independent of pressures for conformity. Therefore, contrary to popular thought and previous studies, peers have the potential to help each other resist conformity rather than always pressuring toward adherence to group norms.

CONCLUSION

Multiple factors were responsible for the etiology of the problems of children in this study. It is likely that the peer relationships described in this section were symptoms rather than causes of the problematic behavior that these children experienced. However, the findings regarding peer patterns suggest the need for further explorations of such areas as the interaction between family and peer influences on behavior, contrasting definitions of *friend*, the effect of negative peer relationships on self-concepts, gender differences in friendship patterns, and the influence of cognitive development and psychological maturity on social relationships.

8

Clinical Issues

This chapter will address several clinical issues concerning the adopted and control adolescents in the sample. In the first section of the chapter, the patterns of symptoms exhibited by the adolescents will be discussed. Second, diagnoses of the adolescents in the two groups will be compared. Finally, the treatment histories of the adolescents in the sample will be discussed, focusing on differences between the adopted and control adolescents.

SYMPTOMS

In a number of studies (e.g., Humphrey and Ounsted, 1963; Menlove, 1965), symptoms exhibited by adopted and non-adopted children in treatment have been compared. A common conclusion is that the symptom patterns of the two groups differ; specifically, adopted children tend to show more behavioral problems that are manifested openly in the family, school, and community than do their non-adopted peers (e.g., Offord, Aponte, and Cross, 1969). In such studies, behaviors of adoptees and non-adoptees are contrasted, and post hoc explanations of why differences occur are offered. Little of this work is theoretically driven, nor does it offer testable hypotheses concerning why these differences appear. Furthermore, these studies vary widely in terms of how symptoms are defined and how symptom data are aggregated.

Data regarding symptoms shown by the adolescents in this study were systematically summarized from the interview data. As indicated in Chapter 2, all symptoms mentioned for each adolescent were recorded on the Adolescent Behavior Checklist (ABC) (Klein, 1982), an instrument that lists eighty-six potential symptoms. Frequency data for the occurrence of each symptom in the adoptive and control samples are noted in Table 8.1. The number of symptoms listed for the adopted adolescents ranged from four to fourteen (mean = 9.1); the number for the control adolescents ranged from one to eighteen (mean = 8.4). In

Table 8.1

Frequencies of Symptoms Exhibited by Adopted and Control
Adolescents on Adolescent Behavior Checklist

SYMPTOM	Frequencies	
	ADOPTED	CONTROL
1. Steals outside of home	21 (42%)	18 (36%)
2. Steals from family	3 (6%)	10 (20%)**
3. Trouble with police/authorities	10 (20%)	8 (16%)
4. CHINS petition, commitment to DYS	3 (6%)	1 (2%)
5. Court offense, arrests, probation	1 (2%)	1 (2%)
6. Anti-social or delinquent behavior	14 (28%)	13 (26%)
7. Withdrawn, alone, seclusive, isolated	11 (22%)	8 (16%)
8. Shy, timid, hypersensitive	0	0
9. Lack of confidence, feels inferior	1 (2%)	8 (16%)**
10. Feelings of loneliness	1 (2%)	0
11. Secretive, uncommunicative	8 (16%)	7 (14%)
12. Absence of close friends	15 (30%)	20 (40%)
13. Alcohol abuse	11 (22%)	14 (28%)
14. Drug abuse	24 (48%)	17 (34%)
15. Drug selling	2 (4%)	0
16. Stomach ache, nausea, vomiting	0	0
17. Headaches, dizziness, faintness	0	0
18. Other recurrent pains, complaints of ill health or discomfort	1 (2%)	1 (2%)
19. Idea something seriously wrong with body	0	0
20. Disobedient and rebellious at home	27 (54%)	22 (44%)
21. Negative, impertinent, etc.	21 (42%)	25 (50%)
22. Staying out late	0	2 (4%)
23. Runs away overnight	32 (64%)	26 (52%)
24. Fears or phobias	0	0
25. Avoidance of situations due to fears	1 (2%)	2 (4%)
26. Nightmares, fear of dark	0	1 (2%)
27. Inadequate guilt feelings	0	0
28. Others are to blame	1 (2%)	0
29. Worrying, anxiety	0	0
30. Chronic fearfulness, etc.	0	0
31. Fear of own impulses	0	0
32. Hysterical or frantic behavior	1 (2%)	1 (2%)
33. Breaks school rules, disobedient at school/work	27 (54%)	29 (58%)
34. Truant from school or work	24 (48%)	16 (32%)
35. Expelled or suspended from school	0	0
36. Difficulty making decisions	1 (2%)	0
37. Obsessions, thoughts or impulses which are ego alien/frightening	2 (4%)	0
38. Compulsions	2 (4%)	1 (2%)
39. Preoccupation with internal events	1 (2%)	1 (2%)
40. Loose temper, easily irritated	4 (8%)	7 (14%)
41. Temper outbursts or tantrums	11 (22%)	17 (34%)
42. Verbally abusive to others	15 (30%)	12 (24%)
43. Lack of impulse control	6 (12%)	6 (12%)

SYMPTOM	Frequencies ADOPTED	CONTROL	
44. Fights with peers, bullies, teases	24 (48%)	16 (32%)	
45. Bad friends, gang member	12 (24%)	2 (4%)	**
46. Feelings of depression/sadness	12 (24%)	20 (40%)	
47. Cries a lot	0	1 (2%)	
48. Apathetic, etc.	1 (2%)	1 (2%)	
49. Discourages, etc.	3 (6%)	2 (4%)	
50. Better to die feelings	0	0	
51. Guilt feelings, blame self	0	0	
52. Feelings of worthlessness, badness	11 (22%)	8 (16%)	
53. Preoccupied with suicide	12 (24%)	5 (10%)	*
54. Suicidal attempts	9 (18%)	5 (10%)	
55. Threatens people with harm	3 (6%)	6 (12%)	
56. Lesser attacks on others	3 (6%)	2 (4%)	
57. Physical attacks on people	20 (40%)	13 (26%)	
58. Reckless behavior which endangers self or others	0	0	
59. Daredevil, braggart, bravado	0	0	
60. Lying	8 (16%)	12 (24%)	
61. Sexual acting out	13 (26%)	8 (16%)	
62. Sleep disturbance	0	3 (6%)	
63. Dependent, clinging, etc.	1 (2%)	1 (2%)	
64. Exploitive relationships	3 (6%)	2 (4%)	
65. Teased, bullied, etc. by others	4 (8%)	5 (10%)	
66. Self-mutilation or minor OD's	6 (12%)	2 (4%)	
67. Can't concentrate	5 (10%)	10 (20%)	
68. Odd or bizarre ideation	0	0	
69. Decreased ability to function	0	0	
70. Distinct periods of elevated or expansive moods	0	0	
71. Delusions	0	0	
72. Hallucinations	0	0	
73. Bizarre behavior	1 (2%)	1 (2%)	
74. Incoherence, illogical thinking	0	0	
75. Inappropriate or blunted affect	0	0	
76. Impairment of functioning	0	0	
77. Other acute psychosis behaviors	0	0	
78. Eating disorder	0	0	
79. Manic-depressive	0	0	
80. Psychosis secondary to drug abuse	0	0	
81. Behavior provoking harm or rejection	0	0	
82. Enuresis	1 (2%)	0	
83. Encopresis	0	2 (4%)	
84. Blackouts, dissociative states	0	0	
85. Histrionics, self-dramatization	1 (2%)	0	
86. Seizures	0	0	

*p < .10
**p < .05

general, the specific symptoms noted for the adopted and control adolescents seem to occur with roughly equal frequency. Exceptions to this observation occurred for only four of the eighty-six behaviors on the ABC: control adolescents showed higher frequencies of stealing from their families (p = .034) and lacking confidence and/or feeling inferior (p = .011) than did adopted adolescents. Adopted adolescents showed higher frequencies of having bad friends and/or being a gang member (p = .001) and preoccupation with suicide (p = .059) than did control adolescents.

In their review of studies of childhood symptomatology, Achenbach and Edelbrock (1978) concluded that two broad-band syndromes commonly emerge that may be more meaningful ways to understand disturbance than individual symptoms. The first, the externalizing syndrome, has been alternatively labeled undercontrolled behavior, conduct problems, hostile-aggressive behavior, or aggressive behavior. The second, the internalizing syndrome, has also been referred to as overcontrolled behavior, personality problems, anxious-fearful behavior, or inhibited behavior. These broad-band categories are useful in the present investigation, because the literature suggests that these dimensions index key behaviors along which adopted and non-adopted adolescents in treatment appear to differ.

Therefore, in a second approach to the symptom data, adopted and control adolescents were compared in terms of the internalizing and externalizing syndromes. Internalizing behaviors involve somatic complaints, depression, inhibition, shyness, anxiety, and personality disorders; externalizing behaviors involve aggression, acting out, drug or alcohol abuse, and conduct disorders. Although Offord, Aponte, and Cross (1969) did not use Achenbach and Edelbrock's (1978) syndromes, they did find that adoptees were more frequently found to exhibit "behavior disorders" (i.e., externalizing) than were non-adoptees; whereas non-adoptees in treatment were more likely to show more "internalized neurotic" symptoms than were adoptees.

The internalizing and externalizing clusters were each represented by thirty-three specific behaviors on Klein's (1982) Adolescent Behavior Checklist. A 2 x 2 analysis of variance (Sex x Adoptive status) was conducted on mean frequencies of internalizing and externalizing behaviors. (Means and analysis-of-variance [ANOVA] tables for internalizing and externalizing symptoms are presented in Tables 8.2 and 8.3, 8.4 and 8.5, respectively.)

No significant effects were found for internalizing behaviors. For externalizing behaviors, a significant Adoptive status x Sex interaction was found [F(1,96) = 4.30, p = .041]. The means indicate that adopted and control males have highly similar levels of externalizing behaviors; however, adopted females have levels above both male means, and control females have levels below both male means.

Table 8.2
Mean Levels of Internalizing Behaviors by Adoptive Status and Sex

		Adopted	Control	Marginal
Sex	Male	1.58 (N=26)	1.81 (N=32)	1.71 (N=58)
	Female	1.58 (N=24)	0.94 (N=18)	1.31 (N=42)
	Marginal	1.58 (N=50)	1.50 (N=50)	1.54 (N=100)

Table 8.3
Analysis of Variance on Internalizing Behaviors by Adoptive Status
and Sex

Source	Sum of Sq.	df	Mean Sq.	F	p
Sex	4.10	1	4.10	2.43	.122
Adoptive Status	.41	1	.41	.25	.622
Sex x Status	4.58	1	4.58	2.72	.103
Residual	161.99	96	1.69		

Although the mean levels of internalizing and externalizing symptoms resembled Klein's (1982) means, the ANOVA results did not correspond fully. Klein found that non-adopted adolescents showed significantly more internalizing symptoms than did adoptees, whereas no significant differences were detected in the present study. For externalizing symptoms, Klein found significant main effects for both adoptive status (adoptees higher) and sex (males higher), in contrast to the present study, which instead found a Status x Sex interaction. Discrepancies in the results of these two studies may be due to differences in samples, procedures for recording data, and the

Table 8.4

Mean Levels of Externalizing Behaviors by Adoptive Status and Sex

		Adopted	Control	Marginal
Sex	Male	6.38 (N=26)	6.63 (N=32)	6.52 (N=58)
	Female	7.38 (N=24)	5.17 (N=18)	6.43 (N=42)
	Marginal	6.86 (N=50)	6.10 (N=50)	6.48 (N=100)

Table 8.5

Analysis of Variance on Externalizing Behaviors by Adoptive Status and Sex

Source	Sum of Sq.	df	Mean Sq.	F	p
Sex	0.82	1	0.82	.10	.754
Adoptive Status	15.07	1	15.07	1.80	.182
Sex x Status	35.92	1	35.92	4.30	.041*
Residual	801.78	96	8.35		

treatment settings in which the data were collected. Klein's subjects were all in-patients in McLean Psychiatric Hospital in Boston, whereas the subjects in the present study were in a variety of less restrictive residential treatment settings.

DIAGNOSES

Caseworkers were asked for information concerning the diagnoses of each adolescent in the study. Frequencies of diagnoses for the adopted and control adolescents are presented in Table 8.6. Frequencies

Table 8.6
Frequencies of Diagnosis Assigned to Adopted and Control Adolescents

Diagnosis	Adopted	Control
Conduct Disorder	27	25
Undersocialized, Aggressive	8	6
Undersocialized, Nonaggressive	3	4
Socialized, Aggressive	3	8
Socialized, Nonaggressive	13	7
Borderline	14	9
Developmental Disorder	5	7
Bipolar Disorder	3	10 *
Attention Deficit Disorder, Hyperactive	6	4
Schizophrenic	5	3
Oppositional Disorder	6	2
Adjustment Disorder	2	7
Other Disorders	13	23

*$\chi^2(1) = 4.33, p = .034.$

in each column sum to greater than 50 because a number of adolescents had multiple diagnoses.

The most frequent diagnosis for adolescents in both groups was conduct disorder (twenty-seven adopted and twenty-five control adolescents). According to the *Diagnostic and Statistical Manual of Mental Disorders* (DSM-III) (APA, 1980), four subtypes of conduct disorder are recognized: undersocialized aggressive, undersocialized nonaggressive, socialized aggressive, and socialized nonaggressive. The undersocialized types show a failure to establish normal degrees of affection or bond with others. Peer relationships are lacking, superficial, or manipulative. There is a lack of concern for the feelings or well-being of others. The socialized types show evidence of attachment to at least one other person but may be manipulative or unconcerned toward others to whom they are not attached. The aggressive types are characterized by persistent patterns of aggressive conduct that may include physical violence and theft. The nonaggressive types do not show physical violence but do evidence age-inappropriate behavior, such as violations of rules, running away, persistent lying, or truancy.

There were no significant differences between the frequencies of adopted and control adolescents in the conduct-disorder diagnosis or in its four subtypes. As can be seen in Table 8.6, the only actual diagnosis for which a significant difference in frequencies emerged was for bipolar disorders, with control adolescents more frequently receiving this diagnosis than adopted adolescents ($\chi^2(1) = 4.33$, $p = .034$). This finding concerning the bipolar disorders is consistent with studies by Klein (1982) and Weiss (1985), both of whom found fewer diagnoses of psychotic symptoms among adoptees than in control groups of non-adopted adolescents.

Each adolescent's caseworker was asked to evaluate his or her prognosis, which was subsequently coded as either "good," "fair," or "poor" (see Table 8.7). Chi-square analysis found that control adolescents were somewhat more likely to receive a prognosis of "good" (N = 26) than were adopted adolescents (N = 17), ($\chi^2(1) = 3.31$, $p = .066$). This might be because more of the control than the adopted adolescents were in treatment because their parents were unable to provide adequate care for them. Had an adequate family setting been available, it is likely that some of the control adolescents could have been dealt with at home rather than in residential treatment. It may also be that adoptive parents delay placing their children in treatment longer than non-adoptive parents, thus contributing to a less optimistic prognosis.

Caseworkers were also asked to outline adolescents' treatment goals (see Table 8.8). The only two goals for which statistically significant differences emerged were for "improving relationship with mother" ($\chi^2(1) = 4.46$, $p = .03$) and "improving relationship with father" ($\chi^2(1) = 3.93$, $p = .04$); in both cases these goals were cited more frequently for adopted than control adolescents. This difference likely emerged because a greater proportion of the control adolescents' parents had had their parental rights terminated by the state; thus, no ongoing relationship was envisioned and other treatment goals were emphasized instead. Another possible interpretation of this finding is that adopted children often express a great deal of anger toward their adoptive mother, thus making an improved relationship desirable and necessary.

Table 8.7
Prognosis of Adopted and Control Adolescents

Prognosis	Adopted	Control
Good	17	26 *
Fair	17	14
Poor	5	5
Unknown	11	5

*$\chi^2(1) = 3.31, p = .066$.

Table 8.8
Treatment Goals Cited for Adopted and Control Adolescents

Goal	Adopted	Control
Improve Self-Image	14	20
Improve Reln w/ Mother	22	12 $
Improve Reln w/ Father	19	10 @
Improve Reln w/ Others	34	22
Develop Insight into Problems	33	28
Reintegrate into the Home	10	11
Other Goals	35	30

$ $\chi^2(1) = 4.46, p = .03$.
@ $\chi^2(1) = 3.93, p = .04$.

TREATMENT HISTORY

The treatment histories of the adolescents in both samples varied widely. For some adolescents, the current residential placement was their first, and they were expected to return home after a relatively short stay. For others, the residential placement was the last in a long series of unsuccessful and sometimes harmful treatment approaches.

Information about the treatment histories of the adolescents in the study may be found in Table 8.9. Five categories were used to summarize treatment histories. An overall chi-square analysis of the frequencies in Table 8.9 was significant ($\chi^2(4) = 9.51$, p = .05), most likely because of the larger number of control than adoptive families who were unable to provide appropriate care for their children.

The largest group in both the adopted (N = 28) and control (N = 22) samples included adolescents who had been in multiple residential settings; they had typically been moved to the current setting because previous approaches had not worked. These adolescents were still in active treatment and were not considered well enough to return home at the time of the interview.

A second category included those fourteen adopted and nine control adolescents for whom the current situation was their first

Table 8.9

Treatment History of Adolescents in Adoptive and Control Families

	Adoptive	Control
Multiple residential placements; still in active treatment	28	22
First residential placement; still in active treatment	14	9
Convenience of parents	0	2
Parents unable to care for child	4	14
Treatment made child's condition worse	4	3
Total	50	50

$\chi^2(4) = 9.51$, p = .05.

residential placement; even so, most of them had first seen a number of private mental health professionals. These adolescents were also still in active treatment and were not considered well enough to return home.

The third group included two control adolescents who appeared to be in treatment for the convenience of their parents rather than because of their own need. For example, in one control family, the caseworker noted that the adolescent had completed her treatment goals at the psychiatric hospital, but her father did not want her home yet because it might jeopardize his precarious marriage.

A fourth category included four adopted and fourteen control adolescents who were in treatment because their parents were unable to take care of them. In many of these families, the state had taken custody away from the child's parents because they had abused or neglected the child.

Finally, there were four adopted and three control families in which the treatment that the child had received appeared to complicate the child's recovery and make him or her worse. The frustration of conflicting professional guidance was expressed by the father of one of the adopted children:

> We've tried everything that the doctor recommended. We've tried — at first, ignoring it, which was the recommendation. And then we tried the reward and punishment process. . . . We'd go to the doctor and the doctor'd say "do this" and we'd do that for a while. And then we'd go to the doctor again and the doctor'd say "try something else," and then we were starting trying something else that was a complete change from what we'd been doing before. . . . I think it [the inconsistency] caused him more problems than it did good.

One adoptive father attributed some of his son's problems to the poor quality treatment he received in one center:

> We moved him to _____, which we now feel real bad about. It's a terrible place. I wouldn't take a sick dog there. He wasn't taken care of or treated. It probably did him more harm. . . . We took him out because of poor conditions — shampoo left in his hair, the kid is half dressed, he looks like he'd been pulled out of a rag sack. They would not let us tour the facility first and see where he'd sleep or the people who were going to take care of him except this little social worker who'd answer the phone.

Another adoptive parent expressed frustration about getting help: "We were rather frustrated through many years of raising her that we couldn't really get the attention of anybody medical about 'Hey, we've got a real problem here; what do we do about it?' . . . It's a little hard to really get anybody's attention and get them to concentrate and acknowledge there really is a problem."

Yet another adoptive mother, whose adopted son is now in his fourth residential placement, stated:

> I think they let him out too early [of his first placement]. He had, I think, a very poor psychiatrist. He was not in tune to anything. [The next place] drugged him up so bad, which they tend to do and would not listen to me. . . . [In the next place] they kept him drugged up against my will and against his will and he just never would really get into the program.

CONCLUSION

Overall, the samples of adopted and non-adopted adolescents in treatment did not differ dramatically in terms of symptoms (specific behaviors), syndromes (internalizing and externalizing), or diagnoses. The prognosis for the control group was considered slightly better, on the average. This difference in prognosis may result from the family situations of the control adolescents: many were in treatment because their parents could not care for them and not necessarily because their behavior was intolerably out of control. The treatment goals were also similar for the two groups, with the exception that more adoptees were attempting to improve their relationships with their parents.

Even though the clinical pictures of symptoms and diagnoses were not substantially different for the two groups, other evidence cited in this study suggests that the dynamics of the emotional disturbance in the two groups are not identical. In Chapter 5, differences in parent-child, marital, and sibling relationships within the two groups were discussed. In Chapters 9 and 10, specific issues concerning how adoption was handled in the family are presented. The similarities in symptoms may be largely a function of the types of treatment centers serving the adolescents in both the adoptive and control groups.

9

Adoptive Family Dynamics: Background Factors and Communication Issues

As stated in the introduction, adoptive family relationships add unique and somewhat complex dynamics to the normal challenges of parenting. Research on adoption has suggested that there may be inherent problems within the adoptive family situation that make adoptive parents and their children especially vulnerable to stress (Goodman and Magno-Nora, 1975; Kirk, 1981; Schechter, 1960). This chapter will include a review of some of the literature on adoptive family dynamics. In addition, specific research findings will be presented on parent and child attitudes about adoption, adoption revelation, and communication issues.

ADOPTIVE FAMILY DYNAMICS

Adoption is often considered "a highly subjective, emotional experience" (Andrews, 1978, 1979) because of prevailing societal attitudes. In a society that prepares and expects adults to have children of their own, adoption is a social institution that has won community acceptance but is still considered the second-best way to build a family (Andrews, 1978). Brinich and Brinich (1982) suggest that adoption is "always painful and potentially traumatic," because it implies two important social failures: 1) a child is unwanted and 2) a couple has been unable to conceive.

Since children represent the real wealth of marriage in most societies, infertility becomes a psychological trauma. Infertile couples may grieve for the loss of their reproductive capabilities in the same way as they would grieve about the death of a family member (Sorosky, Baran, and Pannor, 1978). Such feelings of loss may even be further compounded if the family has also suffered miscarriages or stillbirths. The placement of an adopted child can be viewed as tangible evidence that the couple was unable to have a birthchild (Berman and Bufferd, 1986).

Some families adopt for reasons other than infertility, such as population concerns or a desire to provide a home for a child who needs one. In the present sample of adopted children, eighteen parents already had birthchildren before adopting and eleven had birthchildren after the adoption.

Regardless of their motivation, many adoptive parents compensate for their unique status by being overprotective of the child or attempting to be perfect parents. They might forever question their entitlement to the adopted child (Hartman, 1984). Also, adoptive parents must find ways to not only adjust to their role but to communicate to their children about their adoptive status and to relate information about their birthparents.

Adopted children develop self-concepts that incorporate their perceptions of the reasons their birthparents relinquished them for adoption. Often they express anger, resentment, and a sense of rejection, which they may direct at either their birthparents for not rearing them or toward their adoptive parents for adopting them. They may also face the problem of "genealogical bewilderment" (Sants, 1964), since they must recognize that they were born to a set of parents whom they may never know. They must sort out their feelings toward their two sets of parents, adoptive and birth.

According to Tousseing (1971), anxiety is shared among the family members within adoptive families. First, the mutual knowledge of adoption between parent and child causes anxiety; second, infertile couples may perceive their marriage as being in jeopardy and may have difficulty in believing their child really belongs to them. They may become insecure, which leads to anxiety and tension, which in turn affects relationships throughout the family system. The adopted child then may fear abandonment. Tousseing, like Kirk (1964, 1981), suggests that this anxiety can only be eliminated if adoptive parents accept their lack of biological ties and if professionals, agencies, and society work together to recognize that adoption is inherently different from biological parenthood.

Adoption outcomes seem to be influenced by a variety of child and parental factors, including the parents' reasons and motivation for adoption and their attitudes toward adoptive parenthood. As noted in Chapter 3, preplacement issues such as genetic background and previous placements affect the child prior to coming to the adoptive family. Once the child is placed in the adoptive family, compatibility and other adaptational issues emerge between parent and child. The child's cognitive understanding of adoption and emerging sense of identity are shaped by the family; these in turn contribute to the relationships within the family. This chapter will address these issues from the perspective of the institutionalized adoptees and their families in this sample.

PARENTAL MOTIVATION FOR ADOPTION

Twenty-two of the families in this study adopted because of infertility. Others (six) adopted to provide a sibling for a birthchild, two to help a relative, two because of attachment to a foster child in their home and three because of population concerns. Other reasons included a history of previous stillbirths and problems with the biological child. Half of the parents requested to adopt an infant. All but seven of the families adopted through private or public adoption agencies. Four of these adoptions were identified as independent and were arranged through an attorney or physician, and three were arranged among relatives.

ATTITUDES TOWARD ADOPTIVE PARENTHOOD

Adoptive Parents

Table 9.1 depicts the adoptive parents' feelings about the adoption. Twenty-nine mothers and twenty-five fathers were very positive about the adoption and identified the following major satisfactions from being an adoptive parent: affection, nurturing the child, and watching the child grow. Those who were ambivalent, disappointed, or nervous were generally in situations in which only one parent desired the adoption or the parents were having marital conflict and had thought that perhaps a child would improve the relationship.

Table 9.1
Parental Feelings about the Adoption at Time of Adoption

	Mother	Father
Happy	29	25
Ambivalent	3	5
Disappointed	2	--
Nervous	5	1
No Answer	11	19
Total	50	50

Twenty-five of the adoptive mothers and fourteen of the adoptive fathers felt close to their adopted child at the time of the placement (see Table 9.2). Those who identified their feelings as guarded, distant, or hostile may have been less motivated to adopt. Several possible explanations can be given for these findings. The parents might have requested a particular age or temperament of child and received another. Also they could have been ambivalent about adopting in general and therefore did not feel close to the child at the time of adoption. (It must also be noted that parents were asked to recall their feelings retrospectively; intervening events may have altered those perceptions.)

Parents' feelings about the adoption might have been a function of the process that they have undergone in order to adopt. Many waited for years to have children and only decided to adopt when they realized that they could not have biological children. Therefore, adoptive parents are typically older than birthparents. In this study, the adoptive parents were approximately four years older than the control parents. They usually have had to adjust to the fact that they may be unable to have children biologically. Regardless of the reason for the adoption, these parents have generally spent much time discussing the pros and cons of adoptive parenthood.

Table 9.2
Parental Perceptions of Feelings toward Child at Time of Adoption

	Mother	Father
Close	25	14
Average	--	7
Guarded	2	1
Distant	3	1
Hostile	2	--
Changing	--	1
Did not Answer	18	26
Total	50	50

As mentioned earlier, seven families adopted the child of a relative and/or adopted through an attorney or physician. Most, however, chose to adopt through an agency. Agency applicants must be willing to undergo an evaluative procedure that generally includes assessments of their financial status, emotional maturity, family relationships, social stability, readiness to adopt, feelings about children, and motivation for adoption.

Many families remain on an agency list for at least a year before the home-study process begins. Throughout the process, families are aware that they are being carefully evaluated and must remain hopeful that they will be found fit for parenthood (Kirk, 1981).

If approved for adoption, families might again wait for months before a child is placed with them. This process can be particularly long for parents who wish to adopt a "healthy white infant," since the demand exceeds the supply. Parents adopting older children often find that the process is much briefer. The supply of older children needing adoptive placement is large (Kadushin, 1980). Parents who successfully complete this process are generally relieved and are proud that they have been certified as good parents who have been chosen to adopt a child.

Adoptive parents can feel a greater sense of accountability than biological parents because their role as parents is achieved through a screening process and because adoption may be the only way they will have children. They sometimes feel the need to prove that they are "good parents." Because of these perceptions, adoptive parents might seem to be either overprotective of their children or overpermissive with them (Humphrey and Ounsted, 1963; Pringle, 1967).

Adoptive parents' attitudes are generally considered to be a reflection of the adoption process, their reaction to their infertility, and the attitudes of others toward their status (Melina, 1986). Because of these factors, adoptive parents may try to prove themselves and to demonstrate the significance of environmental factors in child development. Consequently, they might have high expectations for their children as well as for themselves as parents, believing that they can generally overcome any negative situations the child has experienced in the past. They might seek help from therapists or change schools or teachers in order to attempt to overcome problems (Melina, 1986). If the children still fail to conform to their expectations and/or experience serious behavioral difficulties, they tend to attribute the problems to the child's heredity or "bad blood" (Sorosky, Baran, and Pannor, 1984).

Adoptive parents often feel a sense of loss as a result of their inability to have their own biological child. These feelings can be compounded if the family has experienced a miscarriage or stillbirth. The adoption of a child is sometimes viewed unconsciously as an affirmation of that loss and as a result, some parents experience "postpartum blues" after the placement (Berman and Bufferd, 1986; Menning, 1977). Once the parents have accepted their infertility, some tend to become overly attached to the child and become very anxious and fearful about the possibility of separation.

Relatives

Adoptive parents not only have to deal with their own feelings about their status, they must also deal with the reactions of their extended family members and friends to the adoption. Many encounter misgivings among family members about their plans to adopt. They often must respond to many questions about the background of the child and stereotypic statements about adopted children. Others find that their friends and family members are quite accepting of the adoption.

The adoptive parents' relatives in this sample had mixed reactions to their adoption plans (see Table 9.3). Although the majority of adoptive mothers and fathers in the sample recalled that their relatives felt positively about the adoption, twelve mothers and seven fathers believed that their relatives were initially negative. Four of these negative reactions occurred in transracial adoptive family situations, in which the relatives felt they could not accept a minority child in the family. However, almost all of the relatives eventually accepted the

Table 9.3
Relatives' Reactions to Adoption

	Mother	Father
Negative	12	7
Neutral	1	--
Mixed	3	2
Positive	23	21
No Answer	11	20
Total	50	50

adoption. These initial negative reactions did not seem to affect the adopted children in the study. Almost all indicated that their relatives liked them and treated them fairly. Although the parents would have appreciated their relatives' earlier endorsement of the adoption, their displeasure seemed to have had little or no effect on the adoptive parents.

ATTITUDES TOWARD BIRTHPARENTS

Adoptive parents' attitudes toward birthparents are often a reflection of their perception of their social workers' attitudes toward birthparents at the time of the adoption (Sorosky, Baran, and Pannor, 1984). When social workers deemphasized the need for adoptive parents to have extensive information on birthparents to share with their children, the adoptive parents tended to feel similarly. Adoptive parents in this sample had adopted at least eleven years ago. At that time agency confidentiality was considered the rule, and generally very little information was shared with adoptive parents about birthparents. The parents in this study generally had sketchy information about the birthmother and less about the birthfather. Most parents knew something about the birthparents' reasons for relinquishing, marital status, ethnicity, education and medical history. Some knew a little information about the birthmothers' special interests or talents. In most cases, the parents did not initiate the discussion about birthparent background information with the child, but, when asked, provided what limited data they had. In one case, the adoptive mother said she had a chance to get more detailed information about the birthparents from the agency. However, she was afraid to learn anymore about her child's background and declined the offer.

ADOPTION REVELATION

When and How

Although the majority of adoptive parents indicated that their adopted children were "always" told or told before the age of four years about the adoption, the mothers and fathers expressed differing perceptions of exactly when the child was told. For example, as noted in Table 9.4, twenty-seven mothers, as compared with only fifteen fathers, stated that the child was "always told about the adoption." Discrepancies also existed between the parents' and child's recollection of the time of the adoption revelation. Only six children in the study indicated that they were always told of the adoption. Eight indicated that they had been told between the ages of two and four, and twenty-eight said that they had been told between four and eleven.

Table 9.4
Family Members' Recall of Age When Told about the Adoption

Age When Told	Mother	Father	Child
Always	27	15	6
Before Age 2	3	2	--
Between 2 & 4	5	9	8
Between 5 & 7	3	4	16
Between 8 & 11	1	1	5
After Age 11	--	--	7
Can't remember	2	2	7
No answer	9	17	6
Total	50	50	50

All of the parents stated that they had intended to tell the child about the adoption as soon as they thought the child was old enough to understand. In one case the parents waited until the child was eight (the child reported that she was ten) to tell of the adoption. In several instances the child raised questions before the parents had introduced the subject. In three families the questions were stimulated by the adoptive mother being pregnant or by a friend's mother's pregnancy. In another case, the parents had planned to wait until they thought their child was mature enough to understand about the adoption. However, they were forced to tell him at age five when he started quizzing them about his adoption papers he had found.

Three adoptive fathers stated that they had never discussed the adoption with their child. Thirteen mothers and eight fathers reported that siblings, friends, or relatives actually first told the child about his/her adoptive status.

The discrepancy between the parents' and child's perceptions about the time when they were told about their adoption is consistent with recent research (Brodzinsky, Singer, and Braff, 1984) on children's understanding of adoption. In this study, 200 adopted and non-adopted children, ranging in age from four to thirteen, were first interviewed to evaluate their understanding about the adoptive family experience and then given a Q-sort task to evaluate their perceptions of the appropriateness of motives underlying adoption. Brodzinsky and colleagues identified six levels of understanding, as well as children's beliefs, about reasons for adoption. Clear developmental changes were found in children's knowledge about adoptive family relations and in their awareness of motives for adoption. For instance, preschool children were not likely to understand adoption (Level 0) even if they had been told about their adoption by their parents. By the age of five, children frequently tended to fuse the concepts of birth and adoption (Level 1). By age six, most children began to differentiate between birth and adoptive parenthood and could acknowledge the permanence of the adoptive family relationship (Level 2) but didn't understand why.

Between the ages of eight and eleven the children's conception of adoption started to broaden. At Level 3, children could differentiate between birth and adoption but were unclear about the permanence of the relationship. At Level 4 children began to give quasi-legal reasons (i.e., signing papers) for the permanence of the adoptive family relationship. Some children continued to fantasize that their birthparents could reclaim them. Toward the end of Level 5, children regained their certainty in the permanence of the adoptive family relationship. When they reached early to middle adolescence they began to understand that adoption involves a permanent, legal transfer of parental rights and responsibilities. These findings suggest that successful adoption revelation is not measured by what, how much, or even when the information is revealed. Rather, it hinges upon the way in which a child understands adoptive status and on the parents' realistic expectations about his or her understanding at different points in the child's development.

Children's Reactions

The adoptive parents' perception of the children's reaction to the adoption and the children's reaction to knowledge about the adoption varied, according to reports by the adoptive parents (see Table 9.5). Although a large percentage of the sample did not respond to this question, a number of trends were noted among the parents and children who did respond. Almost equal numbers of parents and children perceived the child's reaction as accepting. Fifteen mothers and twelve fathers felt that their child's reaction was neutral, and two mothers and three fathers reported that their child was puzzled by the revelation. Only five adoptive mothers and one adoptive father stated that their child's reaction was angry or sad. However, when compared

Table 9.5
Family Members' Perceptions of the Child's Reaction to Learning about
Adoption

	Mother	Father	Child
Accepting	8	9	9
Neutral	15	12	5
Puzzled	2	3	12
Sad	2	1	2
Angry	3	--	5
Mixed	2	1	--
No Answer	18	24	17
Total	50	50	50

to the children's responses, two major differences were noted. Children were more likely to report that they were puzzled by the news than neutral as parents seemed to suggest. Five children indicated that they were angry. The inconsistency in parental perceptions and the children's reactions to being told may be because of either some denial on the part of the adoptive parents or their differential recollection about when the children were first told about the adoption.

The following quotes from children in the study illustrate the variety of reactions to the revelation. Three adopted children recalled, "I had no strong feelings about it," "I felt wonderful," or "Adoption is neat." However, nineteen in this study were either puzzled or expressed confusion, anger, disbelief, or feelings of rejection or embarrassment upon learning about their adoption. Four ran away from home when told that they were adopted.

According to one fourteen-year-old adopted child,

> When I was eight years old I was looking through my baby book and asked my parents about it [my adoption]. I couldn't handle it. I went out on my own. I got real rebellious because I wanted nothing to do with my family. I was

real different from everybody — I started hanging out in the streets. I didn't like it because all my parents had to do was sign a couple of forms and I was theirs.

An adoptive mother stated, "She was five when she first understood about the adoption. She ran away. She was angry. She called everybody in the phone book to see if they left a kid at the hospital for adoption. She hated her birthparents. She ran away from home again at 12 or 13. She hated herself because her parents gave her away," while another mother recalled, "I think she learned about her adoption when she was seven. Until then, she had lived with the fantasy that she was Mom and Dad's little girl. When our son was born, she felt rejected. She resented me. I think she transferred her anger towards her birthmom to me. She started running away and skipping school."

Although these parents seemed to be aware of their child's adverse reaction to being told of the adoption, few followed up with additional discussions on the topic. Some parents, especially fathers, suggested that their children's negative reactions could be a result of their having been too young to understand the meaning of adoption.

In general, children's reactions to being told of their adoption were quite varied in both direction (positive or negative) and intensity. Further research is needed to identify predictors of individual children's responses.

Communication about the Adoption

As mentioned in Chapter 1, Kirk (1964, 1981) has suggested that adoptive parents experience a role handicap because they are not culturally prepared for the special situations that may occur in raising children not born to them. Adoptive parents must tell their children about the adoption and help them to understand its social and personal implications. This revelation can be problematic for both adoptive parents and children. It conflicts with the adoptive parents' desire for full and exclusive parenthood and with their goal to have a stable and cohesive family. Adoptive status gives children a unique position in the family that can interfere with their feelings of belonging or integration into the family. Some adoptive parents are hesitant to communicate facts about the adoption to their adopted children and often keep it a secret for as long as possible. In this way, adoptive parents and adopted children affirm their identities by means of a myth that fate has created. This myth is that the child and parents were meant to be a real family; thus, the biological parents of their child can be discounted.

Furthermore, Kirk contends that the adoptive family situation at the interpersonal level is objectively different from the biological family, and therefore, to ensure family solidarity and cohesiveness, this difference must be acknowledged. Adoptive family stability is dependent on the interpersonal skills of its members. However, adoptive parents suffering from role handicap usually begin to cope with this handicap by rejecting the differences between adoptive and biological families. This rejection-of-difference coping mechanism is often unconsciously supported by social workers even though it leads to poor communication between parent and child and can adversely affect adoptive relationships. Kirk tested his theory (1964, 1981) by using a questionnaire for adoptive parents, which indicated the amount of acknowledgment of difference, empathy, communication, and trust existing within the family. Kirk found that when parents acknowledge the difference between their own adoptive parenthood and that of biological parenthood they can more readily empathize with their child and listen to questions from their child about his or her background. Empathy and communicative abilities are mechanisms of social solidarity enabling families to become more cohesive.

Kaye and Warren (1986) have recently reexamined Kirk's notions of acknowledgment and denial of difference in adoptive families. They suggested that limited acknowledgments and assurances about non-differences are not necessarily pathological. Accordingly, few acknowledgments may be actually a healthy communication pattern in some families.

As stated in Chapter 2, adoptive parents in this study were administered Kirk's Acknowledgment of Differences, Empathy, and Communication scales. Parents were asked to respond to Kirk's questions twice, pertaining once to the child's early years in the family and once to the present time. The results are presented in Table 9.6. Concerning acknowledgment of difference between adoptive and birth parenthood, significant differences were found at the two points in time. Both mothers and fathers were more likely to acknowledge the difference in the early years than in the child's adolescence. Although the mothers were more empathic than the fathers at both points in time, they were significantly more empathic now. Finally, both mothers and fathers communicated more with their children about the adoption in the early years than now.

Several possible explanations can be given for these findings. Upon assuming the role of adoptive parents, these couples were cognizant of the difference between adoptive and birth parenthood. However, after being in the parenting role for a number of years, they are less likely to feel that adoptive parenting is much different from birth parenting. It may be that as the child grows older, adoptive parents acknowledge the difference less, think less about their child's background, and

Table 9.6
Parents' Responses to Kirk Scales

	Mothers		Fathers	
	Early Years	Now	Early Years	Now

Acknowledgement Of Differences, Scale

	Mothers Early Years	Mothers Now	Fathers Early Years	Fathers Now
Mean	6.1	4.6	5.9	4.6
Std. Dev.	3.1	3.4	4.2	4.2
Range	0-12	0-15	0-16	0-15
N	37	37	31	30

$t = 2.31*$ $t = 3.44**$

Empathy Scale

	Mothers Early Years	Mothers Now	Fathers Early Years	Fathers Now
Mean	7.8	8.1	6.4	5.9
Std. Dev.	2.9	2.2	2.6	3.3
Range	0-12	4-12	0-12	0-12
N	37	36	30	29

$t = 2.62*$

Communication Scale

	Mothers Early Years	Mothers Now	Fathers Early Years	Fathers Now
Mean	4.3	3.1	3.8	3.0
Std. Dev.	1.9	2.2	2.1	2.3
Range	1-9	0-8	0-10	0-8
N	37	35	31	30

$t = 3.18**$ $t = 2.48*$

Notes: Acknowledgment of Differences scale includes six items; potential range: 0–18. Empathy scale includes four items; potential range: 0–12. Communication scale includes four items; potential range: 0–12.

*p < .05.
**p < .01.

communicate less about the adoption to their child. However, this early time-frame emphasis may be dysfunctional, because as adopted children mature they have a greater need and capacity to understand their adoption (Brodzinsky et al., 1984). Mothers scored slightly higher than fathers on all three indexes and were significantly more empathic now than the adoptive fathers, perhaps reflecting more contact with their children. However, even though the mothers were more empathic now than the fathers, both mothers and fathers communicated less about the adoption to the child currently than in the past.

Communication about the adoption could have decreased because parents had been concentrating more on the child's symptomatic behavior and its impact on the family than on the adoption per se. Also, the decreased communication finding is in keeping with Brodzinsky, Singer, and Braff's finding that as adopted children grow older, their parents are less likely to continue to communicate about the adoption (Brodzinsky, Singer, and Braff, 1984). Many parents indicated that they had discussed adoption with the child when he or she was young and that further discussion was unnecessary. As one adoptive mother stated, "We made a special effort, part of the time, about two, three and four (to discuss adoption) and then there's no reason to just keep hounding it and hounding it."

CONCLUSION

In addition to normal family adjustment issues, adoptive parents and their adopted children must deal with additional concerns that can be potentially traumatic. Although many reasons are given for adopting older children (concern about population control, desire to provide a child a home who might otherwise have none, etc.), parents who adopt infants generally do so because they are unable to have birthchildren. They may enter into the adoption experience with a set of attitudes and concerns about being infertile and having to conform to rigid criteria in order to qualify for adoptive parenthood. The parents may have experienced a sense of loss of the fantasy birthchild (Bourguignon and Watson, 1987) they will never have. Often, after waiting for years to become parents, they are finally approved to receive an infant who may not have ever known his or her birthparents but carries their genetic traits. The adoptive parents may know very little about the child's background but must learn to accept the adopted child as their own. The adoptive parents often must answer the queries of relatives, friends, and curious onlookers about the child's origins. Moreover, the child's adoptive status is a constant reminder of the adoptive parents' unsuccessful attempts to become biological parents.

As the child matures, the adoptive parents search for appropriate ways of telling the child the adoption story and helping the child understand why his or her birthparents did not choose to parent. If the child has been in other placements before coming to the current adoptive family, these early life experiences may also affect the child's understanding of the adoption and adjustment in the family. As Kirk (1964, 1981) has suggested, most adoptive parents decrease the amount of discussion about the adoption as the child grows older, a time in which the child's interest in the topic may be heightened. Adoptive families therefore must deal with complex and often very sensitive interactional issues, and outcomes are often influenced by the degree to which parents and children can resolve these communication discrepancies and attitudes toward adoptive status.

10

Adoptive Family Dynamics: Adjustment and Identity Issues

The interviews of all adoptive family members were examined in order to determine whether adoption issues appeared to contribute to the etiology of the adolescents' emotional disturbance. In this sample, twenty-seven of the fifty adopted adolescents were identified as having significant problems adjusting to their adoptive status. In all six cases of minority children transracially adopted by Anglo families, adoption also seemed to play a major role in their disturbance. An additional nine adolescents seemed to have had some problems with their adoptive status, but adoption did not appear to play as major a role in the emotional disturbance as it did for the first group mentioned above. Finally, in eight cases adoption did not seem to be contributing to the adolescents' problems in any way. Age at time of placement did not seem to be associated with the seriousness of the problems associated with adoption (see Table 10.1). Twenty-five of the thirty-three children who experienced significant adoption issues (inracial plus transracial) were placed before the age of one year, and the remainder had been placed between one and three years. Although the relation between severity of problem and age at placement was not statistically significant, children who had minor or no adoptive issues all had been placed before one year of age. This chapter illustrates the kinds of adoption-related problems each of the four groups of children in this study exhibited.

SIGNIFICANT ADOPTION ISSUES

Twenty-seven (44 percent, fifteen males and twelve females) of the inracially adopted children in the study were identified as having problems adjusting to their adoptive status. The four independent adoptions and the three relative adoptions in this sample were included in this group. In twelve of the cases problems began when, or soon after, the child learned of the adoption.

Table 10.1

Relationship between Age at Placement and Severity of Adoption
Problems: Frequencies

Age at Time of Placement	Serious*	Moderate	None
birth - 3 months	17	5	6
4 - 12 months	8	4	2
over 1 year	8	0	0
Totals	33	9	8

*Includes transracial adoptions; $\chi^2 = 5.8171$ and $p = .2132$.

Among the adoption-related problems that this subgroup of
adolescents experienced were the following: feelings of being rejected
by their birthmother, anger toward birth and/or adoptive parents,
using adoptive status for revenge or to hurt adoptive parents,
rootlessness, self-hatred, and resentment about being adopted. Many of
these adoption problems occurred in combination with some of the
other factors, such as preplacement, early childhood characteristics,
family events, and peer and sibling relationships, which have been
discussed in earlier chapters.

In nine cases treatment began while the child was less than five
years of age, and in twelve cases parents in this group initially sought
help for their children during the early school years. In only five cases
did the family initially seek help after the child reached junior high,
and in one case treatment began after the child reached high school age.
Therefore, since most of the problems began during the early years, the
typical adolescent identity conflicts were most likely not the cause of
these problems. To illustrate some of these issues, vignettes and quotes
will be provided from the study cases.

Feelings of Rejection and Anger

Sixteen children in this subgroup expressed the feeling of being
rejected by their birthmothers. For example, one adopted boy stated, "I
was shocked when I found out [about my adoption]. I felt my
birthmom never loved me — that's why she gave me up — that's what
my brother used to tell me also. We had lots of fights over it. Maybe it's

true — she didn't love me." An adoptive mother recalled, "When Tammy found out about her adoption, she just cried. She still cries whenever it comes up. She doesn't want to be adopted. She wants to come out of my stomach."

The adoptive mother of a sixteen-year-old girl recounted this:

> Margaret was a very difficult baby who would never sit still. The doctors denied she was hyperactive. She found out about the adoption when she was five and she felt she was given away because she was bad. Her behavior just got worse. At six she said "I'm terrible and everybody hates me." When Margaret was older she threatened to kill me and herself with a butcher knife.

Another parent stated, "At three, we read Sara a story about her adoption. She wasn't interested — she got up and walked away. Even though we've answered all her questions over the years she still feels rejected."

Sara recalled, "I used to ask them questions but I always felt bad because I didn't want to hurt them. I felt like I was a flower shop reject — the one no one wanted. I just kept running away from home."

Adoptees have a natural tendency to try to understand why they were placed for adoption. They sometimes become depressed or angry and guilty as they try to determine what caused them to be given up for adoption. Some believe that they must have somehow been imperfect or in some cases bad, since their birthparents did not raise them. Some are very hostile toward their birthparents for placing them for adoption. For example, according to a caseworker, one adopted child expressed his intent to find his birthmother and kill her.

Adopted children can feel very rejected if they do not receive adequate information about the reasons for their relinquishment. If the adoptive parents have very limited information, the children might either believe that the adoptive parents are withholding something very negative from them or are just unwilling to tell them about their birthparents.

For example, lack of sufficient information proved to be particularly troubling for one child in the study. According to her caseworker, "Sally was not given proper information about her birthparents. She wasn't told about her birthmother — just told she was adopted. She had an original name and they changed it to theirs. She has never been able to accept not knowing."

Sally stated, "Sometimes I feel like if I would have been with my real parents they'd understand and communicate better. I would have felt more secure."

Self-hatred

Nine children expressed feelings of self-hatred as a result of being adopted. According to the parents of one of these children, Jimmy was a very bright child who never actively inquired about adoption. His parents stopped talking with him about it at a very young age because they thought he understood it well enough. His caseworker reported that Jimmy "thinks his [birth]mother's lousy, for having placed him for adoption, and especially because he ended up in such a screwed-up family." Jimmy had numerous school problems and had failed all but one class since eighth grade. His mother stated that he "got his girlfriend pregnant and tried to get her an abortion and she wouldn't, so he flipped her off. She has recently, by the way, put her baby up for adoption." Although Jimmy did not mention the baby in his interview, he stated that he wouldn't recommend adoption, because "in my case it didn't turn out to be all that constructive to the family that I had." Just prior to his placement in residential treatment, Jimmy attempted suicide. This is an example of a child who seems to have internalized his image of himself as a bad person. His desire to abort the child he fathered may have been a symbolic indicator of his negative self-feelings. Other children in this category referred to themselves as "being no good." One parent said, "Jerry hates himself because he's adopted. He is always talking about how bad he's turned out." When asked about her feelings about adoption, one girl stated, "I tell people not to adopt because the child might turn out like me." Caseworkers generally described these children as having very low self-esteem and feeling unworthy. They may have internalized the rejection they felt because their birthparents had placed them for adoption.

Expression of Hostility

Twenty-one children in this subgroup expressed overt hostility toward their adoptive parents. This is not surprising, as adoptees often assume that if their birthparents rejected them, their adoptive parents will do the same. Since they believe that there must have been something inherently wrong with them, they set out to prove that this is true. They sometimes write their own rejection scripts and engage in rejection producing behaviors (Wilson, 1985). These adoptees, expecting rejection, choose to renounce the adoptive parents before they can be rejected again.

The following quotes illustrate the rejecting, hostile attitudes and behavior of some of the adoptees in this sample:

> I just don't like the idea of the adoption. I was picked up while I was still in the hospital. I am angry at my real mother for putting me up for adoption

and angry at my parents for taking me in the first place. I used to run away and try to find my birthparents. I didn't know what I was doing or where I was going.

One of the biggest things in my life was to know why my mother gave me up. I couldn't understand it. I stopped doing anything my parents said. I became real distant from my Mom. Sometimes I tackled her and called her a bitch.

An adoptive mother recalled, "My daughter and I were never close. When she was a baby, she would scream if a woman came near. Since she's been older she still hasn't had anything to do with me. She fantasizes that her mother was rich and that she was going to see her. She can't accept the adoption. I don't think she still can understand why we haven't given up on her."

The troubled adoptees expressed hostility toward their birthparents, especially their birthmothers, and appeared to displace these angry feelings on their adoptive mothers. In several instances, adoptive mothers were blamed for presumably taking the children from their birthmothers.

Many of the troubled adoptees believed that their adoptive parents would eventually reject them just as their birthparents had. Therefore, they might have tested their parents' love and commitment by deliberately defying their wishes. The overprotectiveness of many adoptive parents may have resulted in the escalation of acting-out behavior among the adoptees (Berman and Bufferd, 1986).

Use of Adoption to Seek Revenge

About ten of the troubled adoptees used their adoptive status as a means to seek revenge or hurt their adoptive parents. For example, Sam stated,

When I was told I was someone else's child, it freaked me out. It's like a black hole. I felt like sh_____ because I didn't know why I was given up and I wanted to know. I still have lots of questions. I started having problems when I was ten or 11. When I got into fights with my parents, I'd say, "I can go back to my real Mom and Dad." One day my [adoptive] Dad said, "You don't even have a father." When I heard that I tried to leave the house and they wouldn't let me. Ever since that day me and my Dad have gotten into really big fights.

Sam's mother said,

Sam always tries to use what he thinks would hurt us the most or get us the angriest. He'll say, "You should never have adopted me, anyway. I hate you, you're not my parents." He would make up his own story about why he was given up for adoption. When we would tell him the information we were given about the reasons he was placed, he would always get physically wild, and scream "You're lying, you're lying, you're lying."

Dwight, another adopted child, mentioned, "I knew my Mom would get real upset when we would talk about it [the adoption]. I would use it to get back at them. When I'm mad at my Mom, I'd say, 'Why don't you give me up for adoption?' It's still a big thing in my family."

The following statements, made by adoptive parents in the study, illustrate the use of adoption as a threat:

> Megan's been curious about the adoption — she's threatened to leave home and go find her mother whenever we argue. I think my feelings were hurt that she'd leave us and go look for her mother. We thought we were her full parents.

> Melissa used adoption as an excuse not to go along with our limits — she would say that we were not her real parents. At age five, Melissa said to her father, "You're not my father anyway." Her father shouted, "You're right." She ran away.

Some of the children's perceptions of rejection could have resulted from early negative interactional experiences that they encountered with their birth, foster, or adoptive parents. Most of the children who used their adoptive status to express anger or revenge had also experienced problems in preplacement environments and/or exhibited problematic early childhood characteristics. These early problems may have resulted in their having difficulty developing attachment or trust with their adoptive parents. Their parents could also have had unrealistic expectations of their adopted child's behavior and relationships within the family and might have found it difficult to adjust to the realities of a child who may have been hyperactive, continually pushing away, or otherwise not conforming to their wishes. It is possible that their feelings of disappointment or even rejection could have been overtly or covertly transmitted to the child.

Lawder (1970) reviewed seventy-one troubled adoptive family case histories and suggested that adoption and its implications complicated family relationships. She hypothesized that inflexible expectations and unrealistic demands of adoptive parents cause their adopted children to act aggressively as they try and fail to meet these demands. These parental needs included school achievement, affection, and emotional feedback. Sometimes demands grew out of pathological fantasies and wishes. Thus, these parents tend to attribute their children's unacceptable behavior to adoption. The children then feel rejected and in turn reject their parents. She concluded that adoption outcome depends on the capacity of parents to grow with their adoptive children, recognizing likenesses and differences.

Feelings of Rootlessness

Four of the adopted children ran away immediately upon being told of the adoption. Others ran away later, presumably to find their birthparents. It may be that in reality these children were not searching for their fantasized birthparents but for a sense of stability and identity (Tousseing, 1962). Running-away behavior may also have been a result of the children's need to capture parental attention, testing whether their parents really care for them or whether they really matter (Wilson, 1985).

Illustrative of the feelings of rootlessness that adoptees in this study experienced, an adoptive mother recalled,

> Gerald was adopted at the age of 13 months. He had been malnourished and unattended in foster homes prior to the adoption. When he was three, he would tell people he was "Momma's adopted boy." He really didn't understand what adoption meant. When he was 13, he asked about his mother. It kind of hurt me. I didn't understand why he would even ask. I told him I didn't know where his mother was. I told him if his mother wanted him, she would find him. Mothers have given up kids and gone back and found them. Now, when he's angry — he'll say, "I'm going to find my mother." I say, "Go find her." He does that to upset me — it does. When he runs away he says he's doing it to find his mother. He never says anything about his father.

Heath, adopted at three days old, indicated that "a lot of my rebelling was — you know — you're not my real parents, so you can't punish me. That used to hurt my parents' feelings a lot and they used to get angry with that. My main thing was rebelling against my adoptive parents."

His adoptive father said, "Heath figured if he could find his mother he could go live with her and she would do for him what we wouldn't do. Once he knew he could find his parents, he backed down."

The behavior described in the preceding example may also be interpreted as the child's attempt to test limits set by his adoptive parents. The literature suggests that adoptive parents may be overly permissive and have difficulty establishing firm consistent limits for their children because of an unconscious fear of losing the child's love or because they are trying so hard to be good parents (McCranie, 1965; Rautman, 1959; Wilson, 1985). The children in turn continue to test their parents' limits to see if they will be rejected.

Several adoptive parents in this study suggested that special efforts are often needed to help children overcome their feeling that they will be rejected by their adoptive parents. For example, an adoptive mother suggested that "adoptive parents must continually try to convince the child that, even though you're not his real parent, you still love him every bit as much." Another stated, "He's feeling he's your child, and he was somebody else's also — so he's missing out on his real parents

— so you gotta compensate for that." An adoptive father suggested, "Adopted children are super sensitive. Little arguments which parents may see as normal parent-child interaction, may be very significant to the child."

Parents' and Children's Advice to Adoptive Parents of the Future

The children who were having problems related to the adoption offered the following kinds of advice to adoptive parents:

> Go get sterile so you won't have any birthkids. One of the worst things is being around birthkids after you're adopted. It's really ignorant, stupid, because you know automatically who's going to matter to them.

> If you adopt — adopt young — and be sure and tell the child when he's old enough to remember about its real parents, but not so old that it upsets and shocks them. If they want to find their real parents help them. Don't stop them as much as it may hurt — help them. Give them the extra love they need to feel secure and welcome and that they can talk to you and be honest with you about everything. And don't expect the child to be perfect. Or if you have natural kids, don't expect the adoptive one to make the same accomplishments as your child. Because he or she won't.

The adoptive parents of children who had had particular problems with the adoption were also very cautious in their advice to others: An adoptive father of a child abused prior to the adoption said, "Make sure you can't have any first — get yourself a cat. Then consider a newborn. Don't consider an abused child unless you have all the special talents required — time, money, etc." A mother who attributed her child's problems to heredity stated, "You're so caught up in joy that you don't think of the things that you want and need to know. Of all of our kids, we don't know enough about them (adopted children) biologically or emotionally or physically." Others stated,

> I feel that you have to give them more love than you would give your own child, I do. I believe that because you got to love him for being your child and love him for being somebody else's child.

> Well I'd certainly say go for it, it has been a real joy for us, even discounting the problems we've had in the past couple of years with her, we certainly have enjoyed our daughter from birth on. We really didn't look upon her as an adopted child, but upon her as our own. There were even times that we had totally forgotten that she was adopted.

> Had I known then what I know now, I don't know that I'd have gone through with this. I'm not sure I really feel that way about the natural childbirth thing, because I believe Jerry would be different if he were mine because, you know, I know what my wife would have done during the pregnancy. There would have been no booze, there would have been no cigarettes, not that

there are now, but you know. There would have been no medicine, there would have been no drugs. I come from tremendous stock, if my family were horses, we'd all be, you know race horses, you know, look at your teeth. So I would have those things under my control.

Think very hard before you do it. Because I think they're going to grow up throwing it back at you sooner or later that you're not their real parents so therefore you can't tell them what to do and don't care anything about them.

Thus, these twenty-seven families had experienced many problems associated with their child's adoption and realized that special efforts were needed. Many tended to attribute the child's problems to genetic factors. However, regardless of the extent of the negative adoption experiences, all appeared dedicated to the children and determined to obtain the best therapeutic help available to resolve their children's emotional difficulties.

TRANSRACAL ADOPTION CONCERNS

Transracial adoption, the adoption of children from one race by families of another race, presents some unique adjustment issues for adoptive parents as well as their children. Transracially adopted children not only have to understand and accept their adoptive status, they must also work toward the development of an appropriate racial identity. Studies of transracial adoptive families have found that parents anticipate that as their children mature they may experience identity problems associated with having been transracially adopted (Grow and Shapiro, 1974; Ladner, 1977; McRoy and Zurcher, 1983).

Six (four males and two females) of the children in this study had been transracially placed. Specific issues related to the transracial nature of the adoption seemed to have contributed to some of the problems that led to the placement of this group of children in residential treatment. Three of the children were black, one black-white, one Native American-white, and one Canadian Indian; all had been adopted by Anglo families. Three had been placed before nine months of age and three had been placed between one and three years. All of the children placed after one year had lived with their birthparents or foster parents prior to being adopted. One had been neglected by the birthmother prior to the adoptive placement. In four families, problems developed during the early school years; in one family, problems were first noted during the preschool years; and in one family, trouble began when the child reached junior high.

The adoptive parents indicated that they adopted transracially for the following reasons: population control, desire for another child, limited number of available white children, as an experiment, and to give a child an opportunity. Four of the families had adopted more than two non-white children. At the time of the study, all six of the adoptive families were intact.

Four families had experienced initial negative reactions from their relatives to the transracial adoption, but all relatives later accepted the adoption. As one adoptive father reported, "My mother was really anti-minority but Jason [adopted child] won her over. I remember when he was seven, my mother said 'I think Jason's getting lighter' — well, he wasn't — she was just getting used to him." The study findings regarding parental motivation for adoption and reactions of extended family members are consistent with previous studies of transracial adoptees (Falk, 1970; Grow and Shapiro, 1974; Ladner, 1977; McRoy and Zurcher, 1983; Zastrow, 1977).

Findings of previous research suggest that the formation of a positive and unambiguous racial identity may be particularly problematic for minority children in white families (McRoy and Zurcher, 1983). Children as young as three are aware of racial differences and soon become aware of the social distinctions between members of his or her racial group and members of the majority group. By the age of seven, all children appear to be aware of the concept of *black,* and many tend to assign undesirable traits to that identity. By the time they reach the second grade, many children have developed prejudicial attitudes, and sometimes they express these through teasing or refusing association with peers who are racially different from themselves (McRoy, Zurcher, Lauderdale, and Anderson, 1984).

The social situation associated with transracial adoptions is obviously complex, since children want to be liked and accepted by their peers and family members but may be impeded by obvious differences in physical appearance. They often lack the system of social supports from other minorities that may be useful in developing a sense of belonging and positive racial self-feelings.

Studies of transracial adoptive families have revealed that the majority often live in predominantly white areas and tend to minimize the significance of race (Grow and Shapiro, 1974; McRoy and Zurcher, 1983; Shireman and Johnson, 1986; Simon and Alstein, 1987). Transracial adoptive families often take color-blind attitudes to racial differences between the child and family. Children growing up in this kind of family situation tend to experience an exaggerated feeling of differentness. They may not feel comfortable discussing their concerns about racial issues. In order to cope, many try to reject or dismiss the significance of their minority identity and may develop negative stereotypes of minorities (McRoy and Zurcher, 1983).

As one caseworker for a transracial adoptive family indicated, "I think he first tried to resist thinking that he did notice skin differences. He now says that he always felt like there was something quite different there — that he wasn't really part of his family. He now wishes he could grow up in a black culture. It would be easier for him to have roots."

All of the transracially adopted children in the study had been teased or taunted by their peers about their minority racial heritage. One mother reported that

> in kindergarten, when Paul passed the milk out, boys wouldn't take it from him because he was black. One white kid told him each day that whites hated blacks. He was afraid to come home and tell us what was happening because we were white, and the kid got him convinced that whites didn't like blacks and he couldn't figure it all out. He used to have real bad asthma attacks when he was upset. Fortunately, his Godparents were black and they used to talk with him about race. After a while his asthma cleared up.

Another transracially adopted black child recalled, "It all started when I went to second grade. People started calling me names and stuff. I had a hard time dealing with that. I talked to my parents a little bit, but I didn't really know how to speak to my parents about it very much. They would tell me not to let it bother me. Sometimes I think my parents are embarrassed of me." This child was institutionalized after pouring alcohol over his head and threatening to set himself on fire. According to the caseworker, this child feels that he was placed for adoption because he wasn't worth anything.

The transracially adopted adolescent of racially mixed parentage (black-white) reported having been subjected to racial teasing as well. His mother indicated that he denies his racial heritage and refers to himself as American Indian.

The two adoptive families of Native American children in the study expressed their belief that Native American heritage and culture may have accounted for the problems the child was experiencing. Both children were adopted around two years of age and lived with their birthparents during the first few months of their lives. One adoptive mother stated,

> Denise's tribe has the lowest self-concept of any Indian group. She normally looks down, like many Indians, and she functions on Indian time. She is real slow and has typical Indian traits. I know other Indians with the same problems. It's hard for people to know what she is though. Everywhere we have moved she's been considered a member of a different racial group. For example, when we were in Minnesota, people thought she was Korean and when we were in Colorado, people thought she was Mexican. We've tried to work with her on her Indian heritage. We have involved our whole family in Indian pow wows, art exhibitions, and we bought moccasins from her tribe. We tried to give her pride in what she is.

An adoptive father of an Indian child recalled, "I'll never forget when we first saw him — we knew we were adopting a minority child — but he was the blackest thing I ever saw in my life. Just for a second, those were my true feelings. It didn't change anything though. I could have cared less if he would have been green." According to the adoptive mother,

Jerry is so dark though that some people tease him about being black. We've tried to teach him pride in being Indian. There are major mismatch issues with our family. His father wants him to be great and famous and Jerry is very laid back. He's not futuristic oriented. He's like Indians — very family oriented. He doesn't act independently. I remember one occasion when he was about five, Jerry kept coming in to get some food and taking it outside. I followed him and found that he was taking it to some drunk Indian sitting in the yard. When I asked him what he was doing he said that he had been talking Indian with his friend. I don't know what he meant because he never talked Indian in his whole life.

Problems with racial identity development were also noted by the transracial adoptive parents of black children in the study. For example, an adoptive mother stated,

Our black daughter will not accept that she will be classified as black. None of our children have seen blacks. Our Korean child is the same way. We have encouraged her to read as much as she can about her heritage. She will not. She said that whenever she sees another Oriental walking down the street she would walk across the street to avoid walking by the person. All our transracially adopted kids have a hang up. We've given them books and done everything we can do other than living in a multi-racial community.

The preceding quotes illustrate many of the kinds of problems that transracially adopted children experienced. Although most of the parents had attempted to acquaint their children with their heritage and respond to their concerns, the children still tended to have difficulty adjusting. Most families had chosen not to live in racially integrated communities or to develop close social relationships with persons of the same racial background as their adopted children.

The greater the physical dissimilarity to the parents, the more problems the children seemed to experience. The black transracially adopted children had suffered more intense racial teasing than the Native American children. The parents often expressed negative stereotypic attitudes toward the minority heritage of their children and seemed to believe that they could help the child overcome these cultural limitations. Most parents had adopted color-blind attitudes toward the children. However, when the children exhibited behavior that was totally counter to parental expectations regardless of their special efforts, they then attributed the behavior to negative characteristics associated with their ethnic background.

Although other factors, such as preplacement environment, age at placement, family events, and parental pathology, may have contributed to the behavioral problems these children experienced, it seems as if racial-identity concerns may have been particularly troubling to transracially adopted children. Reflecting on the problems of transracial adoptive families, one caseworker suggested,

White parents don't have the same experiences as blacks and can't help the child cope with negative racial experiences. Transracial adoptive families find that their children experience adolescent identity crises, adoptive identity crises and racial identity crises. Children who are transracially adopted can have severe racial identity crises and the parents often don't know how to deal with it.

It is important to note that the transracial nature of the adoption by itself did not necessarily lead to the behavioral problems that necessitated residential treatment. Some parents and children have successfully adapted to the transracial situation and have had few, if any, difficulties resulting from differences in racial background. Others have racial-identity issues, but the children have never engaged in behaviors that would necessitate their being institutionalized (McRoy and Zurcher, 1983).

The transracially adopted children in this study exhibited some of the same behaviors (i.e., stealing, running away, etc.) and some of the same angry, rejecting attitudes toward their birth and adoptive parents as the inracially adopted children. However, they also may have experienced exaggerated feelings of differentness because of the nature of their adoption.

FAMILIES WITH MODERATE ADOPTION CONCERNS

Nine children (four males and five females) experienced some problems associated with their adoptive status, but these concerns were less salient in the decision to place the child into residential treatment. These children had experienced at least three major problems other than adoption. Problems began before the child reached school age in three families, during the elementary school years for four families, and during junior high for the other two families in this group. Issues such as illness of the adoptive mother, parental alcoholism, divorce, parenting issues, feeling unwanted by an adoptive parent, and genetic and preplacement factors seemed more salient causes of later problems. However, all of the adopted children in this group mentioned some concerns about their adoptive status and feelings about their birthparents. Notably absent, however, were the rejection statements that characterized the adoption-issues group previously discussed.

The following case vignettes illustrate the problems these families experienced:

Darryl, 12, had been in six different foster homes before being adopted at the age of six. We think he may have been abused and know he was neglected. His birthmother was schizoid. I remember when he was a little over a year old, he was hostile toward us, hit us. If he knew something was yours and it meant a lot and you had to get on to him, he would tear it up. I had told him to get away from the TV and he did, but he walked into the living room and got my white milk fruit dish and brought it back in and looked at me, smiled and just dropped it. He was two then. Friends would say that he's just a boy until they baby-sat for him. He was a terror. Once he bit a hunk out of a kid. He ran away from school in second grade. He used to fantasize that his adoptive father was his birthfather. He has absolutely no affect when he talks about his birthmother who is a patient in a mental hospital.

My wife always wanted to have children and she found out she couldn't. She wanted to adopt and I went along with the plan just to make her happy. Jesse was five days old when we got him. I could never discipline him because my wife and her mother doted on him. He was a battleground — everybody vied for his attention. When he was five, his grandmother told him he was adopted. She said he was special. It went to his head that he was a very special child. She told him that his birthmother did not want him. I've never said anything to him about his adoption. My wife was sickly the first five years of his life. Every time I turned around she was in the hospital. For about two years everything was fine, then she went downhill and she was in the hospital more and more. When Jesse was about seven years old his adoptive mother died of cancer. That was when he really started messing up. He started stealing and becoming unmanageable. His grandmother felt sorry for him and always took up for him when he stole. He would lie — say he's going one place and then go another. I think he was just born with those traits and there's nothing you can do about it. Adoption is like buying a pig in a poke. It's really hard to comprehend what you're getting into.

Although Jesse's father did not talk with him about his adoption, it is evident that Jesse did have some concerns about his birthparents. When his caseworker asked him, if he had three wishes, what would they be, he could only name one — to find his birthmother.

An adoptive mother recalled,

I just couldn't get pregnant, but I found it very difficult to get my husband to adopt. He finally did though. But he was upset all the time while Kim was a baby. Kim was very colicky and cried all the time. I was really uptight and nervous because when you adopt a child you have to be very much on your toes. They're watching you and checking up on you. It's not exactly like a baby you have biologically. Anyway, I had to try to keep him quiet all the time because my husband couldn't stand the crying. He always thought Kim was an intrusion. He felt competitive toward the child. We used to have fights all the time. Eventually we divorced. But then, my husband would try to spoil Kim all the time because I had legal custody. He didn't want to seem too harsh. Kim has never really asked us any questions about his adoption. Of course I told him when he was a little baby that we adopted him because his mother couldn't take care of him. He's really never been accepted by other family members because he's adopted. Kim has said he thinks about his adoption sometimes. However, he doesn't think of it as a big deal because he has never seen his "real parents."

In the preceding examples, the marital relationships, as well as inadequate parenting skills, seem to have had more of an impact on the children's problems than the adoption. However, it must be noted that the parents' and extended family members' attitudes toward the children and their adoptive status may have affected their self-perceptions. Although the child may not acknowledge problems that may have been related to the adoption, the issues may still be present.

Adoptive parents in this group gave the following advice about adoption:

> Well, from my own experience, I would say that the most important thing is you'd better make sure that both of you really want them.

> I feel it's important to let them know they're adopted early on. I don't think you need to treat them any differently than you treat any other child, but I definitely think that you need to watch for signs for emotional trouble or unusual problems. They don't come out as something you can spot, but these kids have some more troubles, maybe trouble in school. If possible, get them some counseling on how to deal with their life. Talk with them as much as possible.

> I guess I don't know if Denise's being adopted is a major factor in our problems. I would probably say that maybe people shouldn't give up their children if there's any other possible way.

> Take each one as it comes. Check into support groups. You don't want these problems. There may be no problems until adolescence. You have a normal, lovable relationship. It's only when you fill out forms do I think about it [adoption]. It's there, but not on top of your brain. Joan reminds me, she says, "Mom, you didn't have me. I can't be that way; I don't have those traits." She still needs that distinction.

This group of parents also suggests caution about adoptive parenthood, and the significance of acknowledging the difference between birth and adoption for the child. As a result of their experiences, they suggest that adopted children know that they are different and may be very sensitive about it. Open communication with the child and an awareness of the need for them to incorporate their adoptive status into their overall identity seems crucial to avoid or minimize adjustment problems.

NONPROBLEMATIC ADOPTION ADJUSTMENT

Among eight families in the sample, adoption was not considered to be a major factor at all in the problems that eventually led to the placement of the child in residential treatment. The children either had such severe problems that it was impossible to discern the impact of the adoption, or the children's statements and behaviors associated with their adoption suggested that they felt very positive about being adopted. Two children had been diagnosed as paranoid schizophrenic. In the remaining six cases the child did not express any anger or rejecting behavior toward adoptive or birthparents. Problems were attributed to such factors as divorce, heredity, death of parent, and extensive drug use. None of these children were "elbow babies." Within this group one family sought treatment during the preschool years, two during elementary school years, two during junior high, and three during high school.

The following vignettes illustrate the attitudes of these children toward their adoptive status:

> I was about five years old when I was told about my adoption. I was really too young to understand they weren't my real parents. I mean my — they are my real parents, I mean my biological parents. I've asked if my parents had any more information on them and they've said that's all they have and I've asked them if I can try to find my mom when I'm 18. My mom told me that she would help me. She also told me that there's a chance my mom might not want to see me. I forget I'm even adopted sometimes. Some adopted children may think that they don't have to take some restrictions because they don't have to listen to their adoptive parents. I think adoptive parents might sometimes be more likely to give up on a kid since they figure its not their kid. I don't feel that way about my parents. They haven't given up on me yet! My parents have told me they care about me, like I'm their real child.

> I was first told I was adopted when I was four, but I don't remember it. I remember I was seven exactly, because I saw baby pictures of my sister, and I go, "Mom!" She says, "Yeah." I go, "How much did I weigh?" She goes, "Goh, you weighed 13 lbs 6 ozs first day of birth." And I sat there and said, "I'm sorry; I didn't mean to hurt you!" She goes, "You didn't hurt me!" She says, "You were adopted." I looked at her; I went "Oh!" You know it really [laughs], you know, it was no big deal to me. "O.K., I'm adopted," you know, it never really bugged me.

> Adoption never made me feel bad or anything. It didn't make me feel like I was unwanted. In fact, it made me kind of feel needed more because it was like these people wanted me, but I got some other people. And it's kind of like — you know, stick my nose up in the air, ha ha. I've thought about finding my birthparents. My mom wants to know about them too. She's real understanding. I'm very close to my mom. She didn't carry me for nine months, but she's still my mother. It's like my mom says — not bone of my bone and not flesh of my flesh, but still miraculously my own. I didn't grow under her heart, but in it. I look back and I'm lucky. I could have been just left — like there was some kid I read about that got left on the doorstep or out in the freezing cold and it died. I deserve as much chance for a life as anybody else I guess.

When asked about whether she would mind if Emma searched for her birthparents, her mother responded, "I don't feel badly about her searching. She's my daughter. I'm very confident in that feeling."

When asked about the role of adoption in Tom's problems, his caseworker responded,

> A lot of his relationship problems are so centered in the here and now and focused on his adoptive parents' divorce, that I'm not sure how much really comes from any of the adoption issues. With some kids [in treatment] it's real

clear that they are looking for their other parents and all that. With Tom, I think that [his adoption] was an issue in the past, but I believe he really has adopted these parents now.

His adoptive mother stated, "He gets a real thrill when people say he looks like me. We're close that way. When the family was all together, Tom looked like me and his brother looked like his father."

Parents of children in this group seemed to feel very confident in their role as adoptive parents and were open to communication with the child about the adoption. Similarly, children in these families were very positive about their adoptive status. An adoptive mother gave the following advice to persons considering adoption: "Love them like your own. Because they are. And I've never thought once or had misgivings or would have changed Karen being my daughter, even with all the trouble it's been. I look forward to happier days with her. I would never change my mind, you know, that kind of thing."

INTEREST IN SEARCHING

Twelve (44 percent) of the twenty-seven adolescents with significant problems related to the adoption were interested in searching for their birthparents, and five of these had actually found at least one birthparent. Only one of the nine adolescents with moderate adoption concerns was interested, and three of the eight adolescents with nonproblematic adoptions planned to search. The literature on adoptee search behavior is controversial, since some authors feel that most adolescents wish to know about or meet their birthparents (Kirk, 1964; McWhinnie, 1967; Pringle, 1967). Sorosky, Baran, and Pannor (1975) suggest that search efforts are more reflective of personality traits than adoptive family relationships. Others, however, believe that interest in searching often results from strained adoptive family relationships (Smith, 1963; Triseliotis, 1973).

The findings from this study suggest that although slightly less than half of the adolescents particularly troubled by the adoption and those with presumably no adoptive adjustment issues were interested in searching, the reasons for searching differed. The former were very angry about their adoptions and wanted to search in order to understand why their birthparents had rejected them or to see if their fantasies about their birthparents' life-styles were true. Communication about the adoption had been strained in all of these families. The latter were more interested in searching out of curiosity and a desire to know more about themselves. These three had parents with whom they could talk freely about the adoption and who expressed their willingness to help them search.

To illustrate the differences in attitudes toward searching, the following vignettes are included:

Children with no adoption-related problems stated:

> I'm just curious. It's just something I've always wanted to know. I just want to know what they're like, and I'm also curious you know, if they got married or something, and if I have any brothers and sisters. It would be kinda neat to see what they look like.

> I've told my Mother that I'd like to know my birthparents. I don't feel uncomfortable talking with her about it. She said, "OK." She's told me that she's even tried before, before I even asked about it. Because she wants to kind of know too.

Children with significant adoption problems stated:

> I've always been interested in who my mother was. I don't really know why. Adoptive parents should know that their children should want to meet their real parents. They should make sure that they have a secure enough relationship with their child, so that when they do want to pursue their natural mom, that its not going to really, you know, you're not going to feel threatened by it. Me and my mom never really had a secure relationship, that's why she was so threatened when I wanted to meet my natural mother.

> I want to find my mother and if she doesn't want to see me I will cuss her out.

An adoptive father recalled, "Carol used to keep telling us she wanted to meet her real mother. When she finally realized she couldn't, she started asking for pictures of her. Once she said that she wanted a picture so she could throw darts at it."

Almost all of the adopted children who talked about searching referred only to their birthmother. The only ones who expressed any interest in their birthfathers were in relative adoptive situations and one of the adoptive parents was related to the birthparents.

CONSIDERATION OF ADOPTIVE STATUS IN TREATMENT

To better discern some of the specific adoption-related clinical issues of children in this sample, as compared with nonadopted institutionalized children, caseworkers were asked to discuss the differences between the two groups. Caseworkers characterized adopted children as having a rebellious, reckless kind of nature. Their own insecurity often leads to exaggerated needs for acceptance, approval, and notoriety. They are very shallow emotionally, manipulators and schemers. They often have an exaggerated need to be independent. Some have more exaggerated sexual and nurturing needs than non-adopted children. One caseworker suggested that

> there is not enough preparation for the adoptive families about what type of problems they might encounter with attachment and bonding; what previous abuse experiences might mean to a child emotionally, where they would get

help for that, normalizing that as an expected problem so that adopted families would come in earlier when they're experiencing difficulties. We've found many cases where they've gone through pure hell for years and the adoptive child has, in a very negative way, controlled the entire family until by the time they reach residential treatment, they're feeling very burned out and very angry. There seems to be an extra belief on the part of adoptive parents that they have something to prove to the community and to the agency that they adopted, that they can handle it, and for some reason they do not see problems developing. The service delivery system in many adoption agencies does little more than provide that post-adoptive session after six months and then a few groups about adoptive identity, but there is nobody there suddenly when the kids are doing things that they don't understand. When that behavior begins to emerge, they're typically just allowing it to continue in the family, toughing it out and then the child, typically, in many cases, does something aggressive against a family member.

As this caseworker suggested, many adoptive families are overdetermined to make the adoption work and are likely to allow behaviors to continue for years before seeking help. Others want so much to be no different than birthparents that they dismiss the importance of the adoption to the child and fail to realize that some of the child's disruptive behaviors may be a sign that he or she is not adjusting to being adopted. Some take the child's angry outbursts extolling his or her "real mom and dad" very personally and feel threatened. Adoptive parents often don't realize that it is normal for children to attack parents where they are perceived to be most vulnerable. Moreover, it is normal for adopted children to feel a sense of loss and to grieve that loss. Oversensitive parents may interpret this behavior as a sign that they have not been good parents to the child. These feelings may aggravate an already tense parent-child relationship.

CONCLUSION

The findings suggest that adoptive status in itself is not necessarily a major cause of problems among institutionalized adoptees. It is difficult to discern exactly why adoption issues were paramount in some families and unimportant in others. Learning about the adoption seemed to trigger problems in some families, and in others the children seemed to accept this status readily. Parental perceptions of their role as adoptive parents and their empathic understanding of the adjustment problems that their children might experience may be related to the outcome. Personality as well as genetic and early background characteristics and experiences may also influence how the child perceives his or her status. Family communication patterns and dynamics as well seem to be associated with the extent to which adoption may become a real issue for a child. Families who openly acknowledge the difference between adoptive and birth parentage and are comfortable with their status as adoptive parents seem more likely to have children who also are more accepting of their adoption. An adoptive father of one child in the study had the following thoughts on the difficult experiences they have had raising an adopted child and gave these suggestions for preventing these problems from arising:

> We didn't realize that she really took the fact that she was adopted more to heart than we expected. It wasn't a big deal to us. You know we didn't think of her as a second rate child, so we never tried to deal with the adoption, specially. But to her, it was something special and we didn't realize that. Adoptive parents need special abilities to raise these children. The first time your adopted kid says, "You're not my real parents and you wouldn't treat me that way if you were," boy, you need to be able to walk out of the house and not come back for a week. They [adoptive parents] need a greater sense of security in their parenthood than biological parents do. Biological parents got something that's given to them from the moment of birth in the hospital. That's their kid. There's no two ways about it. Nobody will ever argue, nobody will ever challenge including the child. When you adopt, you don't have that ownership. As a result, your right to raise that child is questioned; it's threatened by the child himself.

11

Adoption Issues in Non-Clinical Families

Up to this point, comparisons in this volume have been made between the functioning and family backgrounds of adopted and non-adopted adolescents, all of whom are in residential treatment for emotional disturbance of some kind. Although these comparisons permit the reader to disentangle the differential contributions that adoptive and biological parentage might make to emotional disturbance, they are insufficient for clarifying the contributions of adoptive family relationships to normal development. Thus, an additional comparison group was sought.

In addition to data from the samples of fifty adoptive and fifty control families whose adolescents were in residential treatment, data were examined from 115 adoptive families with 185 adopted adolescents in which the children had not been diagnosed or labeled. These families were participants in the Minnesota Adoption Study (Scarr and Weinberg, 1978). It should be noted that the primary purpose of the Minnesota Adoption Study was to examine genetic and environmental contributions to intelligence, personality, and attitudes; consequently, the types of data collected in the Minnesota study and the residential-treatment study were not parallel.

The volunteer families in the sample were Anglo, largely middle and upper-middle class, and had one or more adopted children who were adolescents at the time of the study. Almost all were intact, two-parent families, and only ten families had a biological child as well as adopted children. The adopted children were placed as infants (mean age of placement was 2.6 months) and were between the ages of fourteen and twenty-four at the time of the study. A full description of the sample and methodology may be found in Chapter 2.

Interviews conducted separately with the parents and adolescents were examined with respect to three questions: 1) How has adoption been discussed in these "normal" families over the years? 2) What kinds of problems did the adopted children experience as they were growing up? and 3) Was there any evidence of a link between the problems experienced by these children and the way adoption was handled in their families?

ADOPTION DISCUSSION

Fathers and mothers were asked how frequently adoption was usually discussed in their families. As may be seen in Table 11.1, fathers felt that adoption had been discussed less frequently than mothers had. Almost half of the adoptive fathers felt that adoption had "never or almost never" been discussed, whereas only 30.7 percent of the mothers responded in this manner. Conversely, 28.7 percent of mothers felt that adoption had been a frequent topic of discussion, whereas only 16.2 percent of fathers saw it as a frequent topic of discussion.

This response pattern may be compared with responses obtained in the adoptive families from the residential treatment sample. Both parents and the child were asked how frequently adoption had been discussed within the past year (see Table 11.1). Again, perceptions varied by family member. In general, fathers viewed adoption as being discussed least, mothers more, and adolescents most.

Comparisons of these two samples reveal strikingly similar patterns. In both samples, fathers felt that adoption had been discussed less frequently than did mothers. In addition, the proportions of parents responding with different degrees of frequency were quite similar in the two groups. On the basis of these preliminary comparisons, it does not appear that families with adolescents in treatment differ significantly from non-clinical families with respect to the frequency of discussion about adoption, on the average.

Parents in the Minnesota sample were also asked if their child had requested more information about his or her birthparents. If yes, they were asked how important they felt this information was for the child to have. As may be seen in Table 11.2, most parents did not respond to this question, presumably because their child had not requested more information. Of those who did respond, about equal numbers of mothers thought it was important and not important; the majority of fathers thought it was not important. When the children were asked, almost twice as many thought having the additional information was not important as thought it was important.

Little emphasis was placed on having more information because most parents probably shared the very limited information they had with the child at an early age. There seemed to be a tacit understanding between adoptive parents and their children that not much information was known, what was known had been shared, and little or nothing more could be discovered. This view was probably accurate for most of the families in the Minnesota sample, since the children

Table 11.1
Frequency of Discussion about Adoption

MINNESOTA SAMPLE

Frequency of Discussion	According to Father		According to Mother	
	N	%	N	%
Never or Almost Never	45	45.5	31	30.7
Regularly	38	38.4	41	40.6
Frequently	16	16.2	29	28.7
(No Reply)	16		14	

RESIDENTIAL TREATMENT SAMPLE

Frequency of Discussion in the Past Year	According to Father		According to Mother		According to Adol.	
	N	%	N	%	N	%
Not at All	11	40.7	10	26.3	5	14.3
Once or Twice	8	29.6	13	34.2	10	28.6
Occasionally	5	18.5	8	21.1	9	25.7
Often	3	11.1	7	18.4	11	31.4
(Did not answer)	23		12		15	

Note: Percentages are expressed as a proportion of those individuals who did respond to each item.

had been adopted in the late 1950s and early 1960s, when adoption practice permitted the release of only sketchy, nonidentifying information to the adoptive family.

Children in the Minnesota sample and both parents and children in the residential treatment sample were questioned about parents' responses to children's requests for information about their background (see Table 11.3). In terms of parents' emotional responses, more viewed them as positive (N = 28) or neutral (N = 16) than

Table 11.2

Degree of Perceived Importance of Having Additional Information
about Birthparents

MINNESOTA SAMPLE

Importance	According to Father	According to Mother	According to Adolescent
Important	10	25	47
Neutral	*	*	29
Not Important	38	30	89
Harmful	1	0	*
Info Not Requested	73	94	*
(Did Not Answer)	63	36	20
Totals	185	185	185

*Indicates that this response option was not available for that respondent.

negative (N = 16). In the residential treatment sample, both mothers and fathers stated overwhelmingly that they felt positive about responding to inquiries. Only two fathers and one mother reported that they felt negative about responding. In order to clarify these findings further, responses of parents and adolescents in the residential treatment sample were coded for the presence of several specific attitudes (see Table 11.3). In general, most parents (over 50 percent) viewed themselves as willing to help; 15 to 20 percent indicated that they might feel hurt, and 23 to 27 percent indicated that they were afraid, either for the child's sake, the birthparent's sake, or their own sake. Only 20 percent of the adolescents felt that their parents would be willing to help and many anticipated feelings of hurt (28 percent), jealousy (16 percent), or fear for the child's sake (20 percent), the adoptive parents' sake (8 percent), or the birthparent's sake (8 percent).

In terms of offering information, most parents in the Minnesota sample told their children that they did not know anything more (59.3 percent), 35.8 percent did offer new information, and 4.9 percent refused to give information the adolescent felt they had (see Table 11.4). In the residential treatment sample, two-thirds of the fathers said they told the adolescent everything they knew, while the other one-third

Table 11.3

Parents' Feelings about Answering Inquiries for More Information about
Birthparents

	Minnesota Sample Acc. to Child		Residential Trt Sample Acc. to Father		Acc. to Mother	
	N	%	N	%	N	%
Negative	16	26.7	2	10.5	1	3.2
Neutral	16	26.7	4	21.1	7	22.6
Positive	28	46.7	13	68.4	23	74.2
(No Ans.)	80		31		19	

Perceptions of Parental Attitudes about Responding

Residential Treatment Sample Only

Attitude	Acc. to Child		Acc. to Father		Acc. to Mother	
	N	%	N	%	N	%
Willing to help	5	20.0	15	57.7	22	51.2
Feel hurt	7	28.0	4	15.4	9	20.9
Feel jealous	4	16.0	0	0.0	2	4.7
Afraid / child	5	20.0	3	11.5	5	11.6
Afraid/Ad. Par.	2	8.0	0	0.0	3	7.0
Afraid/Birth P.	2	8.0	4	15.4	2	4.7

Note: Percentages are expressed as proportions of those individuals answering each item.

said they answered questions. None of the fathers reported withholding information. Mothers were somewhat less disclosing: 40 percent told everything they knew, 50 percent answered questions, and 10 percent withheld information.

In both the Minnesota sample and the treatment sample, mothers and fathers appeared to play different roles with respect to adoption. Specifically, in comparison with mothers, fathers seemed to view

Table 11.4
Parents' Actions about Answering Inquiries

Minnesota Sample: According to Adolescent

Response	N	%
Offered Information	29	35.8
Refused to Give Info	4	4.9
Said "Don't Know"	48	59.3
No Answer	76	--

Residential Treatment Sample

Response	According to Father		According to Mother	
	N	%	N	%
Told Everything	8	66.7	8	40.0
Answered Questions	4	33.3	10	50.0
Withheld Info	0	0.0	2	10.0
No Answer	38	--	30	--

Note: Percentages are expressed as proportions of those individuals answering each item.

adoption as being discussed less frequently in the family, to feel that obtaining additional information is less important for the child, and to feel less positive about answering questions but to be somewhat more disclosing. Adolescents in both samples felt that the parents held less positive attitudes about discussing adoption than they did themselves. These findings suggest that discussion of adoption may be viewed as an expressive family task, more appropriately delegated to the mother than the father. The finding that mothers play a more central role than fathers in discussions about adoption may also explain in part why adoptive mothers tend to become targets of more intense anger and bitterness from their children than adoptive fathers do.

PROBLEMS WHILE GROWING UP

Parents and adolescents in the Minnesota sample were asked to describe the types of problems the children had experienced as they were growing up. In order to minimize the reactivity of such a question in a sample of presumably normal families, this question and the follow-up question were worded as follows:

> Of course, all children experience various difficulties as they are growing up. What kinds of difficulties did your child have as he/she was growing up? Did you attribute any of those difficulties to the fact that _____ was adopted?

The total number of problems experienced within these families was surprisingly high, although mothers, fathers, and adolescents often disagreed in terms of what they reported as problems. It should be noted, however, that the behaviors listed as problems differed significantly in severity from the problems experienced by the families in the residential treatment sample. Examples of problems cited by the Minnesota families included the following:

Shyness
Rheumatic fever in third grade
Sensitive to teasing about weight
Fighting with an older brother
Learning disabilities
Felt displaced when biological sister was born
Severely depressed in early adolescence
Felt unpopular
Concern about registering for the draft
Short-tempered
Perfectionistic
Impulsive
Rebellious as adolescent
Problems with mother around "independence"
Strong-willed

Although some of these issues were more serious than others, they tended to be in the range of normal family problems. At the same time, it is interesting to note that some of these same issues (e.g., learning disabilities, strong will, problematic sibling relationships) played a role in the more serious problems ultimately developed by the adolescents in residential treatment.

In Table 11.5, frequency data are presented concerning the presence of problems in six areas: problems with school or learning; physical problems (e.g., medical, handicap, etc.); problems with friends;

Table 11.5

Presence of Problems While Growing Up among Adopted Adolescents in
Minnesota Sample

Problem	Perception of Father		Perception of Mother		Perception of Adolescent	
	Pres.	Severe	Pres.	Severe	Pres.	Severe
School/ Learning	30	3	39	6	25	3
Physical	29	4	32	7	11	1
Friends	15	0	27	1	23	0
Parents	22	2	28	3	50	1
Siblings	9	0	5	1	18	0
Personal	63	8	85	10	59	5

Note: Frequencies may sum to more than the N of 185 children because more than one
problem may have been noted.

problems with parents; problems with siblings; and personal problems
(e.g., self-esteem, depression, etc.). Responses to the rather open-ended
question were coded with respect to these six areas and for two degrees
of severity: 1) the problem was simply mentioned, and 2) the problem
was mentioned as being severe. As indicated in the table, mothers
noted more school, physical, friend, and personal problems than did
fathers or adolescents. Adolescents mentioned problems with parents
and siblings two to three times more frequently than their parents did.
The smaller proportion of family problems reported by parents than by
children may indicate either a lack of awareness or denial of problems
by parents or a hypersensitivity to problems by adolescents. This
pattern of differential perceptions of adolescents and their parents is
consistent with Barnes and Olson (1985), who found that adolescents in
a sample of normal families viewed communication within their
family more negatively than their parents did.

On the basis of the number of problems reported for each
adolescent, a problem severity index was constructed. This index was
computed as the sum of the number of areas in which problems were
noted, scoring each area as 1 for the problems being mentioned and 2 if
the problem was seen as severe. Thus, the severity score could range

from 0 to 12. Because of the differences in parents' and adolescents' perceptions, the problem severity index was computed separately for mothers, fathers, and adolescents. Descriptive statistics for this index may be found in Table 11.6. In general, parents' and adolescents' perceptions of the degree of problems were similar. However, mothers described a greater number of problems than did fathers or adolescents.

Table 11.6
Problem Severity Scores: Perceptions of Fathers, Mothers, and
Adolescents

	Frequencies		
Score	Fathers	Mothers	Adolescents
0	59	32	44
1	70	82	95
2	46	45	31
3	6	13	12
4	1	10	2
5	1	1	1
6	1	1	0
7	1	0	0
8	0	0	0
9	0	0	0
10	0	1	0
11	0	0	0
12	0	0	0
Mean	1.09	1.46	1.11
S.D.	(1.08)	(1.28)	(0.92)

Mothers may have either been more perceptive about problematic behavior, had lower thresholds of designating behaviors as problems, or simply been more disclosing in the interview situation.

LINKS BETWEEN ADOLESCENTS' PROBLEMS AND ADOPTION

Finally, data were examined with respect to potential links between the problems experienced by the adolescents (within the normal families) and the way adoption had been handled within the family. First, mean problem severity scores were compared for those families in which parents viewed adoption as contributing to the child's problems or not (see Table 11.7). A total of twelve of the 115 fathers and twenty-two of the 115 mothers felt that adoption had played a role in the child's difficulties.

Although the mean differences were not statistically significant, the direction of the means for both fathers and mothers suggested that a greater number of problems was associated with attribution to adoption. It should be noted, however, that the average number of problems per child in these non-clinical families was low, at approximately two or fewer.

The problem severity index was also examined with respect to questions relating to how frequently adoption had been discussed in the home. No significant association was found.

Table 11.7
Comparison of Problem Severity Index Means for Families in Which
Adoption Was or Was Not Viewed as a Cause of the Adolescent's
Problems

Perception of:	Adoption Seen as Cause	Adoption Not Seen as Cause
Fathers	2.09 (S.D.=1.76) N=11	1.59 (S.D.=0.74) N=94
Mothers	2.27 (S.D.=2.28) N=15	1.90 (S.D.=1.14) N=83

Note: Parents viewing adoption as causal (actual N = 12 fathers and 22 mothers) are not all represented in this analysis because of missing data.

CONCLUSION

The data collected from the Minnesota sample and the residential treatment sample are not directly comparable because of differences in samples, birth cohorts, and interview questions. However, the similarities rather than the differences between the two samples stand out when comparing their responses concerning how much adoption had been discussed over the years. Families in both samples seem to have discussed adoption approximately the same amount, on the average. As Brodzinsky's work suggests, however, the important factor in discussions of adoption is likely to be how adoption was discussed rather than how frequently.

Some parents in the residential treatment sample claimed to have discussed adoption fairly frequently and openly with their adolescent within the past year. It must be remembered, however, that adoption was being discussed as an aspect of treatment for many of the adolescents. Although not available through our interview data, it would be useful to consider how adoption was discussed before the child began treatment.

Data from both samples also point to the distinctive roles played by mothers and fathers with respect to adoption. Mothers appear to be more centrally involved and concerned with adoption-related matters within the family. Mothers felt that adoption was an important topic of discussion and expressed willingness to help their children obtain information. At the same time, however, their interview responses indicated that they were somewhat more cautious about actually disclosing information than their husbands were. The greater involvement of mothers and their control over information about the adoption may explain in part why they seem to be targets of anger and hostility from their children more than adoptive fathers.

Similarities and differences between the two samples in terms of the types of problems encountered in the families are worthy of note. Families in both the non-clinical Minnesota and residential treatment samples experienced some similar problems with children, such as learning disabilities, depression, sibling rivalry, and difficult temperament. However, the non-clinical Minnesota families were apparently able to handle these problems effectively and prevent them from escalating. For a variety of reasons (including genetically based differences in severity of the disorder, parental pathology, lack of parenting skill, and an unsupportive social environment), families whose children were now in residential treatment were unable to handle the problems. It could also be that the problems manifested by the adolescents now in treatment were more serious from the beginning. An important area of investigation in future studies designed for this purpose would concern how adoptive families effectively cope with such problems and prevent them from escalating.

Although the two samples seem to have responded similarly to questions concerning adoption, much information available on the residential treatment sample is not available from the Minnesota sample. An examination of the model of adoptive family relationships (presented in Figure 1.1) reveals that important data not collected from the Minnesota families concern the genetic and prenatal background of the child, the marital history of the parents, parenting skills, family history and dynamics, the child's cognitive understanding of adoption, and the adolescent's sense of identity as an adoptee. Such information would permit more direct comparisons to be made between the samples.

12

Conclusion: Theoretical Issues

DEVELOPMENT OF FRAMEWORK

The purpose of this investigation has been to identify familial and other contextual factors associated with the placement of adopted adolescents in residential treatment. Although inferences about causality are difficult to draw from a retrospective and correlational study, we will explore possible causal explanations for validation in future research. The predominant level of explanation sought in most studies is of proximal or efficient causes, attempting to understand behavior in terms of the child's immediate context. As Scarr (1985) has demonstrated, theories formulated at this level alone can ignore variables at other levels (i.e., biological, cultural, historical) that explain significant proportions of the variance in the phenomenon under investigation.

In this study, we have contended that there is currently no single theory adequately accounting for relationships and outcomes in adoptive families. A major objective has been to use existing theories and our data in an interactive manner to evolve our own framework of adoptive family relationships. Specifically, seven theoretical perspectives were used to guide the investigation of factors that led to emotional disturbance among the adopted adolescents in the sample. Relevant aspects of each theory are summarized below.

Psychoanalytic theory suggests that the circumstances surrounding the child's birth, including adoptive parents' concerns about infertility and adoptees' concerns about having two sets of parents, may result in emotional disturbance of the adoptees.

Genetic theory states that the etiology of disturbance among adopted children can be a result of their genetic backgrounds and predisposition for certain problems such as schizophrenia, depression, and alcoholism. Genetic differences between adoptive parents and adopted children in terms of intellectual ability and personality might also result in troublesome compatibility problems.

Attachment theory suggests that the preplacement history of the adopted child can influence later adoptive family relationships. Children who have developed insecure or anxious early attachments to foster mothers or birthparents because of abuse, neglect, or frequent moves can have difficulty in forming trusting, secure relationships when placed in a stable family situation.

Goodness-of-fit theory proposes that an individual's development is optimized in those situations in which there is a match between characteristics of the individual and characteristics or demands of the salient environment. In adoptive families, mismatches can occur between intellectual levels or personalities of parents and children, between adopted children, and between adopted and birth children in the same family. Major mismatches can result in serious family problems.

Cognitive-developmental theory claims that the child's understanding of adoption is a constructive process that does not reach a mature level until adolescence. Therefore, communication about adoption must be developmentally matched with the child's ability to understand it. The timing and content of the discussion about adoption can influence the child's acceptance and attitudes toward his or her adoptive status.

Kirk's *adoptive kinship theory* proposes that the experiences of adoptive parenthood are different from birth parenting. Kirk suggests that rejecting this difference can lead to poor communication and in turn adversely affect adoptive family relationships.

Attribution theory suggests the process through which individuals explain current and past behavior and predict future behavior. In troubled adoptive families, parents may disclaim their own responsibility for the child's behavior by blaming the child or may take away the child's responsibility by attributing maladaptive behavior to genetic factors.

These theories were used as a basis for developing a framework (see Figure 1.1) for analyzing the observed adoptive family dynamics among participants. The framework has several distinctive characteristics. First, it is developmental, taking the perspective that emotional disturbance evolves over a lengthy period of time. Second, it is transactional, taking into account the interactions over time between the developing individual and his or her changing environment. Third, it examines the interaction of factors across multiple levels of analysis, as it takes into account more distal factors such as genetic background and societal norms as well as more proximal factors such as the social ecology of the family, the family environment experienced by the child, and the child's psychological treatment history.

To review our framework, factors that appear to place adopted adolescents and their families at risk for disturbance include the following:

A. Parent Background Factors
   1. Parental attitudes about becoming a parent
   2. Parental expectations of the child
   3. Parental personality
   4. Marital relationship
   5. Parental motivation for adopting
   6. Parental willingness to be screened for adoption
   7. Parental attitudes toward adoptive parenthood
B. Child Background Factors
   1. Genetic risk factors
   2. Prenatal environment
   3. Preplacement history (foster homes, etc.)
C. Developmental History of the Child and Family
   1. Early Family Adaptation
      a. Compatibility of the child and family
      b. Early child behavior and interaction patterns
      c. Quality of relationships (e.g., attachment)
   2. Communication about adoption
      a. Cognitive understanding about adoption
      b. Adoptive identity development
      c. Attributions to adoption
   3. Traumatic family events
   4. Family work environments (e.g., military)
   5. Developing adaptation into adolescence
D. Contextual Factors Outside the Family
   1. School
   2. Peers
   3. Community support
E. Treatment
   1. Effectiveness of treatment
   2. Consideration of adoption in treatment

CONCLUSIONS

As we sought to understand factors associated with emotional disturbance in adopted adolescents, we also sought to understand the family processes that might have contributed to the disturbance. As mentioned above, the primary purpose of the study was to begin to identify important processes and not to identify population patterns.

We have drawn several conclusions from our analysis of the data. First, we noted that there appears to be no common denominator underlying the emotional problems of the adolescents in the study. Multiple factors (in different combinations and with different weights) contributed to the disturbance experienced by each adolescent.

Adoption issues appeared to play a major role in about two-thirds of the cases. In the other third, adoption issues played a moderate role or no role at all. Adoption-related problems experienced by some children included the following: feelings of being rejected by birthmother, anger toward birth and/or adoptive parents, self-hatred, rootlessness, and resentment about being adopted.

Although more parents of control adolescents than adopted adolescents evidenced pathology, at least 40 percent of parents in both groups were either alcoholic or abusive. This finding is particularly surprising among the adopted sample, since adoptive applicants are generally carefully screened and evaluated before being approved for adoptive parenthood.

There was a marked difference in the quality of marriages between the two groups; the marriages of adoptive parents appeared to be healthier and longer lasting, with fewer multiple marriages and cohabiting relationships. In the adoptive group, the children were typically the products of much waiting and hoping; in the control group, many of the children were the products of unplanned pregnancies and unstable marriages.

In both samples, parenting skill was problematic for nearly all families. Almost invariably the parents' initial attempts to control problematic behavior became increasingly unsuccessful over time. Some families appeared to lack sources of accurate child-rearing advice; others were given conflicting advice that exacerbated their difficulties; still others appeared to have problems implementing the advice they were given.

One pattern that emerged clearly in the adoptive group but not in the control group concerned the compatibility of the child within the family. As predicted by goodness-of-fit theory, development should be optimized when there is a match between the child's behavioral style and his or her environment. A significant number of adoptive families noted discrepancies between their children's personalities and what was acceptable within the context of their family. Following this discovery, a self-protective attributional process typically began: "It's not our fault, it must be because he is adopted." Abdication of ownership of the problem by the parents often signaled an early stage in the emotional distancing of the adoptive parents from their child. Over time, the distancing served to reinforce the child's feelings of rejection not only by birthparents, but now by adoptive parents as well.

A summary of additional major findings of the study is as follows:

Genetic factors such as schizophrenia or alcohol or drug use by birthparents can place children at high risk for later problems. Genetic contributions to intelligence and personality can set the stage for harmony or disharmony between adoptive parents and child.

Multiple poor foster placements, as well as abuse and neglect prior to the adoptive placement, can obviate the child's development of trust in secure family relationships.

Problematic behavioral styles of children such as hyperactivity or the "elbow baby" behavior patterns, whether a reflection of genetically based temperament or environmental reactions, can cause compatibility problems with the adoptive family.

Stress associated with troubled marital relationships, divorce, and maladaptive postdivorce family relationships seemed to have influenced some of the emotional and behavioral problems experienced by the institutionalized children.

Frequent father absence, relocations, abuse, and distant parent-child interactions seemed to have contributed to some of the children's adjustment difficulties.

Ineffective and inconsistent discipline, inappropriate expectations, lack of adequate nurturance, parental inflexibility, parental pathology, and intolerance of differences seemed adversely to affect the parent-child relationship in many of these families. Overpermissive and overprotective parenting styles also seemed to be problematic in many.

The majority of the institutionalized children had problematic peer relationships that were characterized as being superficial, cold or distant, or nonexistent. Although some parents attributed their children's problems to "bad crowd," the peer problems seemed to be symptoms rather than causes of behavioral difficulties.

Both adopted and control adolescents' problems were most frequently diagnosed as conduct disorders. Specific behaviors included running away, stealing outside of home, antisocial or delinquent behavior, drug or alcohol abuse, disobedient or rebellious behavior at home, truancy, disobedience at work, fighting with peers, and others. The majority of both groups had been in multiple residential settings and had moved to the current setting because previous approaches had not worked.

Open communication with adopted children and an awareness of the need for them to incorporate their adoptive status into their overall identity seemed crucial to avoid or minimize adjustment problems.

Although transracial adoption in itself was not the sole cause of behavioral difficulties, the children seem to have experienced exaggerated feelings of differentness because of the nature of their adoption.

Families with noninstitutionalized adoptees experienced some adjustment problems but to a lesser extent than the troubled adoptive families.

There is no single cause of adolescent institutionalization. The interaction of the child and parental factors specified in our model can all be influential in leading to adaptive or maladaptive behaviors in the adolescent sample.

SUMMARY

This study makes several contributions to the literature. First, the model developed in this investigation will facilitate future research and provide a framework through which the findings of existing studies may be interpreted. Second, through the broad-scale interview procedure used, several risk factors for adoptive families have been identified. Some of them have been mentioned in previous literature; others are new. However, they have not previously been brought together as a coherent group in the analysis of adoptive family relationships.

The discussion of these conclusions must be tempered with caveats and limitations concerning the study. The samples of adoptive and control families were convenience samples. Because no attempt was made to obtain representative or comprehensive samples, the generalizability of these findings must await further investigation. The data were retrospective and probably were colored by family members' selective memories or reconstruction of events. The data obtained in the study were all from self-reports, either through interviews or questionnaires. Because no observational data were included, our conclusions about family processes need further validation. Little information was available about the birthparents and the biological backgrounds of the adopted children in the study. The only information available to us was filtered through what the adoptive parents were willing to share and how well they remembered information obtained at the time of the child's placement. Finally, the study is correlational, and no claims can be made for one direction of effect over another.

IMPLICATIONS FOR RESEARCH

Several interesting research questions and approaches are suggested by the results of this study. A prospective longitudinal approach, following a large and representative sample of adoptive families for placement through adolescence, would clarify many questions about developmental patterns. In addition, further work is needed on the dynamics of successful adoptive families in order to understand the processes of coping and adaptation. How was it that many of the Minnesota Adoption Study families and the adoptive residential treatment study families faced similar problems, yet the outcomes were so different? Studies are needed on identity formation in adopted adolescents. Research on varying degrees of openness in adoption is needed in order to examine the consequences of contact among adopted children, adoptive parents, and birthparents. Further information is needed in order to understand the influence of genetic background factors upon adopted children. Attention should particularly be paid to the role of learning disabilities in the child's school and family adjustment.

Since most of the adopted children had been in several treatment settings before the current institutionalization, it is evident that research is needed to evaluate assessment and treatment approaches currently used with such a population of troubled youth. More accurate, effective early-intervention strategies can eliminate the need for some of the long-term, costly, out-of-home placements that the children in this study were experiencing.

Additional research on such issues as the impact of multiple parental figures on children's adjustment, treatment approaches that have been used to successfully offset the effects of early maltreatment or multiple placements, fear of displacement in the family at the birth of a sibling, and parental attachment issues with rejecting infants are all needed. Further investigation is needed to evaluate whether parental and child denial of difference between adoptive and birth parenthood leads to problems or is in reality a sign of a healthy, positive relationship between adoptive parents and children. We anticipate that research data on each of these topics will increase knowledge about adoptive family dynamics and mental health issues in adoptions and improve agency practices in the selection and preparation of families for adoptive parenthood.

13

Conclusion: Practice Issues

Though limited in generalizability, the findings of this study are consistent with the theoretical issues presented earlier and provoke some important reflections for adoption agencies, adoptive parents, and residential treatment staff.

IMPLICATIONS FOR ADOPTION AGENCIES AND ADOPTIVE FAMILIES

Despite the assumption among many adoption workers that infant adoptions generally are nonproblematic and constitute low-risk placements, problems can arise. In this sample, the majority of the adoptees in residential treatment were placed through agencies rather than independently. The majority of families had sought counseling from family service agencies, school counselors, private psychiatrists or psychologists, or child guidance centers prior to the placement of the child in residential treatment. Most had not sought counseling from the agency where the child had been adopted or from a local adoption agency. This may have resulted from the families' real or perceived assumptions that adoption agencies did not offer post-adoption services, might take the child away if they were found to be having problems, or might view them as some how unfit for adoptive parenthood. Other families may not have attributed the child's problems to the adoption and therefore did not seek adoption counseling services.

However, since the majority of the adoptive families had experienced some problems in adjusting to their adoptive status, it is important for adoption agencies to offer post-placement services especially designed for these children and their families. The seven families in this sample who had undertaken either an independent or a relative adoption were having serious adoption difficulties. Consequently, physicians and lawyers involved in such placements need to be educated about the kinds of problems that can arise.

Adoption agencies must be prepared to offer post-adoption services to this population of adoptive families as well. We recommend individual and group post-adoption counseling services that include both educational and therapeutic counseling for adopted children, their parents, and prospective adoptive parents.

Agency workers need to have a better understanding of the genetic and pre-placement factors that may affect the adjustment of adoptees. Gathering as much information as possible about the child's background is essential for good pre-placement planning. Instead of assuming that a loving family is sufficient to offset negative experiences that a child may have had as an infant, agencies should acknowledge that parenting training and post-adoption follow-up services may be needed. Careful screening of prospective adoptive families is needed in order to evaluate their appropriateness for high-risk children. Children who have been abused, neglected, given negative reinforcement, or are mistrusting of others must be in an environment in which there is predictability, positive interaction, and a reliable attachment figure. These parents must be informed that the child will test them repeatedly and they must be firmly grounded in limit-setting strategies. Not all prospective adoptive parents are capable of handling these unique needs.

Children who have lived in multiple homes before the adoptive placement need time to adjust and to develop attachments in their new families. They will need loving, responsive parents who can provide consistent discipline and who can deal with their fear, uncertainty, and possibly rejecting behavior. Pre- and post-placement counseling should be available to the adoptive parents to help prepare them for whatever problems arise. Parents of children who have schizophrenia or alcohol and drug abuse in the genetic background should receive special training regarding the potential influences on the child's behavior and be aware of resources where help may be obtained if necessary.

Adoption workers should also become more attuned to prospective adoptive parents' concerns about the kinds of children who are acceptable to them in order to avoid the incompatibility problems that were found in this study. Agencies must also more effectively assess prospective adoptive parents to discern their expectations for an adopted child. Social workers must dispel the belief of many adoptive families that love and a positive environment will resolve all problems and must provide counseling services to help families deal with the inevitable difficulties that arise when mismatches occur.

Presently, suitability for adoptive parenthood is determined partly through an evaluation of the couple's financial status, marital stability, and individual personality. Agencies tend to overemphasize the extent to which the couple has grieved about their infertility. None of the families in the sample mentioned infertility as a problem for them. Many, however, did have marital-relationship problems, and some parents exhibited pathology. Agencies need to develop effective screening measures to assess family interactional patterns, marital relationships, and intrapersonal dynamics.

The current agency evaluation process tends to make adoptive parents perceive themselves as exceptional parents or exceptional people, since they were selected from among many applicants to parent a child. As a result, when problems do arise, the parents often attribute the problem to the child or to the child's background rather than to themselves or to the parent-child relationship. This external attribution of the problem may lead to increased tension between the parent and child. Moreover, families who are led to believe that they are inherently excellent parents may not realize that quality parenting is achieved only through hard work. They must be prepared for the inevitable stresses and learn to be flexible and resourceful in seeking help when needed.

The findings suggest that there is a need to provide ongoing parenting-skill education and support to adoptive parents. Some adoptive parents may be too permissive in their behavior toward the adopted children because of a desire to be loved and appreciated by them. Many children test the limits set by adoptive parents and manipulate them by saying that their "real" parents would be more lenient or that their adoptive parents have no right to discipline them.

Parents should be alerted that manipulative comparisons are often made by adoptees and they should be prepared to handle such communications. Parents should also be trained to handle situations in which their adoptees will displace anger with their birthmothers onto their adoptive mothers. The parents should also be sensitized to the possible feelings of difference or rejection that adoptees sometimes experience when other siblings enter the family by birth.

Since a major parenting problem found in our study was inconsistency between mothers and fathers in disciplining the children, agencies must alert families to the possible consequences of this behavior. They must prepare families through pre-placement counseling and reinforce through post-placement counseling the necessity for consistent discipline. The parents also should be trained in specific strategies for handling difficult behavior. Many of the families in this study engaged in ineffective and punitive disciplinary approaches and would have benefitted from guidance in handling specific problematic behaviors.

One possible vehicle for ongoing parent education would be through a newsletter for adoptive parents, geared to the developmental level of the child. Manufacturers of disposable diapers already do this for parents of infants. Following such a model could perform an important service for adoptive parents and children.

Parents and children in this study exhibited different perceptions of the impact of significant family events on the child. Parents who felt that the absence of a consistent father figure in the home did not have a significant impact on the child had children who sometimes thought such absence had been detrimental to their adjustment. Similarly, parents who thought that numerous discussions about adoption were unnecessary and avoided them had adopted children who interpreted the lack of discussion to mean that the parents did not care about them or were hiding something. Agencies should become aware of these potential differences and encourage parents to keep open communication with their children.

According to the findings of this study, adoptive parents are less likely to think and talk about adoption issues as the child gets older. However, adopted children's need to talk about adoption increases as they mature and as they become more cognitively aware of the meaning of adoption. Adoptive parents should receive ongoing training about the children's understanding of adoption so that they can be prepared to answer questions at each cognitive developmental stage. Parents can also be sensitized to the child's feelings of loss and separation as they relate to his or her adoption. Parental attitudes toward adoption and toward the child's birthparents have a significant impact on the child's self-perception and attitudes toward his or her adoptive status. Counseling for adolescent adoptees is especially needed to give them an opportunity to ventilate their concerns and questions.

IMPLICATIONS FOR RESIDENTIAL TREATMENT STAFF

The findings of the study suggest that residential treatment staff need to be aware of the dynamics of adoptive family relationships in order to provide more effective services to this growing population within residential treatment centers. A child's adoptive status can no longer be viewed as merely an entry on the intake or social-history form. It must be viewed as an essential component in understanding the psychosocial history and functioning of a child and his or her family.

The findings suggest further that each case should be treated individually. Adoption is an issue for some children and not for others. Also, treatment centers should note that some parents might attribute problems to adoption that may really be caused by other factors.

Adoption agencies, through their post-adoption counseling services, might provide in-service training to residential treatment center staff to better prepare them to deal with adoption issues, which can be a crucial part of the treatment plan. Many of the adoptees in the study indicated that they had not discussed their feelings about their adoption with their families and also had not dealt with these concerns while either in treatment at the residential treatment centers or in prior out-patient treatment programs. The majority of the residential treatment staff seemed to be aware of the disproportionately high number of adopted children in treatment but generally failed to focus on adoption issues in treatment. During the course of our research interviews with adopted children, some openly sobbed as they began to talk about their adoption concerns. They indicated that they had felt uncomfortable bringing up adoption issues with their parents and had not discussed such concerns in therapy. However, it is evident that the children would welcome the opportunity to talk about their adoptive status and its significance to them.

Because of the large number of adopted children in treatment, it might be possible for staff to organize groups of adopted children for the purpose of addressing feelings of loss, separation, and rejection. Adoption counseling staff from local agencies might be used as consultants to the group. Some adoptees may need to be helped to deal with their feelings of loss, separation, and rejection.

Residential treatment staff should take complete social histories on children in care to comprehend the etiology of the child's emotional problems. Genetic risk factors, multiple placements, alcohol and schizophrenia in the background can be useful data for practitioners as they assess cases and develop treatment plans. Parent and child assessment schedules are provided in Appendixes E and F for use by clinicians in identifying specific child and parental background factors and salient adoption issues in adoptive families. These questions would supplement the regular intake procedure with adolescents and families seeking treatment. Slight modifications will need to be made on the adolescent questionnaire for use with younger children.

In family conferences, treatment staff should also discuss, when appropriate, adoption-related concerns and encourage communication between adoptees and parents about some of their unresolved dilemmas. Groups of adoptive parents whose children are in treatment might also be formed for both educative and counseling purposes.

In these sessions, staff should assess parenting issues, particularly disciplinary concerns. The majority of both adoptive and non-adoptive families in this study had problems with parenting skills. Providing specific suggestions for guidance and discipline as well as support to parents of troubled adolescents would be helpful. Post-treatment follow-up with the families would aid in evaluating the effectiveness of the intervention as well as providing ongoing assistance and support to the parents.

Appendixes

Appendix A
Participating Residential Treatment Centers

Oaks Treatment Center of the Brown Schools, Austin, Texas

Settlement Club Home, Austin, Texas

Merridell Achievement Center, Austin, Texas

Westwood Boys Ranch, Liberty Hill, Texas

Cherokee Home for Children, Cherokee, Texas

El Paso Children's Center, El Paso, Texas

Waco Home for Youth, Waco, Texas

Methodist Home for Children, Waco, Texas

Archdeacon Gilfillan Home, Bemidji, Minnesota

Austin State Hospital, Austin, Texas

Friendship House, Minneapolis, Minnesota

Gerard of Minnesota, Austin, Minnesota

Mary Lee Foundation, Austin, Texas

Presbyterian Children's Home, Itasca, Texas

Appendix B
Parent Interview

I would like to begin by trying to understand the history of
your family, beginning with your first marriage and
continuing to the present. I would especially like you to
note each major family transition, such as the birth,
addition, departure, divorce, or death of any family member.
I'd also like to explore how each of these events affected
_____ (date, child's age, event, perceived effect on).

How long have you been married to your present spouse?

Is this your first marriage? yes   no

If no, please give dates of marriage and divorce for previous
marriages.

If you are currently divorced...

What were the circumstances or key issues leading to the
divorce?

When did you start having trouble with the marriage?

When did you start having trouble with _____?

Do you feel that _____ had any role in bringing about the
divorce?

What happened after the divorce? (return to family of origin?
development of new friendships?)

How often does the non-custodial parent (NCP) see _____?

Was NCP involved in the decision to place _____ in
residential treatment?

What ongoing role does NCP play in making decisions about
_____?

Has NCP relinquished adoptive rights?

(If remarried) Has the new parent expressed interest in
adopting _____?

Have other friends or relatives stepped in to play parental
roles?

How old were you when _____ was adopted?

Were you adopted? no yes

    If yes, ...

Do any of your friends or relatives have adopted children?
If yes, ...

Are any of the adopted children related to each other
biologically? If so, please specify.

Are any of the adopted children related to either adoptive
parent? If so, please specify.

What do you know about _____'s biological parents: age
at birth of child; occupation; education; marital status
(single, married to each other, to others, divorced,
separated); nationality/racial background; special interests
or talents; medical history; reason for relinquishing
_____; physical or emotional problems; circumstances of
pregnancy and delivery; prenatal care of mother; birth
weight of _____?

How much of the above information does _____ know about
his/her biological parents?

Were there any birth siblings?

Is _____ aware of them?

Is your adoption of _____

   a. step parent adoption

   b. foster parent adoption

   c. transracial adoption

   d. older child adoption

   e. infant adoption

   f. other -- please specify _____

What other placement(s) had _____ experienced before
coming to your family? Begin with biological parents: types
of placement (foster, adoption, etc.); length; quality?

Was _____ ever abused or neglected in any of these
placements? If so, please describe.

Why did you decide to adopt?

What did you expect the adoption process to be like?

Please explain the process you went through to adopt _____?

How did you feel going through the process?

Did you have to prove infertility at the time of your adoption application?

What age or sex preference for a child did you have when you first applied to adopt?

Did you adopt through an agency or independently?

(If adopted through an agency) What was the name of the agency?

(If adopted independently) Explain the arrangements of your independent adoption.

Did you receive post finalization services?

What kinds of services (if any) do you think were needed that were not provided?

How would you describe your feelings about _____'s adoption at around the time of the adoption?

What were some of the satisfactions and problems you encountered in the first three years?

What was your relationship like with _____ during those early years?

How did your relatives react to your decision to adopt?

What is the most satisfying aspect of your relationship with _____?

How old was _____ when he was first told of his adoption?

How did you tell him/her of the adoption?

What was his/her reaction?

To the best of your knowledge, has _____ even been teased or questioned about his/her adoption?

Has _____ inquired about his/her adoption?

How old was he/she when he/she first inquired?

How did you feel about answering these questions?

During the past year how often have you talked with _____ about his/her adoption: (not at all, once or twice, occasionally, often)

Has _____ ever expressed an interest in contacting his/her
  biological parents?

Has _____ ever tried to contact one or both?

How do you feel about this?

Some children seem to be more curious than others about their
  birthparents. Which of the following questions has your
  child asked about mother and about father: Whether birthparent is alive, what he/she looks like, what his/her name
  is, where he/she lives. What other questions has the child
  asked?

Now I would like to ask how _____ has been doing in school
  and with friends.

How are _____'s grades?

What kinds of learning or behavioral problems did _____
  have in school?

What are _____'s achievements and special interests or
  talents?

What does _____ want to do when he/she grows up?

How much education does _____ hope to get?

What would you like to see _____ do?

How about _____'s friends? How many close friends does
  _____ have?

What do they do together?

How does _____ get along with his/her brothers and sisters
  (ASK FOR EACH SIBLING): at the time of adoption, at the
  time when _____ started having problems, and now?

Has _____ ever commented that he/she feels treated
  differently than other siblings (ASK FOR EACH SIBLING): by
  parents, by siblings, and by extended family?

What is your view of this?

How many "parent figures" would you say _____ has now?
  Who are they?

Is _____ closer to one of these people than the others?

How old was _____ when problems first arose?

How did you respond? b. What kinds of discipline did you use?
c. Did this change over time? d. What kind of effect did
these measures have? e. What is your view now of how much
you can change children?

Have you ever sought counseling from an adoption agency or
family service before seeking residential treatment?

What were the problems that led you to seek residential
treatment for _____?

What steps did you encounter in the process of placing
_____ in this present residential treatment center
(i.e., previous placements, etc.)? How did _____ react
each step along the way?

How have your other children responded to _____ being
placed in residential treatment?

Have you ever sought residential treatment for any other
children in your family?

Has any other member of your family sought residential
treatment for one of their children?

How would you describe your feelings about _____ being in
residential treatment?

What do you view as the main cause(s) of _____'s problems?

Do you think that any of _____'s problems resulted from
the adoption? Why or why not? (Ex. something that happened
before the adoption? after the adoption?)

Do you think that adoptive children can really belong to an
adoptive family? Do you feel that _____ really
belongs?

Do you belong to any adoptive parent groups? Why or why not?

Are you active in any community, cultural, or religious groups
that you would view as supports for your role as parent? If
so, please describe.

Do you believe that adoptive parents need to have some
abilities in addition to those needed by good parents
generally?

What joys and difficulties do you think are experienced by:

   a. adoptive parents?

   b. biological parents?

   c. adopted children?

   d. biological children?

Finally, given your experience as an adoptive parent, what sort of advice would you give someone who is considering adoption?

Appendix C
Child Interview

What kind of school situation are you in now? What
   are you studying?

How are your grades?

What are your achievements and special interests or
   talents?

What do you want to do when you grow up?

How much education do you hope to get?

What would your parents like to see you do?

How about your friends? How many close friends do you
   have?

What do you do together?

What kinds of learning or behavioral problems did you
   have in school?

Now I would like you to try to think about the big
   events in your life and how they have affected you,
   beginning with your birth and continuing to the present.
   I would especially like to note each major family
   transition, such as the birth, addition, departure,
   divorce, or death of any family member. (Ask date,
   child's age, event, and perceived effect on you).

How do you get along with your brothers and sisters
   (Ask for each sibling): at the time of adoption, at the
   time when you started having problems, and now? (Probe: How
   close are you? What kinds of things do you do together?)

Have you ever felt that you were treated differently
   than other siblings? Why (Ask for each sibling): by
   parents, by siblings, and by your other relatives?

What is your relationship with your mother like?
   father? (early memory, when first started having problems,
   and now?)

What is the best part of your relationship with your father and
   mother?.

What sort of things did your parents do when you did something
   wrong? Did it work? What could they have done?

Are your parents a) married b) separated c) divorced?

(If married), how happy do you consider your parents' marriage (1 being very unhappy, 5 happy, and 10 perfectly happy)?

(If divorced or separated) Why do you think your parents divorced (or separated)?

When did they start having trouble with the marriage?

What happened after the divorce? Did you have any input into the decision regarding what parent you would live with?

How often do you see your non-custodial parent (NCP)?

What ongoing role does NCP play in making decisions about you?

If your parent(s) has (have) remarried, what role do(es) your new parent(s) play in making decisions about you?

What do you know about your biological parents: age at birth of child; occupation; education; marital status (single, married to each other, to others, divorce, separation); nationality/racial background; special interests or talents; medical history; reason for relinquishing; physical or emotional problems; and circumstances of pregnancy and delivery?

Do you have any birth siblings?

What other placement(s) had you experienced before coming to your present adoptive family? (Begin with biological parents.)

Do you remember what any of those placements were like? If so...

Do you know why your parents decided to adopt?

How old were you when you were adopted?

Do you know any other children who were adopted? If yes, who?

How old were you when you were first told of your adoption?

How were you told of the adoption?

What was your reaction?

Have you ever been teased or questioned about your adoption?

Have you ever inquired about your adoption?

How did you feel about asking?

During the past year, how often have you talked to
anyone about your adoption: (not at all, once or twice,
occasionally, often)

Have you ever been interested in contacting your biological
parents?

Have you ever tried to contact one or both?

How do you feel about this?

How many "parent figures" would you say you have now? Who are
they?

Are you closer to one of these people than the others?

How old were you when problems first arose?

How did you respond?

What were the problems that led you to be placed in residential
treatment? Why do you think you had these problems?

What steps did you encounter in the process of being
placed in this present residential treatment center (i.e.,
previous placements, etc.)? How did you react to each step
along the way?

How have your siblings and friends responded to your being
placed in residential treatment?

Has residential treatment ever been sought for any other child
in your family?

How would you describe your feelings about being in residential
treatment?

Do you think that any of your problems resulted from being
adopted? Why or why not?

Do you feel that you really belong to your family?

Do your parents belong to any adoptive groups? Why or why not?

Do you believe that adoptive parents need to have some
abilities in addition to those needed by good parents
generally?

What joys and difficulties do you think are experienced by:

    a. adoptive parents?

    b. biological parents?

    c. adopted children?

    d. biological children?

Finally, given your experience as an adopted child, what sort of advice would you give someone who is considering adoption?

Appendix D
Caseworker Interview

How long has _____ been in residential treatment here?

What were the precipitating circumstances of his/her admission?

Was there any abuse (sexual, emotional or physical) in
   the background? Explain.

What is his/her diagnosis?

What are the goals of the treatment plan? What is his/her
   prognosis?

How would you describe_____'s relationship with her/
   his: father, mother, and siblings?

How would you describe the relationship between the parents?

How would you characterize_____'s mother? father?

Are _____ parents involved in the treatment plan? In
   what way?

Are you aware of any relevant information on which
   _____'s parents and _____have very
   different views?

How does _____get along with other residents at the
   center?

What problems has _____had here?

What does he/she seem to enjoy most about the center?

Has _____ever discussed his/her adoption? If yes,
   explain.

Has _____ever discussed a desire to find his/her
   birthparents?

During the intake evaluation was adoption identified as a
   problem area? Explain.

To what extent do you believe the adoption has affected
   _____'s current problem?

Approximately what proportion of the children (annually) in
   this center are adopted?

Reflecting on your work with adoptees and non-adoptees
   in this center, what similarities and differences have you

noted in their: a) presenting problems (diagnosis), b) relationship with parents, c) plans for return home, d) and behavior?

(Immediately after interview)
(with child and/or family)

Are there any pertinent aspects of this case which did not come out in the interview(s)? Explain.

(6 weeks after the interview)

What affect do you think this interview has had on the child? the parents?

Appendix E
Assessing Adoption Background Information
(Adoptive Parents)

Birthparent Background Factors:

What information do you have about the child's background:

	Birthmother	Birthfather
Age at birth of child		
Occupation		
Education		
Marital Status		
Nationality/ Racial Background		
Medical History		
Reasons for Relinquishing Child		

To the best of your knowledge were any of these factors present in the child's background:

	Birthmother	Birthfather	Other Rel.
Schizophrenia			
Alcoholism			
Depression			
Other Emotional or Physical probs.			

Prenatal Factors

What information do you have on the following?

Mother's emotional
  state during preg.:

Mother's prenatal care/nutrition:

Alcohol use during pregnancy:

Drug use during pregnancy:

Circumstances of pregnancy and delivery:

Child Background Factors

Child's birthweight:

Birth Anomalies, such as
   fetal alcohol syndrome:

Were there any birthsiblings:
   If so, is the child aware of them?

Child's age at placement with you:

What other placements had _____experienced before coming
   to your family?

Type of home (Birth, Foster, Adopt, etc.)	Length	Quality
a.		
b.		
c.		
d.		

Was _____ever abused or neglected in any of these
   placements?   If so, describe.

Parent Background Factors:

Were you adopted?

Why did you decide to adopt?

Did you have to prove infertility at the time of your
   adoption application?

What age, race and sex preference for a child did you have
   when you first applied to adopt?

What counselling did you receive during the adoption
   process?

What kind of post-adoption counselling did you receive?

What kind of adoption do you have:

Transracial:

Relative:

Agency:

Independent:

How old were you when _____was adopted?

How did your relatives react to your decision to adopt?

In what ways is _____ (child) like you (temperament, appearance)?

In what ways is _____(child) dissimilar to you (temperament, appearance)?

Adoption Issues

Do you have any birth children?

Do you have other adopted children?

What were some of the satisfactions you encountered in the first three years after the adoption?

What were some of the problems you encountered in the first three years?

When did you tell _____s/he was adopted?

What was _____ (child's) reaction?

How often do you talk about adoption with _____?

Does _____ask questions about the circumstances of his/her relinquishment?

How does _____feel about his/her birthparents?

Has _____ever asked to find his/her birthparents?

Has_____ever had any contact with his/her birthparents?

Has_____ever met his/her birthparents?

Do you think any of _____'s problems stemmed from the adoption? (If so, explain.)

If transracial adoption, also ask:

How does _____describe his racial identity?
(To what racial group would _____say he/she belongs?)

How do you describe _____'s racial identity?

Why did you decide to transracially adopt?

Do you live in a racially mixed, mostly white or mostly minority neighborhood?

Does _____attend a racially mixed, mostly white, or mostly minority school?

How often does _____see others of his/her own racial background? (In what context?)

How does _____feel about his/her racial heritage?

Have you adopted other children transracially?

Has _____ever experienced any racial prejudice or discrimination? (If so, describe.)

Do you think any of the problems _____has experienced are partially due to his/her transracial adoption? (If so, explain.)

Appendix F
Assessing Adoption Background Information
(Adolescents)

What does the word "adopted" mean to you?

What does the word "birthparent" mean to you?

What do you know about your birthparents?

	Birthmother	Birthfather

Age at your birth

Occupation

Education

Marital Status

Nationality/
   Racial Background

Medical History

Reason for
   Placing you
   for adoption

How did you get this information on your birthparents?

How old were you when you were placed for adoption?

Do you know if you were in any other placements before
   being adopted by your Mom and Dad?

Do you know any other children who were adopted?

How does it feel to be adopted?

Who first told you that you were adopted? How old were
   you?

What did that person say?
   (If Mom and Dad were not the first persons to tell
   child about adoption, ask) How old were you when your
   Mom and Dad first talked to you about your adoption?
   (Probe: What did they say?)

Have you ever met your birthparents?

If not, have you ever wanted to meet your birthmother;
   birthfather? (Why)

If not, have you ever wanted to talk to your birthmother; birthfather? (Why?)

Do you plan to search for your birthparents when you are older? Explain.

Do you have any biological brothers or sisters who were born to your birthparents?

If so, do you know where they are living? Do you have contact with them?

How many other children are in your adoptive family? Are they also adopted, or were they born into the family? If so, how do you get along with your siblings? If so, do you ever feel you are treated differently from your siblings? Explain.

What do you like best about your adoptive mother?

What do you like best about your adoptive father?

What do you like best about being adopted?

What do you like least about being adopted?

Do you think any of your problems stemmed from your adoption? (If so, explain.)

Would you ever like to adopt a child? Explain.

What advice would you give someone interested in adopting?

If transracial adoption, also ask:

To what racial group do you belong?

To what racial group do your adoptive parents belong?

Do you live in a racially mixed, mostly white, or mostly minority neighborhood?

Do you attend a racially mixed, mostly white, or mostly minority school?

How often do you see others who have the same racial background as you? In what context?

How do you feel about your racial heritage?

Have your parents transracially adopted other children in your family?

Have you ever experienced any racial prejudice or discrimination? (If so, describe.)

Do you think any of the problems you have experienced are partially due to your transracial adoption? (If so, explain.)

References

Achenbach, T. M. 1966. The classification of children's psychiatric symptoms: A factor-analytic study. *Psychological Monographs 80* (whole No. 615).

Achenbach, T. M., and C. S. Edelbrock. 1978. The classification of child psychopathology: A review and analysis of empirical efforts. *Psychological Bulletin* 85:1275–1301.

Achenbach, T. M., and C. S. Edelbrock. 1981. Behavioral problems and competencies reported by parents of normal and disturbed children aged 4 through 16. *Monographs of the Society for Research in Child Development 46.*

Ackerman, P. T., P. T. Elardo, and R. A. Dykman. 1979. A psychosocial study of hyperactive and learning disabled boys. *Journal of Abnormal Child Psychology* 7:91–100.

Agee, V. 1979. *Treatment of the violent incorrigible adolescent.* Lexington, MA: D. C. Heath & Co.

Ainsworth, M. D. S. 1973. The development of infant-mother attachment. In *Review of Child Development Research,* Vol. 3, ed. B. M. Caldwell and H. N. Ricciuti, pp. 1–94. Chicago: University of Chicago Press.

Ainsworth, M. D. S. 1979. Infant-mother attachment. *American Psychologist* 34:932–37.

Ainsworth, M. D. S. 1984. Adaptation and attachment. Paper presented at the meeting of the International Conference on Infant Studies, New York City, April.

Ainsworth, M. D. S., M. Blehar, E. Waters, and S. Wall. 1978. *Patterns of attachment.* Hillsdale, N.J.: Erlbaum.

American Psychiatric Association. 1980. *Diagnostic and statistical manual of mental disorders.* 3d ed. (DSM-III). Washington, D.C.: American Psychiatric Association.

Andrews, R. G. 1978. Adoption: Legal resolution or legal fraud? *Family Process* 17:313–28.

Andrews, R. G. 1979. A clinical appraisal of searching. *Public Welfare* 37 (3): 15–21.

Andrews, G., and C. Tennant. 1978. Life event stress and psychiatric illness. *Psychological Medicine* 8:545–49.

Arend, R., F. L. Gove, and L. A. Sroufe. 1979. Continuity of individual adaptation from infancy to kindergarten: A predictive study of ego-resiliency and curiosity in preschoolers. *Child Development* 50:950–59.

Bachrach, C. A. 1986. Adoption plans, adopted children, and adoptive mothers. *Journal of Marriage and the Family* 48:243–53.

Barkley, R. A. 1982. Guidelines for defining hyperactivity in children. In *Advances in clinical child psychology,* Vol. 5, ed. B. B. Lahey and A. E. Kazdin, 137–80. New York: Plenum.

Barnes, H. L., and D. H. Olson. 1985. Parent-adolescent communication and the circumplex model. *Child Development* 56:438–47.

Baruch, D. W., and J. A. Wilcox. 1944. A study of sex differences in preschool children's adjustment coexistent with interpersonal tensions. *The Journal of Genetic Psychology,* 64:281–303.

Bates, J. 1980. The concept of difficult temperament. *Merrill-Palmer Quarterly* 26:299–319.

Baumrind, D. 1967. Child care practices anteceding three patterns of preschool behavior. *Genetic Psychology Monographs* 75:43–88.

Baumrind, D. 1971. Current patterns of parental authority. *Developmental Psychology Monographs* 4.

Becker, W. 1964. Consequences of different kinds of parental discipline. In *Review of child development research,* Vol. 1, ed. M. L. Hoffman and L. W. Hoffman, pp. 169–208. New York: Russell Sage Foundation.

Bell, R. Q., and L. V. Harper. 1977. *Child effects on adults.* Hillsdale, N.J.: Erlbaum.

Belsky, J. 1978. Three theoretical models of child abuse: A critical review. *International Journal of Child Abuse and Neglect* 2:37–49.

Belsky, J. 1980. Child maltreatment: An ecological integration. *American Psychologist,* 35:320–35.

Belsky, J. 1981. Early human experience: A family perspective. *Developmental Psychology* 17:3–23.

Belsky, J. 1984. The determinants of parenting: A process model. *Child Development* 55:83–96.

Belsky, J., and J. Vondra. 1985. Characteristics, consequences, and determinants of parenting. In *Handbook of family psychology and therapy,* ed. L. L'Abate, pp. 523–56. Homewood, Ill.: Dorsey Press.

Berman, L. C., and R. H. Bufferd. 1986. Family treatment to address loss in adoptive families. *Social Casework* 67:3–11.

Block, J. H., J. Block, and P. F. Gjerde. 1986. The personality of children prior to divorce: A prospective study. *Child Development* 57:827–40.

Bohman, M. 1971. A comparative study of adopted children, foster children and children in their biological environment born after undesired pregnancies. *ACTA Psychiatrica Scandanavica Supplement* 221:1–38.

Bourguignon, J., and K. W. Watson. 1987. *After adoption: A manual for professionals working with adoptive families.* Chicago: Illinois Department of Children and Family Services.

Bowen, M. 1978. *Family therapy in clinical practice.* New York: Jason Aronson.

Bowlby, J. 1969. *Attachment and loss.* Vol. 1. New York: Basic Books.

Bretherton, I. I. 1980. Young children in stressful situations: The supporting role of attachment figures and unfamiliar caregivers. In *Uprooting and development,* ed. G. V. Coelho and P. Ahmed, pp. 179–210. New York: Plenum.

Brieland, D., L. Costin, and C. Atherton. 1980. *Contemporary Social Work.* New York: McGraw-Hill.

Brinich, P. 1980. Some potential effects of adoption on self and object representations. In *The psychoanalytic study of the child,* ed. A. Solnit, R. Eissler, A. Freud, M. Kris, and P. Neubauer, pp. 107–31. New Haven, Conn.: Yale University Press.

Brinich, P., and E. Brinich. 1982. Adoption and adaptation. *The Journal of Nervous and Mental Disease* 170 (8): 489–93.

Broderick, C., and J. Smith. 1979. The general systems approach to the family. In *Contemporary theories about the family,* Vol. II, ed. W. R. Burr, R. Hill, F. I. Nye, and I. L. Reiss. New York: The Free Press.

Brodzinsky, D. M., D. E. Schechter, A. M. Braff, and L. M. Singer. 1984. Psychological and academic adjustment in adopted children. *Journal of Consulting and Clinical*

Psychology 52 (4): 582–90.

Brodzinsky, D. M., L. M. Singer, and A. M. Braff. 1984. Children's understanding of adoption. *Child Development* 55:869–78.

Campbell, S. 1979. Mother-infant interaction as a function of maternal ratings of temperament. *Child Psychiatry and Human Development* 10:67–76.

Campos, J. J., K. C. Barrett, M. E. Lamb, H. H. Goldsmith, and C. Stenberg. 1983. Socioemotional development. In *Handbook of child psychology*, Vol. 2, ed. M. M. Haith and J. J. Campos, pp. 783–916. New York: Wiley.

Chambers, D. 1970. Willingness to adopt atypical children. *Child Welfare* 49 (5): 275–79.

Cochran, M. and J. Brassard. 1979. Child development and personal social networks. *Child development* 50:601–16.

Cohen, N. J., and K. Minde. 1983. The "hyperactive syndrome" in kindergarten children: Comparisons of children with pervasive and situational symptoms. *Journal of Child Psychology and Psychiatry* 24:443–56.

Coleman, J. C. 1984. *Intimate relationships, marriage, and family.* Indianapolis, Ind.: Bobbs-Merrill.

Coopersmith, S. 1967. *The antecedents of self-esteem.* San Francisco: W. H. Freeman.

Costin, L. 1972. *Child welfare: Policies and practices.* New York: McGraw-Hill.

Crockenberg, S. 1981. Infant irritability, mother responsiveness, and social support influences on the security of infant-mother attachment. *Child Development* 52:857–65.

Dahl, A. S., K. M. Cowgill, and R. Asmundsson. 1987. Life in remarriage families. *Social Work* 32:40–44.

Darnauer, P. 1976. The adolescent experience in career army families. In *Families in the military system*, ed. H. I. McCubbin, B. B. Dahl, and E. J. Hunter, pp. 55–71. Beverly Hills, Calif.: Sage.

Davids, A., and S. DeVault. 1962. Maternal anxiety during pregnancy and childbirth abnormalities. *Psychosomatic Medicine* 24:464–70.

Davids, A., S. DeVault, and M. Talmadge. 1961. Anxiety, pregnancy, and childbirth abnormalities. *Journal of Consulting Psychology* 25:74–77.

Delameter, A. M., B. B. Lahey, and L. Drake. 1981. Toward an empirical subclassification of "learning disabilities": A psychophysiological comparison of "hyperactive" and "nonhyperactive" subgroups. *Journal of Abnormal Child Psychology* 9:65–77.

Dielman, T., K. Barton, and R. Cattell. 1977. Relationships among family attitudes and child rearing practices. *Journal of Genetic Psychology* 130:105–12.

Dinges, D. F., M. M. Davis, and P. Glass. 1980. Fetal exposure to narcotics: Neonatal sleep as a measure of nervous system disturbance. *Science* 209: 619–21.

Dix, T. 1984. Social cognitive processes during parent-child disciplinary episodes. Paper presented at the meeting of the American Psychological Association, Toronto, August 1984.

Dix, T. H., and J. E. Grusec. 1986. Parent attribution processes in the socialization of children. In *Parental belief systems: Psychological consequences for children*, ed. I. Sigel, pp. 201–33. Hillsdale, N.J.: Erlbaum.

Dontas, C., O. Maratos, M. Fafontis, and A. Karangelis. 1985. Early social development in institutionally reared Greek infants: Attachment and peer interaction. In *Growing points of attachment theory and research*, ed. I. Bretherton and E. Waters. Monographs of the Society for Research in Child Development, Vol. 50, nos. 1–2. Chicago: University of Chicago Press.

Douglas, V. I., and K. G. Peters. 1979. Toward a clearer definition of the attentional deficit of hyperactive children. In *Attention and the development of cognitive skills*, ed. G. A. Hale and M. Lewis, pp. 173–247. New York: Plenum.

Dukette, R. 1962. Discussion of thoughts regarding the etiology of psychological difficulties in adopted children. *Child Welfare* 41 (February): 66–71.

Dunn, J., C. Kendrick, and R. MacNamee. 1981. The reaction of firstborn children to the birth of a sibling: Mothers' reports. *Journal of Child Psychology and Psychiatry* 22:1–10.

Ebbin, J. 1979. Battered child syndrome at the Los Angeles County General Hospital. *American Journal of Diseases of Childhood* 118:660–67.

Egeland, B., and E. A. Farber. 1984. Infant-mother attachment: Factors related to its development and changes over time. *Child Development* 5:753–71.

Eiduson, B. N., and J. B. Livermore. 1953. Complications in therapy with adopted children. *American Journal of Orthopsychiatry* 23:795–802.

Elonen, A., and E. Schwartz. 1969. A longitudinal study of emotional, social and academic functioning of adoptive children. *Child Welfare* 48 (2): 72–78.

Emery, R. E. 1982. Interparental conflict and the children of discord and divorce. *Psychological Bulletin* 2:310–30.

Emery, R. E., and K. D. O'Leary. 1983. Marital discord and child behavior problems in a normative sample. Unpublished manuscript, University of Virginia, Charlottesville.

Erikson, E. H. 1950. *Childhood and society*. New York: Norton.

Falk, L. L. 1970. A comparative study of transracial and inracial adoptions. *Child Welfare* 49:82–88.

Fanshel, D. 1972. *Far from the reservation: The transracial adoption of American Indian children*. Metuchen, N.J.: Scarecrow Press.

Fellner, I. 1968. Recruiting adoptive applicants. *Social Work* 13 (1): 42–100.

Freeman, E. M. 1985. *Social work practice with clients who have alcohol problems*. Springfield, Ill.: Charles C. Thomas.

Freud, S. 1986. *Paradoxes of parenthood: On the impossibility of being a perfect parent*. Clara Pope Willoughby Memorial Lecture in Child and Family Services, University of Texas at Austin (unpublished lecture).

Friedrich, W. N., and J. A. Boriskin. 1976. The role of the child in abuse: A review of the literature. *American Journal of Orthopsychiatry* 46:580–90.

Frodi, A. 1981. Contribution of infant characteristics to child abuse: A review of the literature. *Journal of Mental Deficiency* 85:341–49.

Fullerton, C. S., W. Goodrich, and L. B. Berman. 1986. Adoption predicts psychiatric treatment resistances in hospitalized adolescents. *Journal of the American Academy of Child Psychiatry* 25:542–51.

Gal, P., and M. K. Sharpless. 1984. Fetal drug exposure-behavioral teratogenesis. *Drug Intelligence and Clinical Pharmacy* 18:186–201.

Garmezy, N. 1983. Stressors of childhood. In *Stress, coping, and development in children*, ed. N. Garmezy and M. Rutter, pp. 43–84. New York: McGraw-Hill.

Garmezy, N. 1986. Developmental aspects of children's responses to the stress of separation and loss. In *Depression in young people: Developmental and clinical perspectives*, ed. M. Rutter, C. E. Izard, and P. B. Read, pp. 297–323. New York: Guilford.

Gersten, J. C., T. S. Langner, J. G. Eisenberg, and O. Simcha-Fagan. 1977. An evaluation of the etiological role of stressful life-change events in psychological disorders. *Journal of Health and Social Behavior* 18:228–44.

Gil, D. G. 1970. *Violence against children*. Cambridge, Mass.: Harvard University Press.

Goodman, J. D., and R. Magno-Nora. 1975. Adoption and its influence during adolescence. *Journal of Medical Sociology* 72:922–28.

Goodman, J. D., R. M. Silberstein, and W. Mandell. 1963. Adopted children brought to child psychiatric clinics. *Archives of General Psychiatry* 2:451–56.

Gottesman, I. I., and J. Shields. 1976. A critical review of recent adoption, twin, and family studies of schizophrenia: Behavioral genetics perspective. *Schizophrenia Bulletin* 2:360–400.

Grotevant, H. D., S. Scarr, and R. A. Weinberg. 1977. Patterns of interest similarity in adoptive and biological families. *Journal of Personality and Social Psychology* 35:667–76.

Grow, L. J., and D. Shapiro. 1974. *Black children, white parents*. New York: Child Welfare League of America.

Hallinan, M. T. 1980. Patterns of cliquing among youth. In *Friendship and peer relations in children*, ed. H. C. Foot, A. J. Chapman, and J. R. Smith, pp. 110–18. New York: John Wiley & Sons.

Hartman, A. 1984. *Working with adoptive families beyond placement*. New York: Child Welfare League of America.

Hartup, W. W. 1978. Children and their friends. In *Issues in childhood social development*, ed. H. McGurk, pp. 130–70. London: Methuen.

Hartup, W. W. 1984. The peer context in middle childhood. In *Development during middle childhood: The years from six to twelve*, ed. W. A. Collins, pp. 240–82. Washington, D.C.: National Academy Press.

Harvey, J. H., and G. Weary. 1981. *Perspectives on attributional process*. Dubuque: Wm. C. Brown.

Hazen, N., and M. E. Durrett. 1982. Relationship of security of attachment to exploration and cognitive mapping abilities in 2-year-olds. *Developmental Psychology* 18:751–59.

Heider, F. 1958. *The psychology of interpersonal relations*. New York: Wiley.

Heisel, J. S., S. Ream, R. Raite, M. Rappaport, and R. D. Coddington. 1973. The significance of life events as contributing factors in the diseases of children. Part III: A study of pediatric patients. *Journal of Pediatrics* 83:119–23.

Herrenkohl, R. C., and E. C. Herrenkohl. 1981. Some antecedents and developmental consequences of child maltreatment. *New Directions for Child Development* 11:57–76.

Hess, R. D., and K. A. Camara. 1979. Post-divorce family relationships as mediating factors in the consequences of divorce for children. *Journal of Social Issues* 35:79–96.

Heston, L. L. 1966. Psychiatric disorders in foster home reared children of schizophrenic mothers. *British Journal of Psychiatry* 112:819–25.

Hetherington, E. M. 1979. Divorce: A child's perspective. *American Psychologist* 34:851–58.

Hetherington, E. M. 1984. Stress and coping in children and families. *New Directions for Child Development* 24:7–33.

Hetherington, E. M., M. Cox, and R. Cox. 1976. Divorced fathers. *Family Coordinator* 25:417–28.

Hetherington, E. M., M. Cox, and R. Cox. 1979. Play and social interaction in children following divorce. *Journal of Social Issues* 35:26–49.

Hetherington, E. M., M. Cox, and R. Cox. 1982. Effects of divorce on parents and children. In *Nontraditional Families*, ed. M. Lamb, pp. 30–49. Hillsdale, N.J.: Erlbaum.

Hoffman, M. L. 1970. Moral development. In *Carmichael's manual of child psychology*, Vol. 2, ed. P. H. Mussen, pp. 261–359. New York: Wiley.

Holland, J. L. 1973. *Making vocational choices: A theory of careers*. Englewood Cliffs, N.J.: Prentice-Hall.

Holland, J. L. 1985. *Making vocational choices: A theory of vocational personalities and work environments.* 2d ed. Englewood Cliffs, N.J.: Prentice-Hall.

Horn, J. M. 1983. The Texas adoption project: Adopted children and their intellectual resemblance to biological and adoptive parents. *Child Development* 54:268–75.

Horn, J. M., and R. G. Turner. 1976. Minnesota Multiphasic Personality Inventory profiles among subgroups of unwed mothers. *Journal of Consulting and Clinical Psychology* 44:25–33.

Hudgens, R. W. 1974. Personal catastrophe and depression: A consideration of the subject with respect to medically ill adolescents and a requiem for retrospective life event studies. In *Stressful life events: Their nature and effects,* ed. B. S. Dohrenwend and B. P. Dohrenwend, pp. 119–34. New York: Wiley.

Humphrey, J., and C. Ounsted. 1963. Adoptive families referred for psychiatric advice: Part I. *British Journal of Psychiatry* 109:599–608.

Hunt, J. M. 1961. *Intelligence and experience.* New York: Ronald Press.

Hunter, E. J., and D. S. Nice, eds. 1978. *Children of military families: A part and yet apart.* Washington, D.C.: U.S. Government Printing Office.

Huttenen, M. O., and P. Niskanen. 1978. Prenatal loss of father and psychiatric disorders. *Archives of General Psychiatry* 35:429–31.

Jackson, L. 1968. Unsuccessful adoptions. *British Journal of Medical Psychology* 41:389–98.

Jacobvitz, D., and L. A. Sroufe. In press. The early caregiver-child relationship and attention deficit disorder with hyperactivity in kindergarten: A prospective study. *Child Development.*

Janes, C. L., V. M. Hesselbrock, D. G. Myers, and J. H. Penniman. 1979. Problem boys in young adulthood: Teachers' ratings and twelve-year follow-up. *Journal of Youth and Adolescence* 8:453–72.

Johnson, J. H., and S. M. McCutcheon. 1980. Assessing life stress in older children and adolescents: Preliminary findings with the Life Events Checklist. In *Stress and anxiety,* Vol. 7, ed. I. G. Sarason and C. D. Spielberger, pp. 111–25. Washington, D.C.: Hemisphere.

Jones, E. E., and K. E. Davis. 1965. From acts to dispositions: The attribution process in person perception. In *Advances in experimental social psychology,* Vol. 2, ed. L. Berkowitz, pp. 219–65. New York: Academic Press.

Josselson, R., E. Greenberger, and D. McConochie. 1977. Phenomenological aspects of psychosocial maturity in adolescence. *Journal of Youth and Adolescence* 6:145–67.

Justice, B., and R. Justice. 1976. *The abusing family.* New York: Human Sciences Press.

Kadushin, A. 1962. A study of adoptive parents of hard-to-place children. *Social Casework* 53 (5): 227–33.

Kadushin, A. 1967. A follow-up study of children adopted when older. *American Journal of Orthopsychiatry* 37:530–39.

Kadushin, A. 1974. *Child welfare services.* New York: Macmillan.

Kadushin, A. 1980. *Child welfare services.* 3d ed. New York: Macmillan.

Kaye, K., and S. Warren. 1986. *Family discourse and the acknowledgement or denial of differences in adoptive families.* Manuscript submitted for publication.

Kaye, S. 1982. Self-image formation in adopted children: The environment within. *Journal of Contemporary Psychotherapy* 13:175–81.

Kazak, A. E. 1986. Families with physically handicapped children: Social ecology and family systems. *Family Process* 25:265–81.

Kelley, H. H. 1971. *Attribution in social interaction.* Morristown, N.J.: General Learning Press.

Kelly, H. H. 1972. *Causal schemata and the attribution process.* Morristown, N.J.: General Learning Press.

Kennell, J., O. Maratos, D. Kontos, M. Klaus, and A. Bogomolny. 1986. The attachment process in adoptive dyads. Paper presented at the meeting of the International Conference on Infant Studies, Los Angeles.

Kety, S. S., D. Rosenthal, P. H. Wender, and R. Schulsinger. 1968. The types and prevalence of mental illness in the biological and adoptive families of adopted schizophrenics. *Journal of Psychiatric Research* 6:345–62.

Kety, S. S., D. Rosenthal, P. H. Wender, F. Schulsinger, and B. Jacobson. 1975. Mental illness in the biological and adoptive families of adoptive individuals who have become schizophrenic: A preliminary report based on psychiatric interviews. In *Genetic research in psychiatry,* ed. R. Rieve, D. Rosenthal, and H. Brill, pp. 147–65. Baltimore, Md.: Johns Hopkins University Press.

Kimmel, D. C., and I. B. Weiner. 1985. *Adolescence: A developmental transition.* Hillsdale, N.J.: Erlbaum.

Kirk, H. D. 1964. *Shared fate.* New York: Free Press.

Kirk, H. D. 1981. *Adoptive kinship.* Toronto: Butterworths.

Klein, A. A. 1982. Adopted adolescents who are psychiatric in-patients: Prevalence, characteristics, and symptomatology. Unpublished doctoral dissertation, Boston University.

Ladner, J. 1977. *Mixed families.* New York: Anchor Press.

Lamb, M. E., ed. 1981. *The role of the father in child development.* 2d ed. New York: Wiley.

Lamb, M. E., and K. E. Gilbride. 1985. Compatibility in parent-infant relationships: Origins and processes. In *Compatible and incompatible relationships,* ed. W. Ickes, pp. 33–60. New York: Springer-Verlag.

Lanier, D. Jr. 1978. Child abuse and neglect among military families. In *Children of military families: A part and yet apart,* ed. E. J. Hunter and D. S. Nice, pp. 103–19. Washington, D.C.: U.S. Government Printing Office.

Lawder, E. A. 1970. Postadoption counseling: A professional obligation. *Child Welfare* 49 (8): 435–42.

Lerner, R. 1985. *On the origins of human plasticity.* Cambridge: Cambridge University Press.

Lerner, R., and J. Lerner. 1983. Temperament-intelligence reciprocities in early childhood: A contextual model. In *Origins of intelligence.* 2d ed., ed. M. Lewis, pp. 139–56. New York: Plenum Press.

Lifshitz, M., R. Baum, I. Balgur, and C. Cohen. 1975. The impact of the social milieu upon the nature of adoptees' emotional difficulties. *Journal of Marriage and Family* 37:221–28.

Little, R. E. 1979. Drinking during pregnancy: Implications for public health. *Alcohol Health and Research World* 4:36–42.

Lloyd, C. 1980. Life events and depressive disorder reviewed. Part II: Events as precipitating factors. *Archives of General Psychiatry* 37:541–48.

Long, P. 1986. Growing up military. *Psychology Today* 20:31–37.

Lynn, D. B., and W. L. Sawrey. 1959. The effects of father-absence on Norwegian boys and girls. *Journal of Abnormal and Social Psychology* 47:258–62.

Maas, H. 1960. The successful adoptive parent applicants. *Social Work* 5 (1): 14–20.

Maccoby, E. E. 1980. *Social development: Psychological growth and the parent-child relationship.* New York: Harcourt, Brace, Jovanovich.

Maccoby, E. E., and J. Martin. 1983. Socialization in the context of the family: Parent-child interaction. In *Handbook of child psychology,* Vol. 4, ed. E. M. Hetherington, pp. 1–101. New York: Wiley.

Marks, S. R. 1986. *Three corners: Exploring marriage and the self.* Lexington, Mass.: Lexington Books.

Mash, E. J., and C. Johnston. 1983. Parental perceptions of child behavior problems, parenting self-esteem, and mothers' reported stress in younger and older hyperactive and normal children. *Journal of Consulting and Clinical Psychology* 51:86–99.

Matas, L., R. A. Arend, and L. A. Sroufe. 1978. Continuity of adaptation in the second year: The relationship between quality of attachment and later competence. *Child Development* 49:547–56.

McCall, R. B., M. I. Appelbaum, and P. S. Hogarty. 1973. Developmental changes in mental performance. *Monographs of the Society for Research in Child Development* 38.

McClearn, G. 1973. The genetic aspects of alcoholism. In *Alcoholism: Progress in research and treatment*, ed. P. G. Bourne and R. Fox, pp. 337–58. New York: Academic Press.

McCranie, M. 1965. Normal problems in adapting to adoption. *Journal of the Medical Association of Georgia* 54:247–51.

McCubbin, H. E., C. B. Joy, E. A. Cauble, J. K. Comeau, J. M. Patterson, and R. H. Needle. 1980. Family stress and coping: A decade review. *Journal of Marriage and the Family* 42:855–71.

McRoy, R. G., and L. A. Zurcher. 1983. *Transracial adoptees: The adolescent years.* Springfield, Ill.: Charles C. Thomas.

McRoy, R. G., L. A. Zurcher, M. L. Lauderdale, and R. E. Anderson. 1984. The identity of transracial adoptees. *Social Casework* 65:34–39.

McWhinnie, A. M. 1967. *Adopted children: How they grow up.* London: Routledge & Kegan Paul.

McWhinnie, A. M. 1969. The adopted child in adolescence. In *Adolescence,* ed. G. Caplan and S. Lebovice, pp. 133–42. New York: Basic Books.

Melina, L. R. 1986. *Raising adopted children.* New York: Harper & Row.

Menlove, F. L. 1965. Aggressive symptoms in emotionally disturbed adopted children. *Child Development* 36:512–22.

Menning, B. E. 1977. *Infertility: A guide for the childless couple.* Englewood Cliffs, N.J.: Prentice-Hall.

Miles, M. B., and A. M. Huberman. 1984. *Qualitative data analysis.* Beverly Hills, Calif.: Sage.

Milich, R., and J. Loney. 1979. The role of hyperactive and aggressive symptomatology in predicting adolescent outcome among hyperactive children. *Journal of Pediatric Psychology* 4:93–112.

Miller, E. A. 1978. Cerebral palsied children and their parents. *Exceptional Children* 24:149–53.

Millon, T. 1981. *Disorders of personality.* New York: Wiley.

Minuchin, S. 1974. *Families and family therapy.* Cambridge, Mass.: Harvard University Press.

Napier, A., and C. Whitaker. 1978. *The family crucible.* New York: Harper & Row.

National Committee for Adoption. 1985. *Adoption factbook.* Washington, D.C.: NCFA.

Newcomb, M., C. Huba, and P. Bentler. 1981. A multi-dimensional assessment of stressful life events among adolescents: Derivation and correlates. *Journal of Health and Social Behavior* 22:400–14.

Newman, B. M., and P. R. Newman. 1984. *Development through life: A psychosocial approach.* 3d ed. Homewood, Ill.: Dorsey Press.

Nice, D. S. 1978. The androgynous wife and the military child. In *Children of military families: A part and yet apart,* ed. E. J. Hunter and D. S. Nice, pp. 25–37. Washngton, D.C.: U.S. Government Printing Office.

Norton, R. 1983. Measuring marital quality: A critical look at the dependent variable. *Journal of Marriage and the Family* 45:141–51.

Offord, D. R., J. F. Aponte, and L. A. Cross. 1969. Presenting symptomatology of adopted children. *Archives of General Psychiatry* 20:110–16.

O'Leary, K. D. 1984. Marital discord and children: Problems, strategies, methodologies, and results. *New Directions for Child Development* 24:35–46.

Parke, R. D., and C. W. Collmer. 1975. Child abuse: An interdisciplinary review. In *Review of child development research*, Vol. 5, ed. E. M. Hetherington, pp. 509–90. Chicago: University of Chicago Press.

Pastor, D. L. 1981. The quality of mother-infant attachment and its relationship to toddlers' initial sociability with peers. *Developmental Psychology* 17:326–35.

Paternite, C. E., and J. Loney. 1980. Childhood hyperkinesis: Relationships between symptomatology and home environment. In *Hyperactive children: The social ecology of identification and treatment*, ed. C. K. Whalen and B. Henker, pp. 105–41. New York: Academic Press.

Patterson, G. 1976. The aggressive child: Victim and architect of a coercive system. In *Behavior modification and families: Theory and research*, Vol. 1, ed. L. A. Hamerlynck, L. C. Handy, and E. J. Mash, pp. 84–100. New York: Brunner/Mazel.

Paykel, E. S. 1974. Life stress and psychiatric disorder: Application of the clinical approach. In *Stressful life events: Their nature and effects*, ed. B. S. Dohrenwend and B. P. Dohrenwend, pp. 135–49. New York: Wiley.

Paykel, E. S. 1978. Contribution of life events to causation of psychiatric illness. *Psychological Medicine* 8:245–54.

Paykel, E. S., J. K. Myers, and M. M. Dienelt. 1969. Life events and depression: A controlled study. *Archives of General Psychiatry* 21:753–60.

Paykel, E. S., and J. Tanner. 1976. Life events, depressive relapse, and maintenance treatment. *Psychological Medicine* 6:481–85.

Pedersen, F. 1966. Relationships between father-absence and emotional disturbance in male military dependents. *Merrill-Palmer Quarterly* 12:321–31.

Pedersen, F. A., and E. J. Sullivan. 1964. Relationship among geographic mobility, parental attitudes, and emotional disturbance in children. *American Journal of Orthopsychiatry* 34:575–80.

Pino, C. 1980. Research and clinical applications of marital autopsy in divorce counseling. *Journal of Divorce* 4:31–48.

Pringle, M. L. K. 1967. *Adoption: Facts and fallacies*. London: Longmans, Green.

Privitera, C. R. 1978. The preschool child and the military family. In *Children of military families: A part and yet apart*, ed. E. J. Hunter and D. S. Nice, pp. 5–7. Washington, D.C.: U.S. Government Printing Office.

Rautman, A. 1959. Adoptive parents need help too. *Mental Hygiene* 33:424–31. Reprinted in *Readings in Adoption*, ed. E. Smith. New York: Philosophical Library, 1963.

Reece, S. A., and B. Levin. 1968. Psychiatric disturbances in adopted children. *Social Work* 13:101–11.

Rienerth, J. G. 1978. Separation and female centeredness in the military family. In *Military families: Adaptation to change*, ed. E. J. Hunter and D. S Nice, pp. 169–84. New York: Praeger.

Rutter, M. 1970. Sex differences in children's response to family stress. In *The child in his family*, ed. E. J. Anthony and C. Koupernik, pp. 165–96. New York: Wiley.

Rutter, M. 1971. Parent-child separation: Psychological effects on the children. *Journal of Child Psychology and Psychiatry* 12:233–60.

Rutter, M. 1979. Maternal deprivation, 1972–1978: New findings, new concepts, new approaches. *Child Development,* 50:283–305.

Rutter, M. 1980. The long-term effects of early experience. *Developmental Medicine and Child Neurology* 22:800–15.

Rutter, M. 1981a. *Maternal deprivation reassessed.* 2d ed. Harmondsworth: Penguin.

Rutter, M. 1981b. Social/emotional consequences of day care for preschool children. *American Journal of Orthopsychiatry* 51:4–28.

Rutter, M. 1983. Stress, coping, and development: Some issues and some questions. In *Stress, coping, and development in children,* ed. N. Garmezy and M. Rutter, pp. 1–41. New York: McGraw-Hill.

Rutter, M., and N. Garmezy. 1983. Developmental psychopathology. In *Handbook of child development,* Vol. 4, ed. E. M. Hetherington, pp. 775–911. New York: John Wiley & Sons.

Rutter, M., P. Graham, O. Chadwick, and W. Yule. 1976. Adolescent turmoil: Fact or fiction? *Journal of Child Psychology and Psychiatry* 17:35–56.

Sameroff, A. 1975. Transactional models in early social relations. *Human Development* 18:65–79.

Sameroff, A. J., and M. Chandler. 1975. Reproductive risk and the continuum of caretaking casualty. In *Review of child development research,* Vol. 4, ed. F. Horowitz, pp. 187–243. Chicago: University of Chicago Press.

Sameroff, A. J., and R. Seifer. 1983. Familial risk and child competence. *Child Development* 54: 1254–68.

Sants, H. J. 1964. Genealogical bewilderment in children with substitute parents. *British Journal of Medical Psychology* 37:133–41.

Scarr, S. 1985. Constructing psychology: Making facts and fables for our time. *American Psychologist* 40:499–512.

Scarr, S., and K. K. Kidd. 1983. Developmental behavior genetics. In *Handbook of child psychology,* Vol. 2, ed. M. M. Haith and J. J. Campos, pp. 345–433. New York: Wiley.

Scarr, S., E. Scarf, and R. A. Weinberg. 1980. Perceived and actual similarities in biological and adoptive families: Does perceived similarity bias genetic inferences? *Behavior Genetics* 10:445–58.

Scarr, S., and R. A. Weinberg. 1978. The influence of "family background" on intellectual attainment. *American Sociological Review* 43:674–92.

Scarr, S., and R. A. Weinberg. 1983. The Minnesota adoption studies: Genetic differences and malleability. *Child Development* 54:150–267.

Schachter, F. F. 1985. Sibling deidentification in the clinic: Devil vs. angel. *Family Process* 24:415–27.

Schachter, F. F., G. Gilutz, E. Shore, and M. Adler. 1978. Sibling deidentification judged by mothers: Cross-validation and developmental studies. *Child Development* 49:543–46.

Schachter, F. F., E. Shore, S. Feldman-Rotman, R. E. Marquis, and S. Campbell. 1976. Sibling deidentification. *Developmental Psychology* 12:418–27.

Schechter, M. D. 1960. Observations on adopted children. *Archives of General Psychiatry* 3:21–32.

Schechter, M. D., P. V. Carlson, J. Q. Simmons, and H. H. Work. 1964. Emotional problems in the adoptee. *Archives of General Psychiatry* 10:109–18.

Schnall, S. M. 1978. Characteristics and management of child abuse and neglect among military families. In *Children of military families: A part and yet apart,* ed. E. J. Hunter and D. S. Nice, pp. 141–62. Washington, D.C.: U.S. Government Printing Office.

Schneider-Rosen, K., K. G. Braunwald, V. Carlson, and D. Cicchetti. 1985. Current perspectives in attachment theory: Illustration from the study of maltreated infants. In *Growing points of attachment theory and research,* ed. I. Bretherton and E. Waters. Monographs of the Society for Research in Child Development, Vol. 50, nos. 1–2.

Selman, R. L., and A. P. Selman. 1979. Children's ideas about friendship: A new theory. *Psychology Today* 13:71–80.

Senior, N., and E. Himadi. 1985. Emotionally disturbed, adopted, inpatient adolescents. *Child Psychiatry and Human Development* 15:189–97.

Shaver, K. G. 1975. *An introduction to attribution processes.* Cambridge, Mass.: Winthrop.

Shireman, J. F., and P. R. Johnson. 1986. A longitudinal study of black adoptions: Single parent, transracial, and traditional. *Social Work* 31:172–76.

Simon, N. M., and A. G. Senturia. 1966. Adoption and psychiatric illness. *American Journal of Psychiatry* 122:858–68.

Simon, R. J., and H. Alstein. 1987. *Transracial adoptees and their families.* New York: Praeger.

Singer, L. M., D. M. Brodzinsky, D. Ramsay, M. Stein, and E. Waters. 1985. Mother-infant attachment in adoptive families. *Child Development* 56:1543–51.

Slager-Jorne, P. 1978. Counseling sexually abused children. *Personnel and Guidance Journal* 57 (October): 103–5.

Smith, E., ed. 1963. *Readings in adoption.* New York: Philosophical Library.

Smith, S. M., and R. Hanson. 1975. Interpersonal relationships and child rearing practices in 214 parents of battered children. *British Journal of Psychiatry* 127:513–25.

Sontag, L. W. 1966. Implications of fetal behavior and environment for adult personalities. *Annals of the New York Academy of Sciences* 134:782–86.

Sorosky, A. D., A. Baran, and R. Pannor. 1975. Identity conflicts in adoptees. *American Journal of Orthopsychiatry* 45:18–27.

Sorosky, A. D., A. Baran, and R. Pannor. 1978. *The adoption triangle.* New York: Doubleday, Anchor Press.

Sorosky, A. D., A. Baran, and R. Pannor. 1984. *The adoption triangle.* Garden City, N.Y.: Anchor Books.

Sroufe, L. A., and M. Rutter. 1984. The domain of developmental psychopathology. *Child Development* 55:17–29.

Sroufe, L. A., and J. Fleeson. 1986. Attachment and the construction of relationships. In *Relationships and development,* ed. W. W. Hartup and Z. Rubin, pp. 51–71. Hillsdale, N.J.: Erlbaum.

Sroufe, L. A., and D. Jacobvitz. 1987. Diverging pathways, developmental transformations, multiple etiologies, and the problem of continuity in development. In *Conceptualizing continuity, change, and transformations in individuals: Some lessons from longitudinal studies,* chaired by E. E. Maccoby. Symposium presented at the meeting of The Society for Research in Child Development, Baltimore, Md., April.

Sroufe, L. A. and E. Waters. 1977. Attachment as an organizational construct. *Child Development* 48:1184–99.

Stein, L. M., and J. L. Hoopes. 1985. *Identity formation in the adopted adolescent: The Delaware family study.* New York: Child Welfare League of America.

Sullivan, H. S. 1953. *The interpersonal theory of psychiatry.* New York: Norton.

Swearingen, E. M., and L. H. Cohen. 1985. Life events and psychological distress: A prospective study of young adolescents. *Developmental Psychology* 21:1045–54.

Sweeney, D. M., D. T. Gasbarro, and M. R. Gluck. 1963. A descriptive study of adopted children seen in a child guidance center. *Child Welfare* 42:345–49.

Tennant, C., P. Bebbington, and J. Hurry. 1982. Social experiences in childhood and adult psychiatric morbidity: A multiple regression analysis. *Psychological*

Medicine 12:321–27.

Tew, B., and K. Laurence. 1975. Some sources of stress found in mothers of spina bifida children. *British Journal Preview of Social Medicine* 29:27–30.

Tew, B., J. Payne, and K. Laurence. 1974. Must a family with a handicapped child be a handicapped family? *Developmental Medicine and Child Neurology* 16:95.

Thomas, A., S. Chess, and H. G. Birch. 1968. *Temperament and behavior disorders in children.* New York: New York University Press.

Thompson, W. R. 1957. Influence of prenatal maternal anxiety on emotionality in young rats. *Science* 125:698–99.

Thomson, E. M. 1971. *Child abuse: A community challenge.* Ease Aurora, N.Y.: Henry Stewart.

Tousseing, P. W. 1962. Thoughts regarding the etiology of psychological difficulties in adopted children. *Child Welfare* 41 (2): 59–65.

Tousseing, P. W. 1971. Realizing the potential in adoptions. *Child Welfare* 50 (6): 322–27.

Triseliotis, J. B. 1973. *In search of origins: The experiences of adopted people.* Boston: Routledge & Kegan Paul.

Tsukada, G. K. 1979. Sibling interaction: A review of the literature. *Smith College Studies in Social Work* 49:229–47.

Turner, E. K. 1956. The syndrome in the infant resulting from maternal emotional tension during pregnancy. *The Medical Journal of Australia* 1:221–22.

Vincent, C. 1961. *Unmarried mothers.* New York: Glencoe, Free Press.

Wallerstein, J. S., and J. B. Kelly. 1976. The effects of parental divorce: Experiences of the child in later latency. *American Journal of Orthopsychiatry* 46:256–69.

Wallerstein, J. S., and J. B. Kelly. 1980. *Surviving the break-up: How children and parents cope with divorce.* New York: Basic Books.

Walsh, E. D., and F. S. Lewis. 1969. A study of adoptive mothers in a child guidance clinic. *Social Casework* 50 (December): 587–94.

Waters, E. 1978. The reliability and stability of individual differences in infant-mother attachment. *Child Development* 49:483–94.

Waters, E., and L. A. Sroufe. 1983. Social competence as a developmental construct. *Developmental Review* 3:79–97.

Weiss, A. 1985. Symptomatology of adopted and nonadopted adolescents in a psychiatric hospital. *Adolescence* 20:763–74.

Weiss, G., K. Minde, J. Werry, W. Douglas, and E. Nemeth. 1971. The hyperactive child. Part 8: Five-year follow-up. *Archives of General Psychiatry* 24:409–14.

Werner, E., and S. Smith. 1977. *Kauai's children come of age.* Honolulu: University of Hawaii Press.

Wilson, M. R. 1985. Long-term inpatient psychiatric treatment of adolescent adopted children, a population at risk. Paper presented at the seminar of the San Diego Society for Adolescent Psychiatry, San Diego, Calif., November.

Winder, C. L., and L. Rau. 1962. Parental attitudes associated with social deviance in preadolescent boys. *Journal of Abnormal and Social Psychology* 64:418–24.

Winick, M. 1970. Fetal malnutrition and growth processes. *Hospital Practice.*

Winick, M. 1974. *Nutrition and fetal development.* New York: Wiley.

Work, H. H., and H. Anderson. 1971. Studies in adoption. *American Journal of Psychiatry* 127:948–50.

Wyatt, R. J., S. G. Potkin, and D. L. Murphy. 1979. Platelet monoamine oxidase activity in schizophrenia: A review of the data. *American Journal of Psychiatry* 136:377–85.

Zastrow, C. 1977. *Outcome of black children/white parents transracial adoptions.* San Francisco: R & E Research Associates.

Ziatek, K. 1974. Psychological problems of adoption. *Psychological Wychowawcza* (Warsaw) 17:63–76.

Zill, N. 1985. Achievement and behavior problems among adoptive children: Findings from a national health survey of children. Paper presented at the meeting of the Society for Research in Child Development, Toronto, April.

Author Index

Subject Index

abuse/neglect, 34, 36–38, 40, 59, 63–66, 69, 79–80, 85, 87, 92, 166; by adoptive families, 38, 45–46, 57, 59, 63–66, 69, 79–80, 85, 87; by birthparents, 38, 57, 92; in foster care, 38

acknowledgment of differences, 9–10, 13, 51, 120–23, 139–40, 144

Acknowledgment of Differences Scale, 21, 22, 23, 120–21

adjustment issues, 125–44, 154–56, 159–61; hostility, 2, 128–29; rejection and anger, 126–27; rootlessness, 131–32; seeking revenge, 2, 129–31; self-hatred, 128

adolescence: developmental changes, 2–3; identity formation, 3, 71–73

Adolescent Behavior Checklist (ABC), 23, 77, 97–100

adoption: as a treatment issue, 14, 143–44, 168–69; definition, 1; independent, 125, 165–66; relative, 19, 125, 165–66; statistics, 1; transracial, 19, 125, 133–37, 161

adoption agency practices, 54, 87, 115, 165–68

adoption issues: for children, 125–44, 154–56, 159–61; for parents, 1, 2, 8, 11, 110–15, 122, 134. *See also* adjustment issues

adoption revelation, 9, 115–23

adoptive kinship theory, 9–10, 158

advice to prospective parents, 132–33, 139–41; from children, 132; from parents, 132–33, 139, 141

alcohol use, 31, 39, 57, 61–63, 79, 94, 98–99; adoptive parents, 31, 57, 61–63, 79; birthfamilies, 31, 39, 57, 61, 63; children, 31, 94, 98–99

attachment: relationships, 5–7, 13, 34–38, 45–46, 61, 92, 94; theory, 5–8, 49, 158, 166

attention deficit disorder (ADD): *See* hyperactivity

attribution theory, 10–11, 158

attributions: parental, 9, 10–11, 46, 52, 131, 167

birthparents, 1, 4–5, 31–33. *See* specific topics

blended families, 60–61, 72

children: demographic characteristics, 11–13, 19–20, 29–40. *See* specific topics

cognitive-developmental theory, 9, 158

communication: about adoption, 10, 13, 119–23, 141–42, 146–50, 155–56, 161, 168–69; children's requests for birthparent information, 146–47; parents' reactions to requests for birthparent information, 147–50

compatibility, 7–9, 13, 47–52, 67–68, 160, 166. *See also* goodness-of-fit

conduct disorders, 103–4, 161

drug use, 32, 57, 62–63, 94, 98–99; adoptive parents, 62–63; birthfamilies, 57; birthmothers, 32; children, 94, 98–99

"elbow baby," 44–47, 67, 160–61

expectations: parental, 5, 11, 46, 51–52, 63, 113, 130

externalizing behaviors, 23, 100–2, 108

family systems theory, 60–61

father: presence/absence, 36–37, 59,

About the Authors

RUTH G. McROY, Ph.D., is an Associate Professor of Social Work and Ruby Lee Piester Centennial Fellow in Services to Children and Families at the University of Texas at Austin. She coauthored the book *Transracial and Inracial Adoptees: The Adolescent Years* and has published numerous articles and has made presentations throughout the country on such topics as transracial adoptions, post-adoption services, racial-identity development, and open adoptions.

HAROLD D. GROTEVANT, Ph.D., is Professor of Home Economic and Psychology and Head of the Division of Child Development and Family Relationships at the University of Texas at Austin. His research focuses on identity formation, family communication processes, and relationshps in normal and troubled adoptive families and open adoptions. He has published over sixty articles and has presented his work at national and international conferences.

LOUIS A. ZURCHER, Ph.D., was most recently the Ashbel Smith Professor of Social Work and Sociology at the University of Texas at Austin. He is the coauthor with Ruth G. McRoy of a book on transracial adoptions and has authored or coauthored over one hundred articles and fifteen books, including *The Mutable Self: A Self-Concept for Social Change, Poverty Warriors,* and *Social Roles: Conformity, Conflict, and Creativity.*